04

SACRED CONCRETE

Layout, cover design and typography
Reinhard Steger, Proxi (www.proxi.me)

Editorial supervision and project management
Henriette Mueller-Stahl, Berlin

Production
Amelie Solbrig, Berlin

Lithography
Oriol Rigat, Barcelona

Paper
Magno Volume, 135 g/m^2

Printing and Binding
Beltz Grafische Betriebe GmbH,
Bad Langensalza

Library of Congress Control Number:
2013409906

Bibliographic information published by
the German National Library
The German National Library lists this
publication in the Deutsche National-
bibliografie; detailed bibliographic data
are available on the Internet at
http://dnb.d-nb.de.

ISBN 978-3-0356-2171-6

© 2020 Birkhäuser Verlag GmbH, Basel
P.O. Box 44, 4009 Basel, Switzerland
Part of Walter de Gruyter GmbH, Berlin/Boston

9 8 7 6 5 4 3 2

www.birkhauser.com

FLORA SAMUEL – INGE LINDER-GAILLARD

SACRED CONCRETE

THE CHURCHES OF LE CORBUSIER

SECOND AND REVISED EDITION

BIRKHÄUSER
BASEL

TABLE OF CONTENTS

Acknowledgements

Architect on the one hand, and art historian on the other, both with a strong interest in Le Corbusier, the two of us met at a conference at the Fondation Le Corbusier several years ago. The affinities of our interests quickly became clear to us as did the complementary nature of our fields. So first of all thanks goes to the Fondation for unwittingly bringing us together. The book has been developing in the virtual world ever since our first and only meeting, our differences in outlook and geography adding greatly to the mix. Thanks are due to Henriette Mueller-Stahl for seeing its potential and for her hard work in helping us see the project through. Thanks also to Rein Steger for his patience, hard work and skill in graphic design.

There is a wealth of information out there on Le Corbusier's projects for the Church, much of it is still very much "alive" and in circulation. Tracking it down and gleaning it often comes from encounters with those who have strong ties to the built sites. We are very grateful for the help the following people offered in this context. At Ronchamp: Louis Mauvais, Jean-François Mathey, Christian Luxeuil, Dominique Claudius-Petit, Annick Flicoteaux, Benedicte Mathey and all the Notre Dame du Haut group. At La Tourette: Marc Chauveau. At Firminy: Yvan Mettaud, Jean-Louis Reymondier, Jean-Michel Larois and again Dominique Claudius-Petit. Luis Burriel Bielza has been generous in sharing his research with us. We are also grateful for comments from Juan Carlos Sancho and Peter Sassenroth on chapter 7. Marie Gastinel-Jones and Elizabeth Warman have also assisted with translations.

For their input into the manuscript to help us with theological and Church-related questions, we warmly thank Rosemary Crumlin and Charles Pickstone. Kathleen James Chakraborty and Robert Proctor gave us advice at an important moment in the development of the book. Support was gratefully received from the University of Sheffield, School of Architecture research group. For her incredible book on *L'Art sacré* we would like to acknowledge Françoise Caussé. She managed to turn an often considered unglamorous story into a sort of mystery thriller – and more seriously she unearthed a mountain of very important contextual information for us.

Arnaud Dercelles and Delphine Studer at the Fondation Le Corbusier as ever have been extremely helpful in supplying documents and pictures. We remain indebted to Michel Richard for his support.

Our final and most heartfelt thanks goes to our families – our husbands and our children – who have supported this project all the way. More than anyone else it is they that have taught us the meaning of *savoir habiter*.

Reading and Grenoble 2020

Detail, Le Corbusier's grave, Roquebrune-Cap-Martin

Introduction

Faced with the terrifying uncertainties of the world in which he found himself
Le Corbusier spent his life devising a philosophy of architecture that would give order
and meaning to what he saw around him (Fig. 0.1). He was not alone in feeling this
impetus; changes in society, developments in science and the advance of secular
values meant that the Catholic Church in Rome was itself under pressure to modernise.
Our book explores the tense political relationship between Le Corbusier's view of
religion and that of the Church, manifested in the architecture of his religious
buildings, and the work of those who took influence from them.

Le Corbusier was acutely aware of his own mortality, the passage of time and the need
to use it well. It is no coincidence therefore that he spent the last fifteen years of
his life creating the most thought provoking and audacious projects of his career,
including those church buildings that give structure to this book – La Sainte-Baume,
Notre Dame du Haut Ronchamp, Sainte Marie de la Tourette and Saint Pierre Firminy –
each of which encapsulates in built form his desperate search for meaning. This was
explored in intense dialogue with the monks, members of the clergy and communities
that formed his client base, in many ways an early prototype of the participatory
approach to architecture that is coming into vogue today. As Michel Ragon has
observed: "Never more than during those last fifteen years of his old age had Le
Corbusier paid such attention to the world, and the world had probably never paid
such close attention to an architect."[1]

The members of the Church who sought Le Corbusier's assistance for the co-creation
of some of the most remarkable sacred structures of the twentieth century, did so
because they recognised in him a burning faith. Despite the fact that Le Corbusier's
writings are peppered with such words as spirit, soul, truth and unity it is not widely
recognised that Le Corbusier took a deep interest in religion – defined here as an
orderly way of life binding humans with God, refreshed through constant study and
contemplation[2] – largely because historians have had an interest in emphasising other
aspects of his work.

Nikolaus Pevsner was, for example, more interested in Le Corbusier's early buildings,
dismissing later work, such as Ronchamp, as an "attempt to escape out of reality
into a fairy world".[3] The highly influential architectural historian wrote that there
were "reasons to be thankful" that, in the 1920s and 1930s, "the time was not ripe for
Le Corbusier's attempts to bring 'nature in the sense of the irrational' back into
architecture".[4] It may be that Pevsner's disapproval of this more subjective aspect of Le
Corbusier's work has contributed to its neglect as a subject of research until recently.

While rationalistic issues such as mass production, standardisation and technological
advance were of grave concern to Le Corbusier he had a strong abhorrence for
the word "functionalism", a word that denied the "magical" qualities of architecture.[5]

Machines, and the benefits of standardisation and mass production would rather "provide nourishment both spiritual and material" to humankind.[6]

Le Corbusier was obsessed with symbolism (Fig. 0.2). For him it was like "a yearning for a language limited to only a few words."[7] His architecture is designed to stir the imagination:

> Seek and you shall find. Look into the depths of the work and ask yourself questions. There are illuminations and scenes; there are hours of fullness, agonies, radiant or menacing skies, houses and mountains, seas and lagoons, suns and moons … and there are besides all the cries of the subconscious, sensual or chaste, and everything you can imagine.[8]

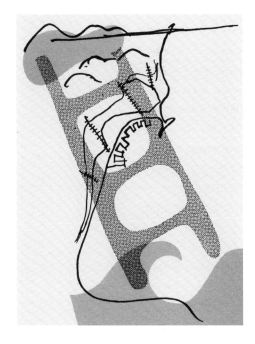

0.1 – Le Corbusier's Jacob's Ladder from *Poésie sur Alger*, 1950

0.2 – The south door of Notre Dame du Haut, Ronchamp

His interest in ancient religion and philosophy has, in recent decades, begun to receive more attention from historians. An article written in 1980 by Richard A. Moore on alchemical themes in Le Corbusier's architecture has paved the way for further investigation into the rich symbolism of his work,[9] for example that of Peter Carl who has done much to advance thinking in this area.[10] More recently Jaime Coll has made a detailed analysis of Le Corbusier's *Taureaux* series of paintings,[11] Danièle Pauly has explored the way he used drawing as a meditative act.[12] Luisa Martina Colli has completed extensive research into the subtleties of his use of colour[13], Nadir Lahiji has explored the issue of sexuality in his work[14], but it is undoubtedly Mogens Krustrup who has done most to reveal the full complexity of the architect's spiritual agenda.

In 2013, architect and photographer Henry Plummer published *Cosmos of Light, The Sacred Architecture of Le Corbusier*. Plummer's introductory essay is followed by a photographic essay with commentary including his own remarkable photographs of Le Corbusier's three built structures. Concentrating on light, the author states "The aim of this book is to consider only this single aspect of Le Corbusier's work, but one that seems to me the most important and, perhaps, the least understood."[15] While we would not disagree with his main assertion that Le Corbusier's manipulation of light allows him to subvert the doctrinal agenda of the Church "in effect using light to consecrate the natural universe", "to activate a universal kind of human reverie" and "bringing us back in tune with the *universe*",[16] as it will be made clear in the development of our narrative, we take this further and study other important aspects of the commissions (liturgical scenography and the architectural promenade to name but two) to identify a much less nebulous agenda on Le Corbusier's part: calling our attention to and making Mary's, that is women's, place more present and compelling – in a word central.

The arcane has often been given precedence over overtly Christian themes in these discussions, perhaps reflecting the backgrounds of the authors or, more likely, the unfashionable status of Christianity as a subject for Western architectural historians. This seems to be changing as greater recognition is being given to the key role of churches in the life of communities, as well as the role that religious structures play in urban conflict.[17]

At the same time Le Corbusier's contribution to religious art and architecture is rarely mentioned in Christian literature which tends largely to ignore the way buildings can facilitate communion with God. A concern with the material seems somehow wrong yet the role of the Liturgy, the way in which ceremony is executed was of central concern to those who wanted to bring religion in line with new developments in society.[18] The configuration of liturgical space and light is interconnected with the liturgical arts, the objects and artworks that contribute to the Roman Catholic Liturgy. They include furnishings, vestments, chalices, and altarpieces. As Catherine de Lorenzo has illustrated, the design of a baptismal font or the layout of the altar can be deeply political.[19] Liturgy, derived from the Greek *leiton* (people) and *ergon* (work) refers to work done by an individual for the good of the people. Hence Le Corbusier's surprising engagement with these issues and his nervousness about their interpretation.

Many have experienced the power and the pull of Le Corbusier's sacred structures. One example is the German artist Anselm Kiefer who visited Ronchamp and La Tourette in 1966 at the tender age of 21. He stayed several weeks at la Tourette and he would have stayed longer if possible. The monastery was to have an enormous impact on him and his work. This story has only recently come to light through Brother Marc's acclaimed exhibition programme including *Anselm Kiefer à la Tourette*.[20]

This and other emergent stories of transformation and change need to be collected, almost as a form of spiritual Post Occupancy Evaluation (revisiting a building to ascertain its impact). This is just one aspect of the constant work carried out by the sites' owners and caretakers: the Association Œuvre Notre-Dame du Haut in Ronchamp; the Dominicans at La Tourette to maintain and grow the relevance of these places; the Metropolitan community of Saint Etienne which includes the town of Firminy for Saint Pierre.[21]

It is a curious thing that, when we began this work there was no single English language book that brought together all of Le Corbusier's ecclesiastical work into one fold. *Le Corbusier: il programma liturgico* (published in 2001) edited by Giuliano and Glauco Gresleri, Italian architects (brothers) who were in contact with Le Corbusier's studio in the 1960s regarding a possible church commission in Bologna was the most comprehensive work in this area.[22] Possibly because Giuliano Gresleri was also the editor and commentator on Le Corbusier's *Voyage en Orient* it places emphasis on the formative influence of Le Corbusier's early travels. We ourselves are more interested in the social significance of Le Corbusier's architecture than in a painstaking analysis of its origins, although they do, inevitably, form part of the discussion. Since the publication of *il programma liturgico*, much work has been undertaken in the field. Le Corbusier and the sacred was the focus of a conference at the Fondation Le Corbusier in the year 2004, the published proceedings of this event being perhaps the most in depth examination of the subject ever achieved up to that moment. There have been several significant anniversaries, each spawning events and publications including the fiftieth anniversaries of both Ronchamp (Fig. 0.3) and La Tourette as well as the construction of Saint Pierre Firminy.

In the early 1960s new developments in Liturgy as well as post-war reconstruction brought about a surge of building and a flow of books on the subject of modern church architecture. A key example is Albert Christ-Janer and Mary Mix Foley's *Modern Church Architecture* of 1962. The Roman Catholic section of the book is divided into "five streams" that well define the, perhaps paradoxical, concerns of church builders at that time: "the renewal of the liturgy that demands new plans and forms in architecture; the investigation of structure by which new plans can be most forcefully

0.3 – The exterior
chapel at Notre Dame
du Haut Ronchamp

expressed in new forms; the regaining of the traditional position of the Church as patron of contemporary arts; the search for simplicity in architecture, which can make of the church building a subordinate background to both liturgy and works of art; and, finally, the expansion of the contemporary philosophy of design to permit suitable decorative enrichment."[23] Christ-Janer and Foley were clearly advocates of Le Corbusier as the structure of the book is informed by a desire to persuade both Church officials and the Church membership "to accept a new and unique solution presented by an informed and gifted architect".[24] Very different sentiments are expressed in a multitude of church books by the English architect Reverend Peter Hammond and by church builders Maguire and Murray whose opinion of Le Corbusier will be discussed in chapter 7. Building on Le Corbusier's term "ineffable space" Karla Britton has more recently examined the role of the ineffable in building design across the globe, broadening the term out into other cultures and faith traditions.[25]

In France Father Jean Capellades' *Guide des églises nouvelles en France* of 1969 provided an overview of the post-war era to the beginning of Vatican II.[26] The same period was treated thematically by Georges Mercier in his *L'Architecture religieuse contemporaine en France: vers une synthèse des arts* which features La Tourette prominently on its cover.[27] More recently, Suzanne Robin's *Églises modernes, évolution des édifices religieux en France depuis 1955*, published in 1980, provided a landmark in the recent history of church architecture.[28]

Like that of Christ-Janer and Mix Foley, Wolfgang Jean Stock's canonical *European Church Architecture 1950–2000* is divided into sections on Protestant and Catholic churches. In it he "emphasises the theological and liturgical demands made on any architectural solution."[29] Stock makes the significant point that the building of churches provides a pure manifestation of the aspirations of their author. It is for this reason that "European church building can be read as a succinct expression of architectural history," a theme that we will return to.[30] Two other recent publications have wider scopes: one gathering international examples – Edwin Heathcote and Laura Moffat's *Contemporary Church Architecture*, 2007 – and the other extending to a wide-range of religions – Phyllis Richardson's *New Sacred Architecture*, 2004.[31] Both acknowledge the significance of Le Corbusier's commissions for the Church.

Back in France, Christine Blanchet and Pierre Vérot's *Architecture et arts sacrés en France de 1945 à nos jours* of 2015 has attempted an overview treatment of seventy years of church building – thousands of them - and commissions of art and liturgical works for churches in France. It pays particular attention to the ever-more present heritage-related and -driven issues regarding the country's churches. Isabelle Saint-Martin's important *Art chrétien/art sacré, regards du catholicisme sur l'art. France, XIXe–XXe siècle* of 2014 also brings these issues to the fore but concentrates on art and not architecture itself. These studies put very little emphasis on Le Corbusier, yet they are landmarks to the context of the era, especially in France, and thus emphasise the singularity of his work.

With *Theology in Stone* Richard Kieckhefer has done much to illuminate the links between the Church and its architecture, but his book is very minimally illustrated and the author is clearly not an architect.[32] As architect and art historian with a strong interest in religious social history, it is our aim to bridge the gap between those architectural books that have very little concern for theology and those theological books that are overpoweringly theological.[33] While neither of the authors is a theologian there are certain theological concepts that will play an important role in the discussion. Are Le Corbusier's churches "theocentric" (focused on God), "christocentric" (focused on Christ) or did he make it his business to create a whole new category of architecture focused on the Virgin Mary (Fig. 0.4)?

The commissioners and parishioners are oddly absent from most histories of church architecture although there is an ever growing movement within the sphere of architectural history and theory away from the veneration of the architect genius towards an acknowledgement of the collaborative processes, including fundraising, that underpin any scheme as built. Le Corbusier himself seems to have wrangled with this issue, for example on the one hand acknowledging his own team and the workmen who came together to build Ronchamp (Fig. 0.5), and on the other, fiercely guarding his name and reputation. There is however no doubt that he drew enormous sustenance from the people around him, whether colleagues or friends. Indeed Le Corbusier's life could be mapped as a series of intellectual leaps from one person to another – his extremely intense relationship with Amédée Ozenfant being a case in point. He could never have achieved what he did without the early partnership of his cousin Pierre Jeanneret. Clearly, more than anyone else, Father Marie-Alain Couturier, co-editor of the highly influential journal *L'Art sacré* played a great part in persuading

0.4 – One of the windows
of the south wall of
Notre Dame du Haut,
Ronchamp

0.5 – The workmen who
built Ronchamp from
Le Corbusier's *The Chapel
at Ronchamp*

Le Corbusier that his ideas were in fact those of an embryonic Christianity as yet untainted by the excesses of religious institutions (Fig. 0.6). Couturier's own calling was to give the Catholicism which he cared about so deeply new relevance by bringing it in line with the changes that he perceived in society (Fig. 0.7). Religious art and architecture would play a primary role in this process of transformation – hence his collaboration with Le Corbusier in whom he perceived a true sense of the sacred.

The question at the heart of all this is why Le Corbusier, who was deeply critical of organised religion, would immerse himself in the business of church building. As the French sociologist Pierre Bourdieu has observed:

> There is no doubt that the climate of spiritual restoration helps to favour the return to forms of art that, like Symbolist poetry or the psychological novel, carry to the highest degree the reassuring denial of the social world.[34]

For Le Corbusier the social and spiritual were not mutually exclusive. Indeed church building was a form of social action. This fitted with a Church that was seeking what Peter Hammond calls "a deeper understanding of its own nature and function in the modern world," an understanding which "breaks through the crust of formal concepts to the underlying social realities." [35] However, Le Corbusier's assistant Jerzy Soltan made the trenchant comment that "Le Corbusier's work for the Dominican order might appear daring and progressive to some (the order was unorthodox enough to have had some difficulties with the Vatican) and a retreat into clericalism for others."[36] It is our aim to explore the social value of Le Corbusier's work in this area. We begin with a discussion of the Catholic Church and its politics before outlining Le Corbusier's own take on religion. These two chapters provide the context for a discussion of each of his church schemes. The final chapter is an examination of the legacy of his work, the way it has been interpreted by others.

Although Le Corbusier anticipated the impact of computers on society it is hard to imagine what he would have thought of a rating of 4.5 stars for the Chapel at Ronchamp on TripAdvisor. In our materialistic and audit driven globalised society the pressure that is on to evaluate, rank and protect such buildings is immense. Can the chapel be measured in tourist souvenirs sold, visitor numbers and selfies taken?[37] We argue that buildings such as Ronchamp, a reminder of our connection to one another and to the environment, have never been so needed as at this time of Climate Emergency.

It is certainly this same élan for connection that inspired the recent project for a welcome centre on the Bourlémont Hill just below the Notre Dame chapel at Ronchamp. The commissions for the Poor Clares' convent and "gatehouse" (as the welcome centre is called, taking cues from monastic architectural typology) were offered to the Italian architect Renzo Piano. The thoughtful landscaping design that ties these new buildings to Le Corbusier's existing complex was executed by Piano's

0.6 – Le Corbusier
and Father Couturier
at Le Corbusier's
apartment, rue
Nungesser et Coli,
1952

0.7 – Cover of *L'Art sacré*,
issue 7–8, March–April 1955
"L'art sacré sa 'mystique' et
sa 'politique'"

friend and long-time collaborator Michel Corajoud. With the tenth anniversary of the project's completion in 2021, the new buildings have become less and less visible, as if receding into the hill, covered by vegetation – subtly reminiscent of the earth built underground houses Le Corbusier conceived for La Sainte Baume. Although deeply controversial the new project has enabled the chapel to maintain its original vocation as a place of worship. Preservation of its original use, the intangible heritage of the chapel, is more important than leaving the hillside intact. Churches are living organisms that have to work with their communities. The gatehouse has simultaneously allowed its owners to remain its caretaker. It also played a major role in achieving the World Heritage status that should protect the chapel for generations to come.

Sainte Marie de la Tourette was included in this successful bid for the inscription of seventeen Le Corbusier buildings as Unesco World Heritage sites in 2016. La Tourette has recently undergone a restoration campaign under the aegis of the French Historical Monuments Council completed in 2013 and the Notre Dame du Haut chapel will undergo extensive refurbishment in the 2020s. The maintenance of original brutalist finishes is notoriously difficult to achieve so we can only hope that this will be done with sensitivity and thus allow the concrete buildings to remain "loyal", as Le Corbusier put it, for a considerable time to come.[38]

MODERNITY AND THE CATHOLIC CHURCH

It is a flaw of many accounts of Le Corbusier's religious architecture that so little attention has been given to the many factors that were influential on its development, not least upheavals within the Catholic Church. This chapter begins with a brief overview of major issues in the early twentieth-century Catholic Church with particular emphasis on events in France. In particular we will focus on its anti-modern campaign which was aimed first at the Church's own renegade theologians and then broadened out to become an attack on society in general.[1] Next key events and realisations concerning early twentieth-century church architecture are laid out together with pertinent examples, first international ones and then French. The Liturgical Reform Movement will be introduced, followed by a discussion of some of the key players in the sacred art and architecture debate that raged at mid-century, coinciding with Le Corbusier's involvement with his own church-oriented commissions. Major issues that emerge in this discussion are: the modernisation of the Church and of life; the application of the ethical, philosophical and theological notions of simplicity, poverty and truth (in a word, asceticism) in church design; the role of space and light as well as the processional route (liturgical questions); and the role of art and artists within or at the service of the Church – all major concerns of Le Corbusier's architecture.

The Catholic Church

It will quickly become apparent that Le Corbusier's churches were aimed at a particular branch of Catholicism, one that did not have an easy relationship with the Church in Rome. The Catholic Church is not a monolithic entity and should not be treated as such. In this section we set out the concerns of the Catholic Church in Rome and show how they differ with that in France. Then, moving to a more granular scale, we will describe some of the factions within French Catholicism that would have a particular bearing on the work of Le Corbusier.

In Rome

The word "modern" is notoriously difficult to define. What was of particular concern to the Church were recent developments in the fields of science, technology, rationalism, the rise of democracy and secular education, and generally, any major breaks with the past that endangered its power and position (Fig. 1.1). In 1864, Pope Pius IX concluded the final, eightieth proposition in his famous *Syllabus of Errors* by condemning any reconciliation of the Church with "progress, liberalism, and modern civilization."[2] Succeeding him in 1907, Pope Pius X condemned modernism outright in his lengthy encyclical *Pascendi dominici gregis* (*On the Doctrines of the Modernists*),

1.1 – Pope Pius X
(Giuseppe Sarto,
1835-1914)

19

in which all modern things were considered heretical, and the modernists themselves, whoever they might be, were named enemies of the Church.[3] Eamon Duffy writes that "characterised by extreme violence of language" this achieved a "lumping" of "a miscellaneous assortment of new ideas together under the blank term 'Modernism'" characterised as a "compendium of all the heresies."[4] It resulted in a period of anti-modernism that was especially vehement. From 1910 all clergy were exhorted to take an Oath Against Modernism, discouraging originality in any form.[5]

Antipathy to modernism was compounded by the advance of Ultramontanism, a doctrine that asserts the authority and importance of the pope in both temporal and spiritual matters (that is, on a real-world, governmental and societal level on the one hand, and a theological one on the other). Its ascendancy was secured during the First Vatican Council of 1870, an event of great importance to the Church hierarchy, instigated by Pope Pius IX. Here the Council declared the dogma of Papal Infallibility, extant today, exerting the authority of the Pope as the legitimate successor of Peter, the Apostle of Jesus considered to be the first Pope by the Roman Catholic Church. As head of the Church hierarchy he leads its bishops, who in turn lead its priests, monks, nuns, and lay-faith community. His decision is final.

Modernity in the nineteenth century – tangled up in social and political phenomena of socialism, communism, atheism and rationalism – was felt to be a threat that the Church simply could not risk. Guidance in this area was urgently needed so Pope Benedict XV, while remaining essentially anti-modernist, took steps to bring the modernist "witch-hunt" to an end.[6] In 1917 a single completed document, the *Code of Canon Law*, presented the body of legislation that would give focussed direction to the Church.[7] It whittled down some ten thousand existing laws and decrees, often contradictory, inadequate or obsolete, to about one thousand seven hundred canons in seven volumes.[8] These were to form the binding laws of the Church.

The issue of modernisation became increasingly intertwined with politics, particularly the growth of communism and developments in industry. In 1891, Pope Leo XIII presented the encyclical *Rerum Novarum*. While rejecting socialism it iterated the Church's stand on the dignity and rights of industrial workers. Later, in 1931, Pope Pius XI issued the encyclical *Quadragesimo Anno* which addressed the social and economic order by calling for greater solidarity.[9] These declarations could be seen as contributing "to hope that in Europe, too, Catholic labour organisations might offset the communist unions."[10]

In 1937 in response to the growing threat of totalitarian rule Pope Pius XI issued two encyclicals, the first denouncing the Nazis with *Mit Brennender Sorge* (*With Burning Anxiety*), the second Communism, with *Divini Redemptoris*. Pius XI died in 1939. While his successor, Pius XII, did what he thought he could to mark his opposition to the Third Reich and save as many Jews as possible – especially those of Rome – the Vatican's actions during World War II remain questionable as were those of Le Corbusier.[11]

After the war in 1947, Pius XII isolated the French Communist Party in his encyclical *Mediator dei*, the main goal of which was to promote a more participatory Liturgy. Then, in 1949, he forbade Catholics to join the Communist Party or support communism in any way.[12] Pius XII himself remained pope until 1958, seeing the start of the Cold War era. He was succeeded by John XXIII, the pope who called for a reconciliation with the modern world via the Vatican II Council of 1962-65, so significant for the development of church architecture at that time.

In France

France has been considered a Catholic nation since Clovis I became the first baptised king of Gaul at the end of the fifth century, but its relationship with the Vatican has not always been easy. In the nineteenth century the vast majority of the population was considered Catholic. France's growing Republican movement was the motor of the country's drive towards secularisation. But definitions were complicated: some Republicans were anti-clerical, others were not; some French Catholics supported the imminent separation of the Church and State, while others were Ultramontane.

In French, the term "moderne" originally evolved in the fifteenth century and received particular attention in the seventeenth century during the "quarrel of the Ancients and Moderns", the debate between old and new prevalent in the arts and sciences at that time. It was only in the nineteenth century that the term "modernisme" began to be used.[13] Given the French government's enthusiasm for modernism it banned the anti-modern *Syllabus of Errors* of 1864 which forbade priests to speak about it in church.[14] The French Church as "the eldest daughter of the Church", a nickname it had earned because of its continual Christianisation since the second century, was rebelling. This rebellion would by turns be tolerated and condemned, according to the leanings of the pope in office and his margins for political manoeuvre.

A Concordat established in 1801 between Napoleon and the Vatican stated that the French government would name the country's bishops who would then in turn be approved by Rome. It also decreed that the government paid the wages of the clergy and were responsible for the building and upkeep of churches. This was to change radically with the 1905 French law imposing separation of Church and State, swiftly condemned by Rome in Pope Pius X's encyclical *Vehementer nos* of 1906. The new law effectively and unilaterally brought to an end the Concordat and meant that all religious edifices built before 1905 became property of the government (cathedrals of the State, churches of the municipalities). This meant that the Church was finally free to build when and what it deemed appropriate and necessary without the constraints of the Concordat and a cumbersome and slow state-run administrative machine.[15] The problem that arose was, of course, funding, as the Church had to pay for any new churches that were to be built.

The separation of Church and State had several other important ramifications. The fact that clergy were no longer paid by the government led to a decline in the number of priests. In villages, their pastoral role was often filled by secular school teachers answering to the mayor, not to the bishop – it was around this time that the Church lost control of French schools. As a spin-off to these developments the majority of religious congregations (monks, nuns, friars and so on) were banned from teaching and many were banished from France or forbidden to live together.[16] However, a law allowing for not-for profit organisations known as *associations*, established in 1901, provided a legal framework for the continued existence of French dioceses and other Church organisations, for example monastic communities.

It is a notable phenomenon that a reduction in Rome's power coincided with a renewal of spirituality in France as well as a growth in socially-oriented activism which was to have a strong influence on Le Corbusier.[17] Several of France's high-profile intellectuals and artists converted to Catholicism, among them: Joris-Karl Huysmans, author of *La Cathédrale* (1898), in Le Corbusier's personal library; Paul Claudel (1868-1955), author of *Lettre à Alexandre Cingria sur les causes de la décadence de l'art sacré* (1919) and *L'Annonce faite a Marie* (1911), in Le Corbusier's collection; Jacques Maritain, author of *Art et scholastique* (1920), also owned by Le Corbusier; and Max Jacob, godson of Pablo Picasso, the painter and writer who would later die at the Drancy internment camp because of his Jewish origin and resistance activity. Some of these authors also took an interest in the arcane.[18] Books on Jesus challenged traditionalist views of the Son of God: from Ernest Renan's *Vie de Jésus* of 1893 – also owned by Le Corbusier – to the *Histoire de la recherche sur la vie de Jésus* of 1906 by future Nobel-prize-winning Albert Schweitzer in which modern methodology was introduced and debated.[19] The influential Father Lucien Laberthonnière's writings were condemned by Rome, including the *Annales de philosophie chrétienne* developed under his directorship in 1913.[20] There was also an emerging interest in democracy developing hand in hand with Christianity, exemplified by the Sillon Movement, founded in 1899 and condemned by Pope Pius X in 1910, because of its modernist tendencies and growing overtly political stance.[21]

These Catholics and their works were observed and tracked by the rising international *Intégrists*, ultra-conservatives. Powerful among them, though not strictly Catholic, was the group *L'Action française*, founded in 1905. Modernist, yet openly monarchist and above all nationalist, it was far-right and anti-Semitic in its leanings leading to its condemnation by Pope Pius XI in 1926, resulting in a crisis within conservative Catholicism in France. The Dreyfus Affair of 1894 – in which Captain Alfred Dreyfus, of Jewish origin, was wrongly accused of treason – cannot be forgotten in this context as it resulted in a scandal that called public attention to and fed the growth of anti-Semitism in France.[22] *L'Action française* continued to exist in defiance of the pope, operating outside of the Church.[23]

Shortly after World War I, in which over 5000 mobilised French priests had died, the territory of Alsace-Lorraine (which remained under the Concordat) was returned to France. In 1919 the French president Georges Clemenceau opened the Paris Peace

1.2 – Antoni Gaudí,
Sagrada Familia,
Barcelona, begun in the
1880s and still ongoing

1.3 – Frank Lloyd Wright,
Unity Temple, Oak Park,
Chicago, 1905-1908

1.4 – Otto Wagner,
Sankt Leopold am
Steinhof, Vienna, 1907

Conference to remap a post-war Europe from which the Vatican was excluded (it was only recognised as a sovereign State in 1929). Despite this, in 1920, the French government established an embassy in Vatican City and Pope Benedict XV sent a bishop as nuncio (a papal ambassador) to Paris. In 1924 Pius XI's encyclical *Maximam gravissimam* finally approved the *association* status that has given legal existence to French dioceses as of 1905.[24]

1920 saw both the official birth of the French Communist Party and the rise of the *Action catholique* movement in Italy and France. Left-leaning, it was concerned with spreading humanist and social ideals and was supported by Pope Pius XI.[25] In France several specialised branches developed for industrial workers, agricultural workers, students, maritime populations and for women. Theologians and philosophers were also associated with the movement, for example Emmanuel Mounier, who founded the review *Esprit* in 1932.

Then, in the opinion of Duffy, came "the most exciting Catholic experiment for generations," the Worker Priest movement.[26] This was instigated in World War II by Cardinal Emmanuel Suhard, the archbishop of Paris, who allowed priests to become employees of factories and the docks and live among the working population. The Dominicans were associated with the movement and its aspirations to "re-Christianise" the lost territories of the working class. Many of the priests had overt Communist sympathies causing the pope to condemn the experiment in 1953 and call the Worker Priests back to the Church. They marked their resistance to this declaration by staying on in their jobs defrocked.[27] Le Corbusier himself would assert the redemptive qualities of industry and collective action.

Church Building in France

Nineteenth-century church architecture in France is dominated by historicist styles.[28] The most famous church built in Paris at the end of the century is the neo-romanesque-byzantine style basilica of the Sacré Coeur, or Sacred Heart (1875-1914, consecrated in 1919), which today dominates the city's skyline.

Meanwhile outside France Antoni Gaudí was working on his extraordinarily innovative Sagrada Familia (begun in 1885, Fig. 1.2), Frank Lloyd Wright had built the reinforced concrete Unity Temple in Chicago (1905-1908, Fig. 1.3) and Otto Wagner had built the functionalist Sankt Leopold am Steinhof in Vienna (1907, Fig. 1.4).[29] In Germany, "free form" expressionist churches were designed by Dominikus Böhm – his "christocentric" church plan of 1922 was built as Sankt Engelbert, Riehl, 1930 (Fig. 1.5) – and Otto Bartning with his famous *Sternkirche*, or star church project of 1922 (Fig. 1.6).[30] Nothing of this nature had ever been built in France before the Perret brothers came on the scene.[31]

1.5 – Dominikus Böhm,
Sankt Engelbert, Riehl, 1930

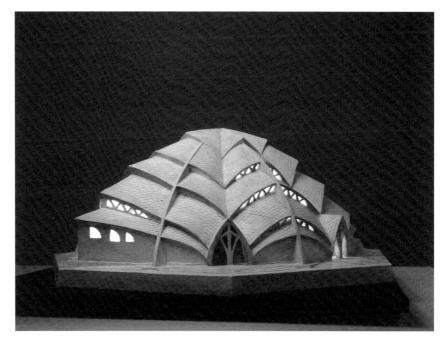

1.6 – Otto Bartning,
Sternkirche, or star church
project, 1922, model

1.7, 1.8 – Auguste and Gustave
Perret, Notre-Dame-de-la-
Consolation du Raincy, 1922-23

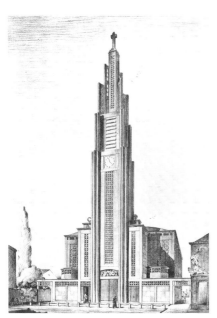

1.9 – Paul Tournon,
church of the Saint Esprit,
Paris, 1928-1935

The Perret Brothers at Raincy

Auguste Perret (1874-1954) and his brother, Gustave Perret (1876-1952), are well known for their innovative use of reinforced concrete. Le Corbusier spent fifteen months working for them in their office in 1908-1909. Their Notre-Dame-de-la-Consolation du Raincy, built in 1922-23 (Fig. 1.7) is described by Peter Collins as "undoubtedly the most revolutionary building constructed in the first quarter of the twentieth century."[32] This one thousand square metre church – essentially a large rectangular box enclosing a single open nave space (Fig. 1.8), its ceiling carried by a series of twenty-eight columns, topped on its main facade by a towering forty-three-metre-high spire – was classified as a historical monument in 1966. At the eastern end the high altar is raised on a choir-platform that crosses the width of the space. Underneath it are the crypt and other parish spaces. Never before had a French church flaunted its concrete structure in such a revolutionary way.[33] Some would complain that an aeroplane hangar, in other words industrial architecture, was an inappropriate building type for a church,[34] while others would argue that *vérité constructive* or *truth in construction* was entirely suitable in this context.[35]

This church is also overtly about light. It boasts walls as grids of concrete, pre-fabricated *claustras* dazzlingly pierced by thousands of pieces of coloured glass, that were designed by painter Maurice Denis (1870-1943), earning it its nickname the "Sainte Chapelle of reinforced concrete". Some windows are figurative, such as one that shows the Virgin Mary on a cloud leading taxis full of soldiers from the Marne to the Ourq in 1914 thus enabling victory in battle. Others are abstract in design. Auguste Perret and Denis had previously collaborated on the Théâtre des Champs-Elysées in Paris (inaugurated in 1913) and on Denis' home and private chapel.[36]

The Raincy church received a substantial amount of good press[37] and was considered a "media success"[38] serving as a model for many other architects doing churches all over the world.[39] The brothers went on to design and build several more churches themselves, but Raincy was the one of which they were most proud.[40]

The Chantiers du Cardinal

Despite its success the Raincy church had very little influence on one of the largest church building programmes ever seen – the *Chantiers du Cardinal* – developed in response to the phenomenal rate of urbanisation that was taking place in France during the nineteenth and twentieth centuries. In the space of the 100 years between 1830 and 1930 the diocese of Paris alone grew in population from seven hundred fifty thousand to over five million. Similarly, between the beginning of World War I and 1931, the size of Paris' suburbs, for the most part places of extreme poverty with no city infrastructure to speak of, doubled from over one million to over two million inhabitants.[41]

In response to this radical expansion Jean-Pierre Verdier, Cardinal and archbishop of the Diocese of the city, set up a massive construction campaign in the Île de France region (that of Paris) in 1931. Verdier was a practical and moral theology professor and a surprise candidate for his new job as he was part of the modern, socially-oriented

Action catholique movement. Officially called *L'Œuvre des nouvelles paroisses de la région parisienne*, but quickly nicknamed the *Chantiers du Cardinal*, its long-term target was to build one church for every ten thousand "souls".[42] One hundred structures were built by 1939, involving over seventy architects, with seventy churches for the suburbs of Paris alone. Several significant exhibition buildings were constructed in its name including the hundredth building, the Pontifical Pavilion made for the historic *Exposition Internationale des Arts et Techniques* world fair of 1937.[43] Over seven million visitors attended.[44] Verdier benefited from his fellow priest Father Pierre Lhande's success of *Le Christ dans la banlieue, enquête sur la vie religieuse dans les milieux ouvriers de la banlieue de Paris (Christ in the Suburbs)*, a series of articles published in the review *Études* and then in book form by Plon in 1926, with thirty five editions produced in just four years. Lhande had also managed to build twenty-seven "emergency chapels", before 1931.[45] Surely the impetus of these initiatives contributed to Cardinal Suhard's decision to support the aforementioned Worker Priest movement in the ensuing decade.

The suburbs were seen as a hotbed of Communism with Maurice Thorez, head of the French Communist Party, presented as a secular saint, "son of the people"[46]. Books such as *Le Christ dans la banlieue* and, later, *France, pays de mission?* of 1943 by two Jesuit priests, Henri Godin and Yvan Daniel (one hundred thousand copies sold in four years), showed concern about the growing Communist population in the ever more "red suburbs" of Paris and about the "de-christianisation" of the country in general.[47] Founded in 1920, it grew partly thanks to its 1925 "extended hand" policy. Although it encouraged Catholics to reconcile their faith with the Party it was perceived as an ever-growing threat to Christianity, culminating in its aforementioned ban by Rome in 1949.[48] Seen in this light the *Chantiers du Cardinal* were a weapon in the Church's fight to keep the population Catholic. It is perhaps unsurprising that funds for the *Chantiers* churches were collected by Parisian personalities, mostly aristocrats, and completed by bank loans. Poster campaigns encouraged financial contributions and giving was promoted as a means to create jobs during a time of social crisis. Verdier's task was to keep the conservative and powerful factions of the Church satisfied while nevertheless trying to employ the new methods of the *Action catholique*.[49] Given the political complexities of the situation it is not surprising that more money was lavished on the churches within the Paris city limits than on their poor relations in the suburbs during his leadership.

Verdier died in 1939. The *Chantiers* came to a standstill during the World War II, but then picked up again, continuing to this day. The *Chantiers* churches' greatest innovation was in terms of materials, especially the frequent, cost-cutting use of reinforced concrete.[50] The vast majority were traditional in their layout, pastiches with little architectural interest, characterised by, in the words of Frédéric Debuyst, "ambient mediocrity".[51] Nevertheless some have since been classified as historical monuments. One of the most noted architects participating in the scheme was Paul Tournon, who built the Saint-Sophia-like church, Saint Esprit in the heart of Paris (1929-36, Fig. 1.9) and Notre-Dame-des-Missions in the Épinay-sur-Seine suburb (1932-33), a remarkable pastiche of Asian architecture, meant to recall important missions taking place at that time (Fig. 1.10).[52]

Few cutting edge artists or architects had any input into the *Chantiers*, perhaps because they had long since distanced themselves from the Church.[53] Father Marie-Alain Couturier, a major figure in our story, wrote, "When Perret, Le Corbusier, Mallet-Stevens will have as many churches to build with the *Chantiers du Cardinal* as Mr. Barbier or Mr. Tartempion, a great part of our task will be done."[54] Robert Mallet-Stevens had designed a project for the Diocese of Paris in 1933, but it was not built.[55] Le Corbusier sketched a church in 1929 for Le Tremblay, in the Île de France region, but then turned down the commission (Fig. 1.11) because he was "persuaded" his innovative proposal would "provoke surprise, protest, violence".[56] The Perrets' sole project for a Paris-city church was a proposal for the 1926 Sainte-Jeanne-d'Arc church competition (including a two-hundred-metre-high spire) which was quickly rejected for reasons which remain unclear, despite their reputation as the most important church builders of the day.[57]

The Liturgical Reform Movement

The Liturgy was of central concern to those who had a stake in trying to make the Church feel relevant to modern times. The first signs of Liturgical Reform began with Pope Pius X who, from 1905 to 1910, made it possible to take communion more frequently and for children to participate in communion; in so doing encouraging family and community involvement. He also reformed the Liturgy itself, especially the use of music, encouraging the use of plainsong and classical polyphony. Further, he reformed the priests' prayer routine, the breviary, to make it simpler and shorter.[58]

The 1920s saw the birth of the Liturgical Reform movement with its vast repercussions for church art, architecture and its interior as well as liturgical spaces all over the world. The Italian-born Romano Guardini (1885–1968) is often cited as its instigator.[59] Guardini's books *Vom Geist der Liturgie*, 1918 (translated into French as *L'Esprit de la Liturgie* and English as *The Spirit of the Liturgy*, both in 1930) and *Von Heiligen Zeichen*, 1922-23 (translated into French as *Les Signes Sacrés* and English as *Sacred Signs*, also both in 1930) were among his most important writings.

Guardini led a Catholic youth centre in Rothenfels am Main, Germany, over the period 1920–39. This was an international gathering place and a breeding ground for a number of important actors in the fields of theology and architecture. Here in 1928, with the help of architect Rudolf Schwarz, Guardini developed a multipurpose space in the former Rittersaal of the castle for celebration of the Mass, meetings, and other gatherings. Modern, sober stools were provided for seating, to be moved around as necessary within an austere space devoid of decoration, the aim being to retrieve the simplicity of the early church (Fig. 1.12). The priest was to celebrate Mass facing the small congregation, gathered around the altar in a horseshoe shape. Here Guardini made liturgical space into something simple and flexible which provided for a greater amount of proximity and participation.

Schwarz's impact on Liturgical Reform is not to be underestimated. With its affinities with the Bauhaus and influenced by Zen, his *Wegkirche*, or path-church, of Corpus Christi, Aachen, 1930, left room for the "invisible" (Fig. 1.13).[60] Schwarz was also an important theoretician. His landmark *Vom Bau der Kirche* was published clandestinely in 1938 and republished in 1947. Mies van der Rohe wrote an eulogistic forword to the English-language edition of 1958 entitled *The Church Incarnate, the Sacred Function of Christian Architecture*.[61] Mies and Schwarz would come to inhabit a very different faction of church architecture to Le Corbusier.

World War II brought church building in war-zone Europe to a near halt. Only clandestine projects were possible, as exemplified by the famous "barn church" at Boust in occupied Lorraine (France), designed by another architect from Guardini's circle, Emil Steffann in 1943 (Fig. 1.14).[62] In 1947 Germany continued to pioneer reform with a highly influential "Guiding Principles for the Design of Churches According to the Spirit of the Roman Liturgy"[63] produced by the German Liturgical Commission,[64] published in French in 1954 and praised by France's own reformers.[65] They also published information and pictures of the Germans' most innovative churches by Schwarz, Steffann, Bartning and the Böhms, father and son.[66] The response from Pope Pius XII, following on from his aforementioned 1947 reform-oriented *Mediator Dei*, was his 1948 Commission for the Reform of the Liturgy.[67]

1.11 – Le Corbusier, church project for Le Tremblay, 1929

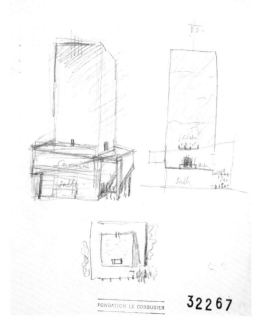

FONDATION LE CORBUSIER   32267

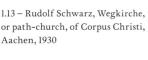

1.13 – Rudolf Schwarz, Wegkirche, or path-church, of Corpus Christi, Aachen, 1930

1.12 – Rudolf Schwarz and Romano Guardini, multipurpose space in the former Rittersaal, Rothenfels am Main, 1928

1.14 – Emil Steffann, "barn church" at Boust in occupied Lorraine, 1943

Ten years later the Vatican II Council in Rome (1962-65) ratified the changes initiated by the Liturgical Reform Movement. Vatican II was presided over by two popes, John XXIII, who had initiated it in 1959, and Paul VI, after his death in 1963. Of utmost importance, Liturgical Reform was the first issue treated by the council, its findings written up in the constitution *On the Sacred Liturgy*. This gave emphasis to the Church as a community and to direct, personal participation in the Eucharist and the Paschal mystery (Christ's crucifixion and resurrection).[68] Such theological and liturgical ideas were expected to be made "readable" via space, light and the positioning of liturgical objects and furnishings – that is, through architecture and interior design.

The altar, symbolic of Christ's sacrifice, was moved out from the wall and made the centre of attention, taking on a new symbolic importance. Behind it, the priest was to face the people (instead of having his back towards the congregation) and include them in the liturgical rites, voiced in the vernacular, the aim being to celebrate the role of the community in the body of Christ. The place and role of the ambo, the pulpit used for reading scripture, was emphasised, giving it new importance. Likewise the tabernacle, the case containing the consecrated host and wine of the Eucharist, was also to be rendered visible and accessible. The baptistery required space around it to allow for communal worship and the place of penance was to be a mix of classic confessional and chapel for reconciliation. These elements constitute a "theology of the assembly" about participation and communication, privileging the person over the object, interiority over exteriority, and the values of hospitality over monumental symbolism.[69]

Three years later the council closed with a message, "To Artists", a bold call for cooperation between artists and the Church, inviting them to rejoin the Church and create works of beauty as they had in the past.[70] This was probably also meant as a *mea culpa* following the sacred art debates of the 1940s and 1950s which, as we shall see, were particularly heated in France, affecting Le Corbusier's own projects in the field. Art in places of worship was to be carefully monitored and the furnishings were to be dignified. The issue of appropriate style was left to place and circumstance since art, and other material things involved in worship, differed from culture to culture. While the veneration of sacred images was maintained, they were not to be given too much importance. Authority in matters of judgement was given to Diocesan committees on sacred art.[71] Sacred furnishings and works of value were to be maintained in good condition by clergy. They were also to be properly educated. At the same time artists trained, so that the quality would be improved, but it was Le Corbusier's mother Marie, who he admired for her "liberty of spirit" and her "individual response to life", who dominated Le Corbusier's education.

The call "To Artists" came too late. It was out of step with the times all over the globe, especially in France. Vatican II had shaken up the Church. In 1967 thousands attended the *International Congress on Religion, Architecture and the Visual Arts* in New York and Montreal. The arts were nearly absent from discussion and churches were discussed as multipurpose spaces meant to blend in with the urban matrix. During the onslaught of the 1968 cultural revolution, art projects for churches, no matter how humble, were considered wasteful; Church money was better spent on social programmes. In France, where most agreed that the majority of churches built during post-war reconstruction were failures, church building did continue, if very humbly. *L'Art sacré* stated in 1968, "Beyond the wave of protest that has hit France after hitting other countries, the construction of churches has these days become questionable in general."[72] From within the Church bishopric hierarchy itself, the question was posed in 1971: should church construction continue?[73]

L'Art sacré

While the Liturgical Reform movement took considerable time to take off in France, major changes were afoot in the field of the liturgical arts. Of great importance to the development of this area was the artist Maurice Denis and his protégé Father Marie-Alain Couturier, instrumental in developing the movement known as *L'Art sacré* which was to be so profoundly influential on Le Corbusier.

Maurice Denis and the *Ateliers d'art sacré*

Rome's anti-modernist stance at the beginning of the century and its hostility towards change posed problems for many artists who struggled to reconcile their religion with their desire to create modern art. Denis, who wanted to make links between Catholicism and modern life, is a prime example. In 1889, when not yet twenty years old, he painted his seminal *Mystère catholique* (Fig. 1.15), a small picture showing an Annunciation scene in a modern salon (his own living room). Another example is the Virgin leading the convoy of taxis depicted in the window of Raincy, described above. Denis, one of the leading members of the avant-garde *Nabis* group, was one of the main protagonists of modern sacred art in France at the beginning of the century.[74] Oddly enough he appears to have been totally ignorant of the pioneering work going on in other countries, for example that of architects Rudolf Schwarz and Emil Steffann in Germany, or Hermann Baur and Fritz Metzger in Switzerland.[75] This is testimony to the somewhat hermetic situation in France which took its cues very largely from Rome.

In 1919, with fellow painter Georges Desvallières, Denis co-founded the *Ateliers d'art sacré* which were to become the most well-known of the many artistic groups that were concerned with promoting modern-style art and architecture for churches at that time. The theological and theoretical groundings for the multi-disciplinary workshop-cum-school based in Paris was neo-Thomism, especially Saint Thomas' theories on beauty and art. Simultaneously here was a revival of interest in medieval aesthetics and workshop-style practice. Neo-Thomism is the renewed interest in the philo-sophical and theological work of Dominican priest Saint Thomas Aquinas (1225–74), one of the foundation Doctors of the Church, considered one of the major thinkers of Christianity and, more generally, of Western philosophy. Since Leo XIII each pope has reiterated Thomas' importance, culminating with Paul VI and the Vatican II Council. The Council gave credence to Thomas in the 1965 decree *Optatam Totius* (*On Priestly Formation*).[76] In the same year at the Sixth International Thomistic Congress, the pope declared Saint Thomas the most important of all the Doctors of the Church.[77] Known as a Scholastic philosopher, his views on ethics, the nature and role of God, humanity and the cosmos have had a considerable impact on Western civilisation, including architects such as Mies van der Rohe and indeed Le Corbusier.[78]

Also influential on the *Ateliers d'art sacré* was theologian Jacques Maritain's *Art et scholastique* (*Art and Scholasticism*) of 1920. Indeed it formed its main intellectual framework, as did several publications by Denis on sacred, modern art and the history of religious painting.[79] There were also connections with the arcane, notably Rosicrucianism.[80] The best known student to emerge from the *Ateliers* was Couturier who helped Denis paint the Raincy windows and went on to work as an artist in his own right.[81]

The *Ateliers d'art sacré* was only one of several sacred art groups formed at the time, each with its specificities.[82] An example is the small but influential Thomist group

L'Arche including the internationally known architect and Benedictine monk Dom Bellot. Members of these groups, with the *Ateliers* at the lead, completed various commissions for churches in and around Paris – some even for *Chantiers du Cardinal* (notably for the aforementioned Saint Esprit church) – and elsewhere in France. Denis remained hopeful that these churches, largely "with no soul", could be "spiritualised", and thus saved, by the artwork commissioned for them.[83] It was rare for modern art, or at least modern-style art, to enter churches in France. Little by little the work of the *Ateliers* began to resemble the kind of tasteless work that it was originally designed to combat. This "Saint Sulpice art", named after the neighbourhood of the Parisian church where kitsch, manufactured, industrially-produced "art" could be purchased, was an object for revulsion in the Catholic intellectual community. (Fig. 1.16)[84]

The *Ateliers* closed in 1948, five years after Denis' death in a car accident. Despite the fact that much of the work was mediocre[85] they played a crucial role in the development of the liturgical arts, for they enabled the next step to be possible – the great commissions granted by, obtained with the influence of, or supported by Couturier.

Father Marie-Alain Couturier and the Journal *L'Art sacré*

Pierre Couturier was born in 1897 in Montbrison, France. As a young soldier wounded in World War I he quickly demobilised and went to Paris to study art at the Grande Chaumière before joining Denis' *Ateliers* in 1919. His transformation into the Dominican monk, Father Marie-Alain, in 1925, did little to stop the advance of his artistic career.

Before the war in 1937, Couturier became director of the review *L'Art sacré* with fellow Dominican Father Pie-Raymond Régamey.[86] Régamey was an art historian trained by the École du Louvre who had worked at the Louvre as a curator. As a Dominican Régamey defended the inclusion of contemporary art – especially abstract art – in churches and was engaged in Liturgical Reform. Couturier, the more charismatic of the two, befriended the great artists of the day and managed to convince many of them to create work for the Church – "We believed that it was our duty to procure for God and our faith the best art of the present."[87] They were complementary in many ways, leading the review together until Couturier's death in 1954.[88] Under their direction *L'Art sacré* became the well-known mouth-piece for defending modern art and modern liturgy for churches from within the Church itself (Fig. 1.17).

Couturier's own stance against mediocre art grew as his ties with artists "outside the fold" became stronger. Time spent in the USA and Canada during the war years reinforced this view. There he came into contact with artists and intellectuals such as Fernand Léger, Salvador Dalí, André Breton, Marc Chagall, also Jacques Maritain, art historian Henri Focillon, scientist Henri Laugier (who later became the United Nations' Assistant Secretary-General and participated in writing the Universal Declaration of Human Rights) as well as others. It was during this period that Couturier opened up

1.15 – Maurice Denis, *Mystère catholique*, 1889

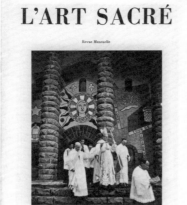

1.16 – Cover of *L'Art sacré*, issue 9-10, May-June 1951, "Les marchands et le Temple", featuring Saint Sulpice art

1.17 – Typical Spartan cover of *L'Art sacré,* issue 9-10, May-June 1952, "Bilan d'une querelle"

to abstract art.[89] His objective became the defence of freedom – indeed, his writings of this post-war period are gathered under the title *Se garder libre* (*Staying Free*).[90] Freedom, a politically loaded term, seems in this case to mean freedom to achieve salvation. As Antoine Lion has also surmised, "Supporting *la France libre* and pushing for contemporary art, for him these were the same inspiration."[91] This emancipatory tendency would receive expression in Le Corbusier's architecture.

In *Art et scholastique* Maritain had already encouraged Christian artists not to make "Christian art", but to "be Christian" and just make good contemporary art. Couturier took this one step further by declaring that because the (so-called) Christian artists of the day were not good enough to make great art for churches, the Church had the duty to call on (so-called) secular artists to create great works. Only in this way could Christian art be revitalised.[92] Couturier called this his "bet on genius", claiming after Saint Augustine that those who often appeared to be within the Church were actually without and vice versa.[93]

Couturier was perceived as problematic by conservatives in the Church hierarchy. He was perfectly comfortable working with artists such as Pablo Picasso, who had a strong interest in the arcane – see for example his mural project *War and Peace* done for the town of Vallauris in the 1950s.[94] Picasso himself was the target of the influential Paul Cardinal Scortesco's text *Saint Picasso, peignez pour nous, ou les deux conformismes* (*Saint Picasso, Paint for Us, or the Two Conformities*, 1953), which was clearly antimodern.[95] His work lends itself to more esoteric readings about discord and harmony in the universe, by turns readable as Christian and pagan.

Couturier's understanding of artists' psychology was that they were on a path towards the divine, by making, not believing, ideas echoed by both Matisse and Le Corbusier.[96] Further Couturier believed that being surrounded by mediocre art would have negative psychological consequences on the clergy and church-goers, pointing out that unbelievers could not understand why Christians put up with such bad art in their churches.[97] We regret that we can only touch upon issues of taste, what Pierre Bourdieu would call "distinction", in church art and architecture as it is an area ripe for exploration.[98]

Notre-Dame-de-Toute-Grâce Assy and the Debate on Sacred Art

Despite the difficulties of being a moderniser in the Church, Couturier remained hopeful. "I believe in miracles," he stated.[99] This sense of hope drove him to solicit a handful of the era's most well-known artists to complete the decoration of Notre-Dame-de-Toute-Grâce on the Assy Plateau in the French Alps, near Mont Blanc (Fig. 1.18). Couturier had begun to oversee the work with Canon Jean Devémy in 1939, but progress was interrupted by the war. Built during the period 1938 to 1946 by the architect Maurice Novarina (1907-2002), it was designed for sanatorium patients in a vernacular chalet style. Its artistic programme was impressive, including work by Fernand Léger, Georges Rouault, Jean Bazaine, Jean Lurçat, Germaine Richier (Fig. 1.19), Henri Matisse, Georges Braque, Pierre Bonnard, Marc Chagall and Jacques Lipchitz, along with a handful of other lesser-known artists from the sacred art circles. The church was blessed by Pope Pius XII in 1946 and was consecrated on August 4, 1950. Considered a sensation, it received much media attention from even the popular international press, featuring, for example, in *Life* magazine in the US in 1950.[100]

While the choices Devémy and Couturier made were "organic", in that they developed over time in response to their work with artists, some were also very strategic. The inclusion of the communist artists Léger and Lurçat in the Assy line up implied toleration of the French Communist Party (condemned by Rome). It also implied support of the Worker Priest movement, still under way. The inclusion of the eminent Jewish artists Chagall and Lipchitz could be read as a modest gesture of reconciliation between the Catholic Church of France and its Jewish population in the aftermath of the Holocaust. Though establishing a detente was not the only motivation for their inclusion, it was certainly important symbolically.[101] It should not be forgotten that Christians and communists found themselves fighting as allies in the Resistance, something which may have contributed to Lurçat's participation, for example.[102]

The Chapel of the Rosary in Vence

One of the greatest achievements of Couturier's career is the Chapel of the Rosary at Vence. Matisse spent several of his final years making what is considered by many, including the artist himself, to be his masterpiece. The tiny *Chapelle du Rosaire,* designed for the Dominican sisters in Vence, just inland of the Riviera, was consecrated on June 25, 1951 (Fig. 1.20). The Rosaire, or Rosary, refers to the prayer beads used in Marian devotion and so points to an edifice dedicated to Mary in the hands of Dominicans. The artist's personal history was at the core of this endeavour. The invitation to make the chapel stemmed from the Dominican Sister Jacques-Marie formally Monique Bourgeois (1921–2005) who, as his nurse and model during the war, had gained the painter's fraternal affection. As a Dominican she was sent to live in Vence, coincidentally across the street from Matisse's famous Villa Rosa. There she convinced him to design the chapel and then accompanied him in its making, along with Dominican Brother Louis-Bertrand Rayssiguier – heavily influenced himself by Le Corbusier[103] – and another friend of Matisse, Couturier.[104]

It was Couturier's suggestion to bring Le Corbusier into the project, but Matisse preferred to work with his old friend Perret who commented on the drawings that had already been produced but did little else that was satisfactory.[105] Despite this Perret's name figured on all the chapel's documents as the supervising architect. But Couturier's input was real and sustained. He gave support to Sister Jacques-Marie and Brother Louis-Bertrand who, as Antoine Lion has pointed out, were both only in their twenties when they ran the project on site.[106]

1.18 – Maurice Novarina,
Notre-Dame-de-Toute-Grâce,
Assy, 1937-1946

1.19 – Notre-Dame-de-Toute-
Grâce, Assy, featuring Germaine
Richier's controversial Crucifix
at the main altar

1.20 – Henri Matisse,
Chapelle du Rosaire, Vence,
consecrated 1951, exterior

The small white rectangular box of the chapel with its terracotta-tiled roof is pierced on two sides by tall thin windows. Matisse designed everything for it, including its windows, liturgical furniture and vestments, the altar, crucifix and other details. Some details are "oriental" (North African) in their aesthetics, for example the forged metal cross with its golden crescent moons on the roof of the chapel – also readable as a sign of Mary. The stained glass, featuring Mediterranean plant motifs, brings in colourful light that fills the otherwise white interior. Monumental drawings, painted in black directly onto shiny white ceramic tiles dominate. In the nave, one shows a *Virgin and Child*. The figures are faceless, leaving it to the imagination of the visitor to provide their own.[107] On the nave's back wall is a highly innovative *Stations of the Cross*, told in one sequential picture. Behind the altar looms the silhouette of *Saint Dominic*. As with the *Saint Dominic* Matisse drew at the same time for the Assy church, Father Couturier served as the model (Fig. 1.21). Unlike Assy, which is crypt-like in atmosphere, Vence is light-filled and bright, airy and uplifting, simple and elegant.

The Scandal of *L'Art sacré*

In 1951, the debate over the role of modern artists in Church art commissions came to a head with an incident provoked by a small but powerful group of arch-conservative *Intégrists* who opposed, among other things considered morally deviant, the participation of modern artists in the decoration of churches. Their *On ne se moque pas de Dieu !* (*Let God Not Be Mocked!*), the so-called Tract of Angers, was distributed on January 4, 1951 when Devémy lectured on the subject of Assy in Angers, France – they also jeered him during his presentation. It particularly condemned Richier's *Crucifix*, which stood behind the main altar in the church, on aesthetic grounds – this organic Christ looking almost like a branch or a twig[108] was too distorted, pained, and "existential" for the group who in 1951, succeeded in causing its removal (only to be restored twenty years later).[109]

The Vatican was also quick to make known, albeit in somewhat shrouded terms, its own reservations.[110] On June 10, 1951, Celso Constantini (1876-1958), its dominant spokesman on the subject of art, published the article "Dell'Arte sacra deformatrice" ("Some Disfiguring Sacred Art") on the first page of the Vatican's newspaper, the *Osservatore Romano*. Assy was his prime target.[111] One year later, in June 1952, the Vatican issued *On Sacred Art*.[112] This instruction acted as a reminder of Pius XI's and Pius XII's disapproval. Couturier simultaneously reprinted the Tract of Angers with a defence of Richier's *Crucifix* in the May-June issue of *L'Art sacré*.[113] Régamey shot back via his own *L'Art sacré au XXe siècle ?* (*Sacred Art in the Twentieth Century ?*) with its significant question mark – was it even possible for sacred art to continue?[114] This heightened Rome's suspicion of the Dominicans in Paris, including Couturier and Régamey who were already under scrutiny. Couturier came close to excommunication while Régamey, after Couturier's death in 1954, left the journal and devoted himself mostly to his purely theological writings.

1.21 – Henri Matisse,
Chapelle du Rosaire,
Vence, consecrated
1951, interior
featuring altar,
windows and Saint
Dominic (Father
Couturier)

Summary

The picture here is of the Vatican struggling to maintain authority in the face of
radical societal, technological and artistic change. Architectural historians have
had a tendency to carelessly lump the Catholic Church into a one-dimensional and
monolithic entity. One thing that this chapter has made very clear is the importance of
recognising the fact that the Catholic Church was a cluster of groups, some with very
divergent and unruly political leanings.

For the Dominicans of *L'Art sacré* there was a move away from excessive unwarranted
decoration towards simplicity and a renewed concern for light as a carrier of meaning.
Truth to materials, as it emerged in the work of nineteenth century architects such as
Eugène Emmanuel Viollet-le-Duc was a moral business. To criticise existing church
production for its dishonesty in this area was to criticise the Catholic Church itself and
to undermine its traditional authority as an arbiter of taste and culture. The debate
was, of course, steeped in politics – the more conservative desire to maintain existing
power structures and building types pitted against a more pared down, industrial
church for the people. The modernist agenda was undeniably an ecumenical one.
At the same time the call for greater connection with other religions was a direct
response to world unrest, for example, Assy with its inclusion of Jewish artists and
Vence with its "oriental", or Islamic undertones. The recent construction of the
Grande mosquée, built in the heart of Paris in the wake of World War I by the French
government as a thanks and recognition to the North African forces in combat should
be remembered here. This then is the religious context of Le Corbusier's church
architecture, one in which the sacred was deeply political.

LE CORBUSIER AND RELIGION

Devoting yourself to architecture is like entering a religious order.
You must consecrate yourself, have faith and give.
Le Corbusier

Anxiety about the chaos brought about by modern life was to have a strong impact on Le Corbusier. Infected by debates within the Church and by the general dissatisfaction with organised religion that was prevalent at that time he was quick to reject the Protestantism of his birth, spending the rest of his life looking for a form of belief inclusive enough to encompass his vision of how to live, *savoir habiter*[1].

> Knowing how to live is the fundamental question before modern society, everywhere, in the whole world. An ingenuous question and one that could be considered childish. How to live? Do you know reader? Do you know how to live soundly, strongly, gaily, free of the hundred stupidities established by habit, custom and urban disorganization?[2]

This chapter charts the evolution of Le Corbusier's thinking on religion from his upbringing in La Chaux-de-Fonds, through the spiritual hothouse that was Paris in the early twentieth century, to maturity, Orphism and the roots of world religion. As Edward A. Sovik, writes "one can discover in this architecture ... a most intense commitment to a series of ideas which can hardly be thought of except in terms of religion."[3]

Upbringing

Born in 1887 in La Chaux-de-Fonds in the Swiss Jura the young Le Corbusier, then Charles Édouard Jeanneret, was well versed in the Bible. He and his family went to the local Independent Protestant church regularly where, at the age of sixteen, he received six weeks of formal religious instruction.[4] His aunt Pauline contributed to his education in this area, but it was Le Corbusier's mother Marie who he admired for her "liberty of spirit" and her "individual response" to life who dominated Le Corbusier's education, remaining a constant source of inspiration.[5] His memories of this period – mythologised in *My Work* – are of learning strange family words, chivalric or Provençal in origin, of his supposed ancestral links to the Albigensian Cathars, a Manichaen heretical sect prevalent in the Languedoc area of France during the twelfth and thirteenth centuries, and of his introduction to the work of François Rabelais. His challenge was to resolve this heady introduction to the arcane with the formal religious teaching that he received at school and the quasi religious appreciation of nature instilled in him on walks through the mountains with his father.[6]

It was noted in the last chapter that Le Corbusier collected certain key books written at the end of the nineteenth and beginning of the twentieth centuries marking a revival of interest in religion in France following the Separation of Church and State.[7] He also owned some important texts that tried to resolve Christianity, science and the arcane. Of particular note are Henri Provensal's *L'Art de demain* and Edouard Schuré's *Les Grands Initiés*, given to him by his teacher Charles l'Eplattenier.[8] Subtitled *Esquisse de l'histoire secrète des religions,* in it the lives of a number of great spiritual leaders are recorded in turn: Rama, Krishna, Hermes, Moses, Orpheus, Pythagoras, Plato and Jesus. Of particular note is a lengthy description by Schuré of an initiation into the mysteries of Orpheus through the knowledge of Hermes Tresmigistus, the father of hermetic thought.

> Now you have heard, said the hierophant, what old Hermes saw in his vision and what his successors have handed down to us. The words of the wise are like the seven notes of the lyre containing all music, with the rhythms and laws of the universe. (...) The eternal numbers and the magical signs that open up to the secrets are contained in this vision. The more you meditate on it and learn to understand there, the more it will grow in your mind ... You must now take command yourself and choose the path you want to follow in order to reach the pure spirit. From now on you are among the resurrected. Remember that there are two keys that give access to all knowledge. The first is this: human beings are mortal gods, and the Gods are immortal human beings. Happy is the one who understands these words. [9]

Schuré's book made a great impression on the young Jeanneret who wrote to his parents in January 1908:

> I have just finished reading *Les Grands Initiés* a fortnight ago ... This Schuré has opened horizons to me which have filled me with happiness. I foresaw

this – no, that's going too far. More accurately I struggled between, on the one hand, rationalism, strongly imbued in me by an active real life and the little bits of science which I picked up at school and on the other hand, the innate, intuitive idea of a supreme being, which is revealed to me at every step by a contemplation of nature. This struggle prepared the ground to receive that noble harvest with which this 600 page book is full. I am now more at ease, I am happier although I have no solution and hope one day to glimpse it so that I can throw myself into resolving it.[10]

"Resolving" this "noble harvest" was to become his life's quest. It was the task of the "prophet ... who, in the crises of the times, knows how to see events, knows how to read them." One of the less attractive aspects of Le Corbusier's character – his Messianic pretensions – will emerge from time to time in this book.

Paris Milieu

Unable to accept a life free from religion, many of the artists and writers of the Parisian avant-garde, freshly liberated from the rigid Catholicism in which they were raised – the Separation of Church and State must have played a significant role in this – sought to revitalise religion through an exploration of its roots. Jeanneret, the young Le Corbusier, first went to Paris in 1908, spending sixteen months working for the Perret brothers. Much has been made of the knowledge that he would have gained in the office on the technology of reinforced concrete, but little has been made of the fact that Auguste Perret was at the very epicenter of the re-evaluation of religion that was going on at that time. Le Corbusier eventually made the city his home in 1917. In doing so he joined a milieu in which the esoteric ideas instilled within him by his family and education would flourish.

It should be noted that the Theosophical writings of Helena Blatavatsky began to gain currency amongst artists and modernist architects at around this time, particularly in Holland. Parallels can be drawn between theosophical ideas on space and colour and those of Le Corbusier.[11] One strand of the group was organised by Annie Besant who followed the writings of J. Krishnamurti, Buddhism and Eastern religion. Le Corbusier owned one of Krishnamurti's books, but he does not appear to have been a major influence. Le Corbusier was drawn instead to a form of belief classical in origin.

It was at this point that Jeanneret made contact with the poet Guillaume Apollinaire who was to play an important role in his development. He was a great admirer of Apollinaire – indeed *L'Esprit nouveau*, the title of the journal that he set up in the 1920s with Amedée Ozenfant and Paul Dermée, took its title from Apollinaire's lecture "L'Esprit nouveau et les poètes" of 1917.[12] The subject matter of their journal, conceived "to open paths toward that laughing, clear and beautiful sky,"[13] was extremely diverse, ranging across from biology, astronomy, physics and medicine to psychoanalysis, sexuality, history, literature, art and town planning. It clearly represents an attempt to find commonality across a range of fields, some unifying certitude in an increasingly complex world, the task of the "poet" being to establish relationships and show "the new truth".[14]

Apollinaire was very knowledgeable about religion. He slipped comfortably between one sort and another, combining Christian symbolism with that of alchemy and other Orphic forms of spirituality. He played games of association around the traditional Catholic figure of Mary whose name he intertwined with that of his lover Marie Laurencin, just as Le Corbusier was to do with his mother Marie. Apollinaire likened Laurencin to an alchemical alembic. Her body was a place of transformation, the idea being that through contact with this woman he was able to bring his own creative talents to fruition.[15] Most importantly for this book Apollinaire was the instigator of the art movement Orphism, in many ways a form of religion.[16] The Orphist artists, who included amongst their number Le Corbusier's good friend Fernand Léger, wanted to achieve a similar state of harmony through painting, using colour and mathematical form to affect the emotions.

Orphism

Le Corbusier's historical interests were diverse – the Ancient Egyptians, Classical mythology, Gnosticism, Kabbalism, Alchemy, Catharism, Troubadours, neo-Platonism (particularly the work of Pico della Mirandola), the Masons and Rosicrucianism receive repeated mention in his writings.[17] All these areas of concern have shared roots in Pythagoras and the cult of Orpheus. Orphism is a word explicitly used in the La Sainte Baume correspondence to be discussed in the next chapter. We use it here as a useful term to encapsulate a series of concerns that are absolutely central to the evolution of Le Corbusier's thinking on religion: harmony, unity, mathematics and love.

Orpheus was said to be the prophet of a particular type of mystery-religion, traceable back to the sixth century before Christ. W.K.C. Guthrie, a contemporary of Le Corbusier's described it as "a modification of the mysteries of Dionysos"[18] and a "species of the Bacchic".[19] Dionysos, who appeared to his followers in the guise of a bull[20] was, according to the scholar, worshipped under many names including Pan and Apollo.[21] There are frequent allusions to Orphic rites in the writings of the Graeco-Roman period, for example in the work of Plato and also in the work of the Neoplatonists.[22] Orpheus was regarded not as a god, but as a hero, someone with certain superhuman powers, but who lived an ordinary span of life.[23] The son of a Muse, he was identified with the god Apollo who also played the lyre.[24] He is for this reason connected to music and mathematical harmony. The legend tells that when Orpheus' wife Euridice died his mourning music was so beautiful that the gods took pity on him and gave him the power to travel from the light into the dark Underworld to bring her back.[25] His sojourn into the land of death meant that he had unique knowledge of the secrets of Hades and could tell his followers, via initiation, of the best way to prepare for the Afterlife, for the Orphics a cyclical journey of reincarnation culminating in Unity with the higher soul.[26] This process has already been mentioned in the discussion of Edouard Schuré's *Les Grands Initiés* above. The Orphics were highly syncretic in their approach to religion; they were prepared to see all religions as manifestations of one and the same thing.[27] Having been so influential in ancient times, Orphism could be linked to the history of a number of world religions hence, in part, its attraction for Le Corbusier.

Like the Orphics the Pythagoreans, who founded a religious order at Croton in the late sixth century B.C., were ascetic in their approach to life and looked upon Apollo as a figure of veneration.[28] Pythagoras took it upon himself to discover a way to express his essentially Orphic view of the cosmos rationally by means of mathematics and numerical rations.[29] This idea appears to have held strong appeal for Le Corbusier and may have been the root of his investigations into the Modulor, his own system of proportion.

The Modulor had three principal aims: the first practical – to facilitate standardisation through modular manufacturing and building practices; the second aesthetic – linking to well-known standards of beauty such as the Golden Section, and the third more spiritual – to link people and the environment together within a radiant web of number. The principles behind it are set out in cryptic terms in Le Corbusier's books *Modulor* and *Modulor 2* in which he acknowledged his debt to Pythagoras.[30] It seems more than likely that the architect was influenced by his belief that the contemplation of harmony and order in the universe would encourage the development of harmony and order within the soul.[31]

For Plato (c. 427–347 B.C.), strongly influenced by Pythagoras, "Temperance" in all things was the source of "happiness and harmony" making "us friends with the gods" and "with one another".[32] Harmonious balance, a central concern of Le Corbusier, receives expression here. Building on the ideas of Plato, Le Corbusier believed that the primary means to influence thought was by influencing the body at a subconscious level,[33] the "joys of the body" being "interdependent to intellectual sensations."[34] In this way the "emotion leading to action" could then be felt in "our inner depths, before even the formulation of a theory."[35] Such ideas can be further explored through reading the work of the unorthodox French art historian Elie Faure (1873-1937), a strong influence on Le Corbusier.[36] The relationship between body and spirit, often symbolised through darkness and light, is a key theme in Le Corbusier's work.

This leads to another important Orphic concept of fundamental importance to Le Corbusier and indeed Apollinaire's world view – the ideal of the mystical androgyne. In the *Symposium* Plato gives an account of the original three sexes, "man, woman, and the union of the two – the man was originally the child of the sun, the woman of the earth, and the man-woman of the moon, which is made up of sun and earth."[37] So powerful did this race become that it incurred the wrath of Zeus who, in revenge, divided each sex from its other meaning that humankind was destined to spend its life in the pursuit of its other half. When they find each other, "the pair are lost in an amazement of love and friendship and intimacy."[38] For Plato this "desire and pursuit of the whole is called love". The alchemists were to represent it geometrically in terms of the "squaring of the circle", a version of the union of opposites, making an important connection here between mathematics and love (Fig. 2.1).[39] What Julia Fagan-King has called this "Orphic fusion of male and female", was popular in early twentieth century Paris (Fig. 2.2).[40]

Pico della Mirandola (1463-1494) was one of a group of Neoplatonists who revitalised the Kabbala, an ancient form of Jewish theosophy, that went through a rebirth in thirteenth century Provence at the same time that Catharism and philosophical pantheism were being violently attacked by the Church.[41] He too was also a strong influence on Le Corbusier.

2.1 – Squaring of the circle in alchemy from Michael Maier's 1618 *Atalanta fugiens*

2.2 – Fusion of male and female from Le Corbusier's *Le poème de l'angle droit*

According to Pico's syncretic view the Kabbala formed the link between a number of aspects of antique occult thought – Platonism, Neoplatonism, Hermeticism, Orphism. His vision, like that of Le Corbusier, was strongly dualistic and governed by number. The soul before it entered the world was male and female united in one being. When it descended to earth the two parts separated and animated different bodies. If a person lived well they would be lucky enough to meet the other half of their soul.[42] If a person used their life badly their soul, as in Orphism, would return to earth so that he or she could make amends. One day all souls would be united with the highest soul and there would be no more sin, temptation and suffering.[43] It is here that we find clear expression of the doctrine of unity and balance that was to become so central to Le Corbusier's work and belief. It is not surprising therefore that Le Corbusier wrote of Pico:

> The modern age has carved up physics, chemistry, medicine, the army, mechanics, and even education into categories proportionate to the vastness of the human brain, to the availabilities of [certain kinds of] education. Pico della Mirandola is, as his name implies a miraculandolous, exceptional individual summit ... If there is somewhere and someday, some Pico della Mirandola arising on the horizon, he will appear (mirandoling mirandolesque) with his biceps and his head and that's all right! Schools are not turning them out, that's precisely today's great equivocation.[44]

He admired Pico for his ability to bring elements from a number of different religions and philosophies into a unified whole, utilising both his "biceps and his head", his body and spirit to do so.

Orphism thus encapsulated a series of concerns that appears repeatedly in the work of Le Corbusier. Many of these revolve around dualities – a harmonious balance of dark and light, body and spirit, woman and man – connected with the play of number, geometry and music.

Orphic Themes in *Le poème de l'angle droit*

The best representation of these concerns in the work of Le Corbusier is contained within *Le poème de l'angle droit* written between 1947 and 1953 (Fig. 2.3). A combination of paintings and text, Le Corbusier arranged its key, or contents page, into what he called an iconostasis, a sequence of panels in the form of a tree (Fig. 2.4). In *Journey to the East* he wrote of an "intoxicating" iconostasis that he had seen in a church that "shone twenty-nine icons from their golden heavens and the halos of their saints."[45] Traditionally in Eastern churches the iconostasis was a screen separating nave from sanctuary, supporting the icons of Christ, Mary and the saints; Le Corbusier's own version appears to allude to his relationship with his wife Yvonne. The exact meaning of this "pact of solidarity" with nature remains very obscure although it has been subjected to much scrutiny from Mogens Krustup and others.[46]

We do know that the eponymous right angle is loaded with meaning by Le Corbusier. "The vertical gives the meaning of the horizontal. One is alive because of the other. Such are the powers of synthesis," wrote Le Corbusier.[47] The horizontal represented earthly concerns whilst the vertical represented the spiritual.[48] The "right angle" thus symbolised the relationship of spirit and matter, central to the Orphic vision of reincarnation. It may be for this reason that in the last square of the iconostasis – that entitled "Tool" – in which a hand draws a right angle in charcoal, the vertical line dominates over the horizontal. Le Corbusier would in this way be emphasising the importance of the journey up to the higher soul or unity.

Number Symbolism

Pythagorean number symbolism was a subject of some debate in Paris in the early twentieth century. It is our suggestion that Le Corbusier uses it in the structure of *Le poème de l'angle droit*. Louis Réau, a contemporary of Le Corbusier, wrote – with reference to the numerological laws of the medieval cathedral builders (themselves derived from those of Pythagoras) – that seven was a number which was "particularly august".[49] It could be obtained by adding three, symbolic of the Trinity, and four, symbolic of earthly concerns (such as the seasons and the elements). Thus it was expressive of the relationship between the earth and sky, body and spirit, in Corbusian terms the right angle. Émile Mâle, "iconographical consultant" on the scheme for La Sainte Baume wrote:

> The number seven, regarded by the fathers as mysterious above all others, intoxicated the mediaeval mystic. It was observed first of all that seven – composed of four, the number of the body, and of three, the number of the soul – is pre-eminently the number of humanity, and expresses the union of man's double nature. (...) The number seven thus expresses the harmony of man's nature, but it also expresses the harmonious relation of man to the universe. The seven planets govern human destiny, for each of the seven ages is under the influence of one of them. Thus seven invisible threads connect man with the scheme of the universe.[50]

The number seven in this way represented the order of the universe and the union of body and spirit, in other words, Orphic harmony. For Matila Ghyka, a strong influence on Le Corbusier, "in Pythagorean Number-Mystic, seven was the Virgin-Number," linking it to Mary.[51] It therefore seems more than coincidental that the poem has seven layers.

At the top of the tree of the iconostasis there are five squares devoted to "Milieu" corresponding to the five squares on the third level down, which are devoted to the theme of "Flesh". "Milieu" is a complex word expressive of nature in its raw, original sense, humming with life and number. "Environment" is not an adequate translation of this term. Both "Milieu" and "Flesh" have five squares. According to Réau, in Christian art, the number five corresponded to the five senses.[52] This would seem to be appropriate if Le Corbusier was trying to emphasise the links between these layers

2.3 – Cover of Le Corbusier's
Le poème de l'angle droit

2.4 – Iconostasis of Le Corbusier's
Le poème de l'angle droit

and the body. The layer in between "Milieu" and "Flesh" which is devoted to "Spirit" has three squares corresponding, as Réau would have it, to the Trinity. Mathematics, the "spark stolen from the flame the Gods nourished to make the world play," is celebrated here.[53] The top three layers of the poem are thus devoted numerically to this most central concern of Orphism, the relationship of spirit and matter.

The sections devoted specifically to the cause of unity, "Fusion", an image of the alchemical union of opposites (Fig. 2.2), "Offering", an image of Le Corbusier's Open Hand, symbolic of the giving and receiving of love, and "Tool" into which the whole poem is summarised, are each given one square. According to Réau the number one was, for the mediaeval builders, symbolic of unity and of God.[54] By giving each of these layers just one square Le Corbusier gave emphasis to their importance. Thus, through the use of Pythagorean number symbolism, the architect used the structure of the iconostasis to reinforce its message.

Balancing Darkness and Light

Le Corbusier made connections between mathematics, rhythm, the tides and the diurnal movement of the sun. It may be for this reason that the first top left square of the iconostasis is a rendition of his recurring symbol of the 24 hour day, an image of the line made by the sun as it tracks above and below the horizon (Fig. 2.5). This was to be an object of meditation for those "whose mission it is to see clearly and to lead," holding within it the key to "habitation", *savoir habiter*. He wrote: "knowing how to live! How to use the blessings of God; the sun and the spirit that He has given to men to enable them to achieve the joy of living on earth and to find again the Lost Paradise."[55] A similar image occupies a full page spread in Section A1 of "Milieu". It is accompanied by these words:

> Continuity
> is his but he
> imposes an alternative –
> night and day – these two phases
> rule our destiny: a sun rises
> a sun sets
> a sun rises anew [56]

For Pico the sun is our "Father and leader".[57] For Le Corbusier he is our "master".[58] Apollo, Dionysos and the son, Christ – at once man and God – are all intertwined.

The Union of Opposites

The culmination of love, the union of "Spirit" and "Flesh", produces "Fusion", which occurs on the fourth layer down of *Le poéme de l'angle droit* (Fig. 2.2). It occupies just one square and is divided horizontally into two zones, the world of the spirit above and the world of the body below, an image of sexual union based on Le Corbusier's reworking of alchemical texts.[59]

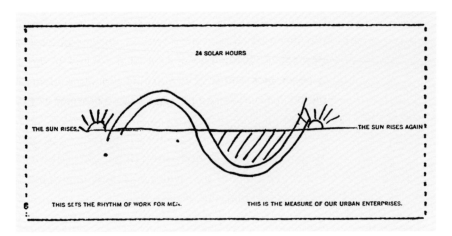

2.5 – Le Corbusier's
symbol of the 24
hour day

2.6 – Siren from
Le Corbusier's *Sketch-books Volume 3,
1954-1957*, sketch 257

Not only is the "Fusion" section a celebration of the union of man with woman,
it is also a celebration of the union of the soul with the body. Above the horizon
is Le Corbusier's winged siren, a symbol of the soul separated from the body.[60]
Plato wrote of the "soul which is ever longing after the whole of things both divine and
human;" in this image the siren is head down, her horn, a phallic element penetrating
the image of the two lovers.[61] The siren inhabits both the celestial and the earthy
sides of life; in doing so she links the lovers with the divine. It seems very strange that
Le Corbusier should portray the siren thus upside down but the image evokes the
words of Pico who wrote that according to Zoroaster, the soul had wings and when her
feathers fell off she was "borne headlong into the body" and that when they sprouted
again she flew back up into the "heights".[62] In other words, the soul gained sustenance
from the body, a message of central importance to Le Corbusier's work.

Le Corbusier took a strong interest in the Bestiary, a symbolic language dating from the early Christian period that was utilised by the builders of the Middle Ages, one that seems to have been a popular subject of discussion in his milieu.[63] It provided him with an excellent way of merging the symbolism of Christianity and paganism into one unified whole, as can be seen from a reading of Émile Mâle:

> The Bestiaries are certainly the most curious of the symbolic works devoted to nature, for in these extraordinary books paganism and Christianity are inextricably interwoven. Fables of animals collected by Ctesias, Pliny or Alian are found side by side with mystical commentaries added by the early Christians.[64]

Mâle wrote of twelfth century representations of a centaur with a siren in which the siren was not represented as a woman fish but as a woman bird, "a tradition long followed by the Bestiaries."[65] He described the siren as a "tradition of antiquity, for the Greeks never represented sirens in any other way." She was borrowed by the Greeks from the art of Egypt as a means to symbolise the soul separated from the body, the relationship of the two being a preoccupation of Orphism.[66] Apollinaire linked the siren with Orpheus in two verses of his *Le Bestiaire ou Cortège d'Orphée*.[67] According to Provensal Plato believed that the soul had an important role in mediating between the terrestrial and the divine.[68] She can be seen, as if copied from a Greek vase painting, in the pages of one of Le Corbusier's sketchbooks (Fig. 2.6).[69] In 1946 he drew a series of studies of the siren, the woman bird, entitled *Garder mon aile dans ta main*[70] (Fig. 2.7), studies for the eventual cover of *Poésie sur Alger*.[71] Given Mâle's interpretation of the woman bird, it is in fact a depiction of a hand sheltering the soul.[72] In one version of this image Le Corbusier drew the image on top of a collage made out of newspaper cuttings. One cutting, deliberately ripped, was from a section devoted to woman's hairstyles. It is as though Le Corbusier was making a connection between the role of the siren and that of modern woman.[73]

The layer below "Fusion", devoted to "Characters", has three squares, again a Trinity, suggesting that it is in some way concerned with the spirit. At its centre is Icône, the feminine deity central to Le Corbusier's painted work and thought, often seen in opposition to the Dionysiac and masculine Taureau, important characters in his Bestiary. That Le Corbusier connected Icône with his own wife Yvonne can be seen from a version of the iconostasis drawn in one of Le Corbusier's sketchbooks (Fig. 2.8).[74] Icône appears to cup a flame in her hands which can be read simultaneously as light and vulva, her reading changing according to the viewer's interpretation.[75] Mary is the bringer of Jesus, often symbolized through light. She is like the figure of Yvonne in the *Icône* paintings, who cups the light in her hand. Krustrup refers to it as the crystal presumably meaning the philosopher's stone, which C. G. Jung links back to the figure of Christ.[76] It is in the form of the *vesica piscis,* well known by Le Corbusier, used by the early Christians to represent the mystery of God's union with his mother bride and is much used in Christian art to represent the womb (Fig. 2.9).[77] The symbol opens up the possibility of a multiplicity of interpretations. Icône is simultaneously sexually inviting and chaste, bodily and spiritual, Orphic and Christian.

2.7 – 'Garder mon
aile dans ta main',
Le Corbusier, sketch
FLC D-4595-R

2.8 – Sketch by Le Corbusier
showing Yvonne at the centre
of the iconostasis

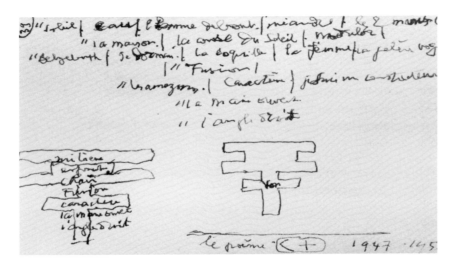

2.9 – Sketch by Le Corbusier
of Christ held in a *vesica piscis*.
Le Corbusier, *Sketchbooks Volume 3,
1954-1957*, sketch 516

The giving and receiving of love receives particular expression in the square entitled "Offering", an image of Le Corbusier's symbol of the Open Hand and a version, it seems, of what Le Corbusier called "the Christian word: 'Love one another'" (Fig. 2.10).[78] The enlightened soul who had experienced the other earlier layers of the iconostasis would understand the true importance of this message. A small diversion into the work of Pierre Teilhard de Chardin brings into focus Le Corbusier's heavily shrouded thoughts on religion and love. It is very possible that Le Corbusier came in contact with his writings via his Jesuit neighbours at his atelier Rue de Sèvres. Born in 1881, Teilhard was, simultaneously, a Jesuit father and a distinguished paleontologist who fell foul of the Vatican because of his modernist leanings. He felt a strong need to create a theory of evolution that would reconcile the phenomenon of religious experience with those of natural science. It is perhaps for this reason that Le Corbusier was so "favourably impressed" with his work.[79]

According to Teilhard the only way that an individual can achieve fulfillment is in opposition with others,[80] an idea that is echoed in *Le Poème de l'angle droit*, and clearly originates in Plato. Woman would play a particular role in all this:

> Woman stands before [man] as the lure and symbol of the world. He cannot embrace her except by himself growing, in his turn, to world scale. And because the world is always growing and always unfinished and always ahead of us, to achieve his love man is engaged in a limitless conquest of the universe and himself. In this sense man can only attain woman by consummating a union with the universe. Love is a sacred reserve of energy; it is like the blood of spiritual evolution. This is the first revelation we receive from the sense of the earth.[81]

The attraction of the feminine, in her human form, was the concentrated form, destined to expand, of cosmic attraction, the force that would inevitably bring man and nature together in unity.[82]

Radiance

It was Teilhard's theory that as people become ever more inward looking or reflective and knowledgeable they would, paradoxically, become better attuned with one another, drawn together through a mutual "sympathy" with no accompanying loss of personality. This process of "planetisation" was not limited to the relationship between people, it also concerned the relationship between people and things, indeed things and things, each sharing a fragment of the divine energy with which they were made – there are echoes here of the "divine spark" of "Mathematics" described by Le Corbusier in *Le poème de l'angle droit*.[83] Such ideas mesh neatly with the Corbusian concept of "radiance" in which mathematics plays a central role in unification. It can be no accident, given Le Corbusier's penchant for word play that God, *Dieu*, is there at the heart of the word – ra*dieu*se.

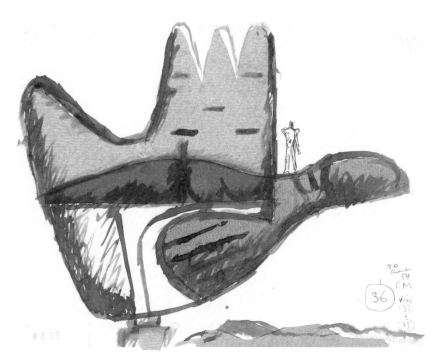

2.10 – Sketch of
the Open Hand,
FLC DE-2339

After the stock market crash in America there was a depression in France as in much of
the rest of the world. During this period Le Corbusier looked to left wing syndicalism
as an alternative to capitalism and parliamentary democracy.[84] From 1931 to 1936 he
acted as both a contributor and editor for two different syndicalist journals, *Plans*
and *Prélude*. It was here that he first outlined his plans for the Radiant City.[85] As Mary
McLeod has illustrated, the *Plans* group was very interested in the culture of the
Mediterranean, its links with ancient Greece and the cult of Apollo. They particularly
admired the work of Frédéric Mistral (1830-1914) who drew the attention of the world
to Provençal literature.[86] Le Corbusier set out his own version of the syndicalist ideal
in an article in *Prélude* (later republished in the *The Radient City*), in response to
contemporary concerns about the relationship between religion and industrialisation
discussed in chapter 1. In it he described the Van Nelle factory in Holland, designed by
the Theosophist architect Karel de Bazel in 1916, as "a proof of love":

> It is to this goal, by means of the new administrative forms that will purify and
> amplify it, that we must lead our modern world. Tell us what we are, what we
> can do to help, why we are working … *Unite us*. Speak to us. Are we not all one,
> within the *serene* whole of an organised hierarchy?
>
> If you show us such plans and explain them to us, the old dichotomy between
> "haves" and despairing "have-nots" will disappear. There will be but a single
> society, united in belief and action.
>
> We live in an age of strictest rationalism, and this is a matter of conscience.
> We must awaken a conscience in the world. Conscience in everyone and about
> everyone.[87]

The pursuit of the collective, an economic and political imperative, was in his mind "a spiritual task". Here "Labour retains its fundamental materiality, but it is enlightened by the spirit."[88]

The concept of the Radiant City received its full expression in the book of the same name published in 1933. A radiant building would influence everything around it, like the Parthenon, which Le Corbusier described thus:

> Effect of a work of art (architecture, statue or painting) on its surroundings: waves, outcries, turmoil (the Parthenon on the Acropolis at Athens), lines spurting, radiating out as if produced by an explosion: the surroundings, both immediate and more distant, are stirred and shaken, dominated or caressed by it. (...) A kind of harmony is created, exact like a mathematical exercise, a true manifestation of the acoustics of plastic matter. It is not out of place, in this context, to bring in music, one of the subtlest phenomena of all, bringer of joy, (harmony) or of oppression (cacophony).[89]

Radiant architecture would be connected with other edifices, both old and new, built in the same spirit and with the same sensitivity to geometry. Furthermore, architecture could be "made radiant" through the use of the Modulor.

Radiance and energy are closely linked. Certainly electricity was a very important theme in Le Corbusier's work, as can be deduced from *Le Poème électronique* designed for the Brussels World Fair of 1958. Like Le Corbusier's symbol of the 24 hour day the electricity wave is cyclical, it represents a flow of energy, from positive to negative and back again. It could be used as a powerful and modern way in which to represent the oppositions central to the architect's ideas.[90]

The cross and arrow symbols that occur in "Tool", the final square of *Le poème de l'angle droit* are also evocative of the positive and negative signs in electricity.[91] At the same time they evoke the sexual symbols of man and woman.[92] Le Corbusier defined "male" architecture as "strong objectivity of forms, under the intense light of a Mediterranean sun," while "female" architecture was described in terms of "limitless subjectivity rising against a clouded sky,"[93] in other words, more nebulous (Fig. 2.11). His architecture became a marriage of these two opposites, in alchemical terms, a highly charged and erotic interplay intended to work upon the inhabitant through what he called a "psychophysiology" of the feelings.[94] The Radiant City itself was "produced by the interplay of two elements, one male, one female: sun and water. Two contradictory elements that both need the other to exist ..."[95] Not only would this interplay occur in the lives of the men and women who occupied his radiant architecture, it would occur in the production of its spaces.

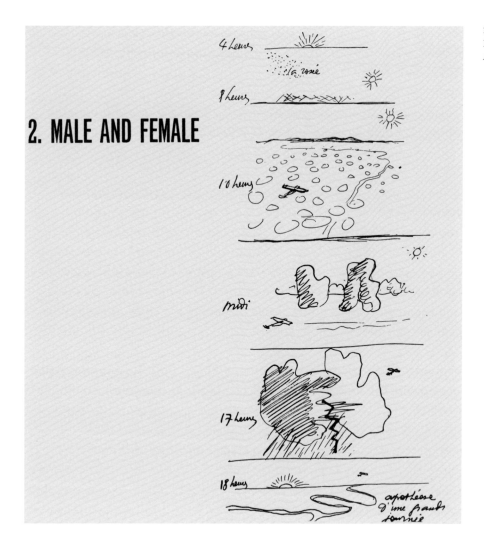

2. MALE AND FEMALE

It is this *espace indicible* or ineffable space that is central to his vision of religion. As Le Corbusier himself observed: "I have not experienced the miracle of faith, but I have often known the miracle of ineffable space, the apotheosis of plastic emotion."[96] Further, "There is no need whatever to take on an exalted or ecstatic air when we speak of these flashes of fundamental truth, which we are entitled to experience sometimes at the crossing of the ways, and which are an authentic fact of religion."[97]

Christianity

Being brought up as a Protestant the deficiencies of the Catholic religion are likely to have been instilled in Le Corbusier from birth. It was politically dangerous for his career to criticise Catholicism too much but his early writings are peppered with sardonic statements about what he perceived as its hypocrisy.[98] This explains, in part, his appreciation of the work of François Rabelais who hid his contempt for this religion beneath a thin layer of bawdiness and comedy.[99] Like Rabelais, he was fond of turning the words of the Bible back against the Church.

Le Corbusier was particularly concerned about the destructive effects of the Church on the lives of women, particularly through its attitude to sex and procreation:

> The biblical dogma that begins by defining as sin the fundamental law of nature, the act of making love, has rotted our hearts, has finished by ending in this twentieth century in notions of honour and honesty that are facades sometimes hiding lies and crimes … Is it not an anguishing sight to see the daily papers describing this "scandalous drama" – an offence to human dignity – of a poor girl who has had an abortion? Do you want to know why she had an abortion? Search: architecture and planning for it expresses the way of thinking of a period and today we are suffocating under constraint.[100]

The importance of woman in the life of the spirit has already been alluded to in the discussion of *Le poème de l'angle droit* above. Le Corbusier, as befits a man with a strong interest in Orphic harmony and what he saw as the "natural law" of gender equality,[101] was interested in any religion that elevated women to a level comparable with men. As Réau observed, "all the Mediterranean religions before Christianity worshipped feminine divinities. A religion without women is against nature."[102] It was for this reason that Le Corbusier sought to reassert the role of woman in religion hence, in part his growing interest in Mary's role in Catholicism. A painting by André Bauchant above Le Corbusier's own bed in the penthouse at 24 Rue Nungesser et Coli showing a horned God crowning Mary provides clear evidence of this ambition (Fig. 2.12).

Le Corbusier adhered to the Platonic idea, introduced above, that it was necessary to get beyond the senses to gain access to the spirit. This seems to have been his main issue with the religion of his birth.

> Protestantism as a religion lacks the necessary sensuality that fills the innermost depths of a human being, sanctuaries of which he is hardly conscious and which are part of the animal self, or perhaps the most elevated part of the subconscious. This sensuality, which intoxicates and eludes reason, is a source of latent joy and a harness of living strength.[103]

Although he held the Roman Catholic Church in contempt he clearly admired the sensory appeal of its services and its engagement with the figure of Mary.

Summary

Le Corbusier's attitude to religion was in many ways the logical product of his upbringing and environment, a desire for order and an enthusiasm for the arcane set within the spiritual hothouse of Paris in the early 1920s. Herein can be found the roots of his ethos of *savoir habiter*, knowing how to live, central concerns of which are the appreciation of nature, harmony, gender equality, love, the role played by the body in the attainment of knowledge, and a quasi religious faith in the potential of mathematics.

In looking to Orphism for the sources of his new religion Le Corbusier was looking back to the sources of Catholicism itself. "I discover in Catholicism the continuation of the most ancient, the most human rites (human scale, and pertinent)."[104]

"Human scale" here refers again to that divine spark of mathematics, present within our bodies, within Jesus (God in human form, the God within) and with God. What then is God for Le Corbusier?

> Who began it: man or woman? Is the eternal feminine? From the belly of what great Mother did you emerge, multiple forms? And what fathering principle fertilized your womb? Inadmissible duality. In this case, God is the child. My spirit refuses to divide God. As soon as I admit the existence of the division there is conflict. Whoever has gods has war. There are no gods but there is one God. God's reign is peace. Everything is absorbed and reconciled in Unity.[105]

These words by Daedalus, the "architect" of the labyrinth in André Gide's *Thésée* (1945), begin to indicate some of the complexity of this issue.[106]

Le Corbusier's vision of Catholicism was very different from that of the anti-modern Vatican. It was different again from that of Couturier and his colleagues, although they share similar rhetoric – a concern with light, with humility, with purity, with geometry, with unity and the transformative possibilities of art. The thing that sets Le Corbusier's Catholicism apart from that of *L'Art sacré* is his fascination with women and what he felt to be the redeeming power of physical love, the focus of the scheme for La Sainte Baume.

2.12 – Bauchant painting over Le Corbusier's bed in the penthouse at 24 Rue Nungesser et Coli

THE
BASILICA
AT LA
SAINTE
BAUME

La Sainte Baume is situated in Provence in the south of France forty kilometres to the east of Marseilles (Fig. 3.1). At the heart of the site is a grotto dedicated to the memory of Mary Magdalene which is set into the north side of a limestone ridge seven hundred metres above sea level. This was to provide the setting for what Le Corbusier described as "an astonishing and perhaps marvellous undertaking"[1], a vast underground Basilica, housing, accommodation for pilgrims and a museum of Magdalenic iconography all designed by Le Corbusier in close collaboration with his client Édouard Trouin, the owner of the land (Fig. 3.2). It was a highly ambitious project, so ambitious that A.-M. Cocagnac wrote in *L'Art sacré* that it would become no less than the third most holy place in the world after the Holy Sepulchre in Jerusalem and St Peter's in Rome.[2] Dominican monks had had a special role in the protection of La Sainte Baume since 1295 which may be why Couturier and his colleagues at *L'Art sacré* felt a special affiliation with the site.[3]

Le Corbusier worked on the La Sainte Baume project, on and off, from 1946 to 1960. It therefore provides the backdrop to Notre Dame du Haut Ronchamp, Sainte Marie de La Tourette and Saint Pierre Firminy-Vert. The discussion here focuses on three projects for the Basilica which were developed largely during the period 1945 to 1950. Although never built, it would be impossible to overstate the importance of La Sainte Baume for the development of Le Corbusier's thinking on the Church, mainly because it was in the course of this project that he developed a strong working relationship with Father Marie-Alain Couturier, their first encounter being on March 24, 1948. Couturier had become interested in Le Corbusier's work whilst working as a painter with Maurice Denis and the *Ateliers d'art sacré* in Paris. Having written, in 1939, of his

3.1 – The grotto at
La Sainte Baume as
it is today

3.2 – Édouard Trouin

desire to involve architects such as Le Corbusier in the work of *L'Art sacré*, La Sainte Baume at last gave him the opportunity to do so. It was while introducing Le Corbusier to the possibilities of Catholicism that Couturier gave him his first real taste of the complexities of Church politics.

Édouard Trouin and the Committee of Support

Another figure crucial to the evolution of Le Corbusier's view of the Church was his client Édouard Trouin, born in 1907[4] in Mazargues, a village on the outskirts of Marseilles and educated by monks, first in Marseilles and then in Italy, before studying law in Aix-en-Provence and being pushed towards a surveying career by his domineering father.[5] From the *Œuvre complète* it can be learnt that Trouin had the "thunder of God"[6] and was "passionate about architecture, construction, the management of land, landscape and geometry".[7] However, as Françoise Caussé has pointed out, he also had a reputation for being a collaborator and a crook.[8] When Trouin informed the local Dominicans of his plans to build a Basilica at La Sainte Baume not long after he bought the land at the beginning of World War II, they refused to take him seriously.

Once the War was over Trouin departed for Paris where, according to his wife, "he lived some bohemian times with his head full of projects!" He asked Auguste Perret to do an abortive sketch design before settling upon Le Corbusier as architect, largely because of his sympathetic attitude to the project and his fees. It was Jean Badovici, editor of *L'Architecture vivante* who made the introduction.[9] Although Trouin and Le Corbusier had a turbulent relationship, they were actually very close to one another as can be seen from a letter written by Le Corbusier in July 1963:

We acknowledge that we are brothers in the face of destiny. We are expert at giving each other a kick up the backside from morning to night, week to week, month to month and year to year. Etc, etc …

Let's not make a drama out of this! We have a very friendly respect for each other. That is what I want to tell you.

Your Corbu [10]

Given the closeness and longevity of their working relationship (almost twenty years) it seems that they must have been largely in agreement about what the project stood for.

While in Paris Trouin managed to persuade a raft of high profile figures, including Jacques Maritain, to join the committee of support for the project, for which Perret was initially named President.[11] Father Régamey, then co-editor of *L'Art sacré*, was included as a member of the patronage committee in 1945 but, as Caussé has pointed out, he was lukewarm in his support. Couturier would join it in 1948. The project also attracted the attention of Fernand Léger who wrote about it to Couturier in November 1943.[12]

Claudel's Basilica Scheme

According to Couturier the scheme for an "underground church" was originally inspired by the writer and diplomat Paul Claudel[13] who, as mentioned in Chapter 1, was dramatically converted to Catholicism on December 25, 1886, after a mystical experience in the cathedral of Notre Dame in Paris.[14] Claudel favoured a dramatic renunciation of modern materialism, the theme of his play *L'Annonce faite à Marie*.[15] He also had an important influence on the development of *L'Art sacré* during the late 1930s and early 1940s. Father Régamey described Claudel's contribution to Christian art as being "without doubt the most decisive that took place between the wars."[16] Expressing exasperation at the domination of religious art by two artists – Maurice Denis and Georges Desvallières – Claudel urged Couturier to be adventurous in his choice of who to support.[17]

Claudel had a long-term interest in architecture which emerged from time to time in his writings. In 1926, whilst acting as ambassador in Tokyo, he devised a scheme for a project for an underground church large enough to accommodate ten thousand people which he hoped to build in Chicago, a place where Christians from all over the world could meet.[18] Couturier, an admirer of Claudel's writings, made it his mission to see the scheme built. Arriving in New York in 1940 Couturier was forced to remain in North America and Canada throughout the War. It was during this period that he began work on Claudel's project with the assistance of the architect Antonin Raymond, who had originally made his name working in Japan, but who was forced to return to America because of the War.[19] Raymond had designed a church in Japan which had caught the attention of Dominique de Ménil, an important French-American arts patron, who had then mentioned it to Couturier who published it in *L'Art sacré* in 1937.[20] Raymond got to know Claudel well in Japan, indeed they were good friends.[21]

Raymond wrote that the main subject of their discussions was the cathedral. Claudel was writing his well-known prose-poem, "Projet d'une cathédrale souterraine à Chicago", and Raymond was to realize it in black and white.[22] The architect included a number of images of the "remarkable" cathedral in his autobiography (Fig. 3.3) in which he described the scheme at some length. Arranged around a route of redemption it would encapsulate "a double Colliseum ... a double cupola, a double amphitheatre, the one adjusted and reciprocating the other, that of the Earth and that of the Sky." These would "be exactly like the two sides of a shell." Also included was an altar "like solidified glass".[23] Claudel had a strong interest in church lighting and a very clear idea about the lighting effects that he hoped to achieve.[24]

3.3 – Antonin Raymond's interpretation of Paul Claudel's Basilica

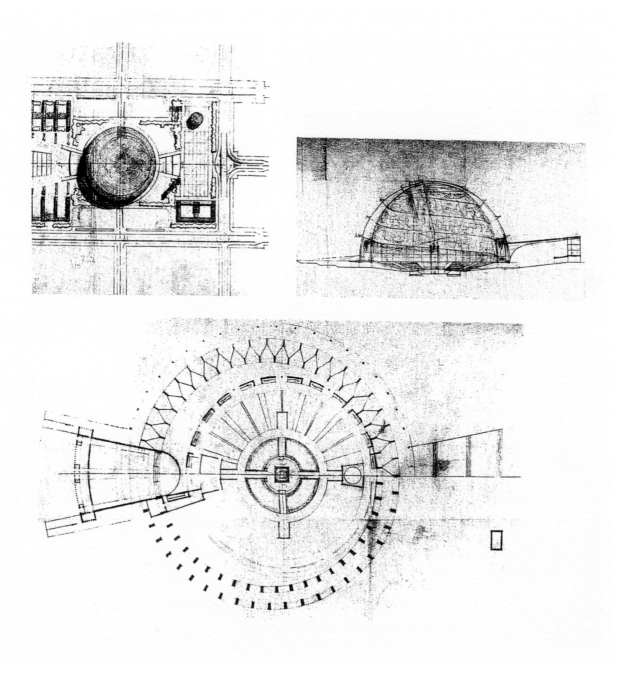

Right in front of the procession everything is obscured but at the end visible from the gallery a striking light has been set up, which turns on and off again further on as God advances, continually managing the same space between it and Him in the darkness. This is the light that precedes day and prepares the way to the Truth.[25]

According to Raymond, the interior of the dome would be covered in an enormous mosaic of a "Byzantine Christ extending his arms" in the middle of which would be an oculus. He added, "or it could be a double spiral, flowing in opposite directions, but meeting at the top of the cupola, signifying in that way the two Catholic churches, the Eastern and the Western, meeting at the apex in Christ."[26] The aim of the scheme was to engender world peace, exactly the same aspiration that Trouin would express for his Basilica scheme.

Claudel set out his conception of a new church in a piece of writing entitled *La Jeune fille Violaine* (1901), a revised version of *L'Annonce faite à Marie*, in which one of the main protagonists, an architect named Pierre de Craôn, was in the process of building a church. Claude Bergeron writes:

> The traditional church is that of the morning, so he said in *La Jeune fille Violaine*. It is the one that was created for the celebration of mass and the one in which the choir is separated from the nave and the clergy, and from the people. Pierre de Craôn added two other churches to this ancient church and united them all under the same roof, or more precisely under one mountain. These two new churches are the church of the evening and the church of the night. They are places of contemplation and illustrate the theme of redemption and forgiveness which are life giving. In the church of the evening the believer is plunged into the heart of what the poet calls an "apocalyptic temple", a whirlwind of monsters and demons. Once he has confronted this vision of the Final Judgement he is led along the ramps and terraces to the church of the night, the "dungeon of Penitence", which is a grotto where repentant sinners are assured of a pleasant night. That is where they find things such as the seed buried in the earth awaiting germination.[27] Nearby the lamp burns in front of the tabernacle and the baptismal fonts rise at dawn. This is therefore the welcoming vision of a new life after the long road to purification. It is like the light from the Mediterranean at the end of a long tunnel in the rock at Sainte Baume.[28]

For Le Corbusier "the compasses" of de Craôn, "The Master of the Rule", ... "explain all that is limitless, esoteric and pythagorean and so forth", which is why *L'Annonce faite à Marie* is discussed extensively in the *Modulor*.[29]

There are three partially conflicting versions of events at this stage in the project. Bergeron has suggested that Couturier chose La Sainte Baume as a suitable site for the Basilica because of Claudel's enthusiasm for the figure of the Magdalene as an exemplification of the power of pardon and has argued that the ideas of Claudel had a profound influence on La Sainte Baume. According to Caussé Couturier came to know about the project via Régamey and Couturier himself acknowledged the role Claudel played in its conception. However, in Le Corbusier's version of events, spelt out in the *Œuvre complète*, Trouin was the driving force behind the scheme and Claudel is not mentioned.[30] When questioned upon this matter Trouin's wife Henriette maintained that the scheme was her husband's alone.[31] There are however uncanny similarities between Claudel and Trouin's schemes.

The Evolution of Trouin and Le Corbusier's Basilica Schemes

When Trouin arrived in Paris he brought with him a set of sketches of his vision of the Basilica (1946-47). They seem to have been translated into a drawing by Le Corbusier which was eventually published in his *Œuvre complète* and credited to Trouin alongside a further, much purified version of the Basilica scheme clearly executed by Le Corbusier himself. For the sake of clarity we refer to the first scheme as Trouin's, the second as Le Corbusier's, but having evolved from the same set of precedents there was clearly much cross fertilisation between the two.

Trouin wrote, "since prehistoric times" La Sainte Baume "has been a highly religious site which has been defended and is still to an extent protected by many TABOOS, the spirit of which have been lost over time, but the words of which exist for me today."[32] Within the landscape and its history he found many links between Christianity and pagan religion, in particular the cult of Mother Earth, something that is likely to have held appeal for Le Corbusier.

The grotto has a rich history and has been visited by many eminent figures including twelve popes, all the kings of France (except two) and a range of saints and poets. The renaissance poet Petrarch (1304-74), famed for his poems of courtly love, also came to visit La Sainte Baume in 1342.[33] For Le Corbusier his songs of chivalry were replete with hidden meaning, Orphic in intent.[34] In more recent years it had been celebrated by a series of eminent artists as well as Frédéric Mistral in his poem *Mirèio*.[35] In March 1931 extracts from the poem were published in Provençal in the Regional Syndicalist journal *Plans,* to which Le Corbusier was also a contributor, as mentioned in chapter 2.[36] La Sainte Baume continued to be a site of great importance to those who climbed the pilgrimage route (Fig. 3.4 and Fig. 3.5) to the grotto to wet their hands in the water of the "Fountain of Penitence", which, according to legend, had miraculous properties.[37]

For Le Corbusier La Sainte Baume formed part of "a brilliant landscape ... capable of allowing you to enjoy its real value, the spirit which reigns over the area," that of Mary Magdalene.[38] The first two pages of the section of the *Œuvre complète* devoted to the project are dominated by images from Trouin's collection of her iconography.[39]

3.4 – The approach to the existing grotto at La Sainte Baume

3.5 – Entrance to the grotto at La Sainte Baume

3.6 – Page from Le Corbusier's *Œuvre complète* including some of Trouin's collection of Magdalenic art

Quelques illustrations de la Maquette établie par Trouin sur l'iconographie de Marie-Madeleine

An astonishing and perhaps marvellous undertaking: inspired by Edward Trouin whose family have been geometers in Marseilles since 1780. He, the last of them, is fifty years old, and is descended from seamen and pirates of St-Malo, and from peasants of Provence. He is a geometer, that is to say that he is devoted to architecture, construction, the management of the land, the countryside and to geometry. He speaks with a Marseilles accent, has the energy of the "thunder of God", as they say in Marseilles, and possesses by chance a million square metres of uncultivated and unproductive land at La Sainte-Baume. He decided to make some use of it. Week-end hunters came and asked him to sell them pieces here and there, but Trouin did not wish to sell, he wanted to realise a noble idea, to save the countryside of La Sainte-Baume from the speculative builder, who had already invaded Le Plan d'Aups. Then began the long search for an architecture worthy of the countryside.

La Sainte-Baume—"a High Place", a formidable wall of rocks on the edge of half a plate (Le Plan d'Aups), the other half, slightly raised, looking to the north as far as

Marie-Madeleine, amie du seigneur

Dans la grotte de la Ste-Baume

The Magdalene's hands, prefiguring "the Open Hand" of the architect's later work, are much in evidence, whether anointing Christ's feet or fervently praying (Fig. 3.6).

There is still debate over the identity of the Magdalene – her relationship with other Biblical Marys remains obscure. Over the centuries the original account of her life has been much altered by those who have used it as a vehicle to express their own ideas about religion, particularly sexuality, as she became linked to that of another New Testament woman, the "sinner"[40] who washed Christ's feet with her hair,[41] clasping her jar of ointment, the Myrophore.[42]

In 1279, about fifteen years before the arrival of the Dominicans in the area, it was announced that the body of Mary Magdalene had been found in the crypt of the monastery church of St Maximin, not far from La Sainte Baume. The relics were exhumed in the presence of Louis IX's nephew Charles of Salerno and put into a golden reliquary in the shape of a head surmounted by a royal crown.[43] The cult of the Magdalene at St. Maximin, the origins of which may never be known, quickly spread across Provence aided by the Dominicans who declared the saint as their patroness. There are several different versions of the Provençal legend of the Magdalene, the best known being that she travelled to France by boat in the company of Saint Maximin, in this way bringing the faith to Provence,[44] spending 33 years[45], the rest of her life, in spiritual retreat at La Sainte Baume.[46]

The master carpenter Antoine Moles, an acquaintance of Le Corbusier's,[47] dedicated a whole chapter to a further version of the Magdalene's story in his book on the cathedral builders of the Middle Ages, the birth of the guilds and of Masonry, *Histoire des charpentiers*.[48] According to Moles, Mary Magdalene arrived in Provence in the company of the first "campagnons bâtisseurs", the companion builders[49] who came from the plateaux of Asia bringing with them a knowledge of geometry. This is why the Magdalene's grotto became an important site of pilgrimage for the "Compagnons du Tour de France", the guild of master craftsmen who were to be involved in the development of the Basilica scheme.[50] Le Corbusier was interested in the connections between these men and "other secrets from the past" as can be seen from the many annotations that he made to Jean Gimpel's *Les Bâtisseurs de cathédrales*.[51]

Le Corbusier gave his own version of the Magdalene's legend within the pages of his *Œuvre complète*:

> Half-way up this massive vertical rock face is the black hole of a cave: here lived Mary Magdalene, the friend of Jesus, who came from Palestine in a small boat, with the other Marys. Every morning angels came to the cave and carried her 200 metres up to the summit of the mountain called "Le Pilon", where she used to pray. From there the mountain falls away as far as Toulon and the Mediterranean. The legend has made La Sainte Baume a divine place, which today is guarded by the Dominicans. On the plain at the foot of the

hills is The Basilica of St Maximin, where the beautiful head (skeleton) of Mary Magdalene is kept in a golden casket.[52]

It is notable that Le Corbusier referred here to the "Marys".[53] According to Provençal tradition the three Marys who travelled to France from Palestine were Mary Magdalene, Mary the wife of Cleophas[54] and Mary, mother of James.[55] Trouin observed that there was also a role played by the fifth-century reformed prostitute "Saint Mary of Egypt in the development of our Magdalene" as he had learnt through discussion with Emile Mâle who he described as knowing "everything".[56]

It seems likely that Le Corbusier was drawing upon the writings of Jacobus de Voragine who described in his *Legenda Aurea* (compiled around 1260) how every day "at the seven canonical hours she [Mary Magdalene] was carried aloft by angels and with her bodily ears heard the glorious chants of the celestial hosts."[57] The thing that is likely to have interested Le Corbusier in this account was her complete immersion into the powers of harmony, both acoustic and geometric. According to Voragine, author of *The Golden Legend* (c. 1260), Mary Magdalene could also be symbolised by light.[58] Like the figure of Icône in Le Corbusier's paintings, the Magdalene was the bringer of illumination, the bringer of Christ.[59]

For Trouin Mary Magdalene had a very particular role in bringing the Christian religion of the east to France.[60] In his opinion her heart was "not that of a lamb nor of an innocent person", it was a "paragon of knowledge".[61] He noted that: "Renan wrote that the vision of this woman in love gave the world a resurrected god and that the church called her the 'APOSTLE of APOSTLES'. Not at all bad for an ex-prostitute."[62] Trouin was here referring to Ernest Renan's description of the Resurrection in which the Magdalene, crazed by love, had a vision of Christ, a vision that had then become the foundation of the Christian religion. Renan, who receives mention in chapter 1, went to Palestine to seek out archaeological proof of Jesus' life because he was sceptical about the contents of the gospels[63] and was interested in making a connection to the story of Jesus' life with more ancient related mythologies.[64] From the number of annotations made by Le Corbusier in Renan's *La Vie de Jésus* it is evident that this work occupied an important position in his own collection of books.[65]

Le Corbusier also reproduced in the *Œuvre complète* two pages from a scrapbook compiled by Trouin as inspiration for the Basilica (Fig. 3.7). As well as suggesting what the interior might be like, the pages set the scene for the kind of religious thought that it might embody, underground in both senses of the word: both beneath the earth and somewhat illicit. That this was the case can be seen from annotations to one of the volumes owned by Le Corbusier, *Esclarmonde de Foix: Princesse Cathare*. In it he underlined a reference to Ornolac, an underground Cathar cathedral, and wrote next to it "Trouin and L.C.".[66] The cave at Ornolac, not far from the Cathar stronghold of Montsegur, is perched high in a long rock wall visible for miles around. Within it a large stone acted as an altar, dramatically lit from cracks in the rock above. It is strikingly

3.7 – Pages from
Trouin's scrapbook
as reproduced in Le
Corbusier's *Œuvre
complète*

similar in aspect to the grotto at La Sainte Baume. Le Corbusier also underlined the
words, "one knows the importance that Catharism gave to women;" next to them he
wrote the initials "MM," presumably standing for Mary Magdalene, who was an object
of veneration for this sect, counted amongst his ancestors by Le Corbusier.[67]

Further inspiration came from the Neolithic caves of Rocamadour and Font de
Gaume.[68] Le Corbusier also made a note to remind himself to do some research on the
catacombs of Paris and of Rome.[69] What the French art historian Louis Réau described
as the "secret language of symbolism" of the catacombs was to have a direct bearing
on his scheme (Fig. 3.10).[70] In Trouin's words, "we do not set ourselves at a distance
from the first prehistoric place of prayer, of which cathedral crypts are remnants."[71]
Such a sentiment would not have been out of place within the pages of *L'Art sacré*.

Further inspiration came from the sacred monuments of India[72] as well as Egyptian
temples, all initiatory routes into the pleasures of harmony. For Le Corbusier "the
Parthenon, the Indian temples, and the cathedrals were all built according to precise
measures which constituted a code, a coherent system: a system which proclaimed
essential unity" – in other words Orphic.[73]

According to Trouin La Sainte Baume was the "Orphic City". He attempted to summarise
the programme for the project through the use of a single cryptic equation:[74]

```
                        – of Rabelais
        City                                  – orphic
                        – of Saint Teresa
```

The juxtaposed presence of François Rabelais and Saint Teresa is significant. Ostensibly these two figures would appear to be in stark contrast with one another – the first a man known for his crude wit, the second a woman known for her extreme piety – but they have more in common with one another than one might at first suppose.

Rabelais' *Gargantua and Pantagruel* was published in 1534. Saint Teresa's works were roughly contemporary, *The Way of Perfection*[75] being finished in 1567 and the *Interior Castle*[76] being written approximately ten years later. Rabelais and Saint Teresa, whose work remains influential today, occupied the hinge of history between the medieval period and the Renaissance, an age of great tension between orthodox Catholicism and other more esoteric versions of Christianity, a time when accusations of heresy were rife and the Counter Reformation was in full swing. In the opinion of Catherine Swietlicki it is likely that Saint Teresa, like Rabelais, was influenced by the writings of the Kabbalists, for example through the use of number symbolism[77], meaning that the writings of both authors are open to two different kinds of interpretation, one orthodox and one Orphic.

Having been so influential in ancient times Orphism could be linked to the history of a number of world religions. It is easy to see why Trouin and Le Corbusier would have thought that this syncretic religion had much to offer their cause as they were concerned with finding a religion that would have universal relevance. An illustration on the reverse of a publicity pamphlet for the Basilica (the front cover of which was designed by Léger) makes clear their objectives (Fig. 3.8 and 3.9). La Sainte Baume is depicted at the centre of the globe linking East and West.[78] In geopolitical terms the scheme was an assertion of minority Provençale culture, a culture with greater links to the Mediterranean than to Paris.

Trouin described how, on his first visit to La Sainte Baume, Le Corbusier "shouted into the wind and with three stones marked the correct viewpoint" for the Basilica.[79] Here on the mountainside they seem to have come to a mutual understanding about the course that the project would take, the embodiment of the word "forgiveness", a place of reconciliation in response to the fragmentation caused by World War II. As such it would share common ground with Couturier's Notre-Dame-de-Toute-Grâce on the Assy plateau.[80] Trouin wrote what he called a "declaration of love for La Sainte Baume",[81] within which he exclaimed, "clearly, Corbu, I will end up believing in the spirit of the place – genius loci, which defends itself, in La Sainte Baume, from change but which we will glorify again, all the same, as violation for enrichment's sake."[82]

3.8 – Front cover of Trouin [Montalte pseud.], *La Basilique Universelle de la Paix et du Pardon,* FLC 13 01 403, by Fernand Léger

3.9 – Back cover of Trouin [Montalte pseud.], *La Basilique Universelle de la Paix et du Pardon*, FLC 13 01 403, showing La Sainte Baume as the epicentre of the world

3.10 – Image of the catacombs from Le Corbusier's copy of T. Rollet, *Les Catacombes de Rome: Histoire de l'art et des croyances religieuses pendant les premiers siècles du Christianisme, vol. 2* (Paris: Morel, 1881), illustrations not numbered

Trouin's Basilica scheme

Trouin's scheme for the "International Basilica for Peace and Forgiveness" could be entered via a myriad of tunnels to be discovered in the forest on the south side of the mountain below the grotto of Mary Magdalene (Fig. 3.11).[83] Tiny numbers can be seen dotted across the entire section of Trouin's drawing of the Basilica indicating the presence of seven asymmetrical entrances, "simple open areas between the great beeches and the old oak trees of the druidical forest." These would "welcome visitors individually" and lead them down to the "Route of Perfection" inside the Basilica.[84] In providing seven entrances Trouin suggests that there are a number of ways to begin the journey to spiritual redemption.[85] It is possible that each entrance could have corresponded to one of the seven deadly sins, but it seems more likely that the number seven would here be used, as it was by the mediaeval cathedral builders, to represent the union of body and spirit as discussed in chapter 2.[86]

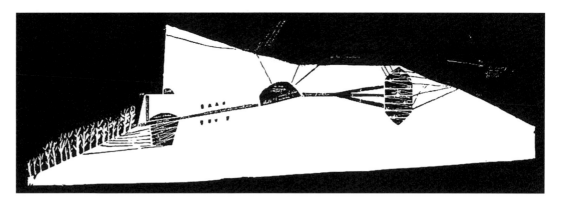

Having gained entrance to the Basilica, pilgrims would then be able to travel up a shaft, through the rock to a ledge, named "the Balcony of the Sky", outside the grotto itself.[87] Alternatively sixty metres below, they could enter the Basilica across a "pont jubé", a kind of gallery or rood screen.[88] Here both believers and non-believers alike were to be brought together in the first stage of the journey along a "spelographic tunnel", three hundred metres long, designed to "push the crowds towards the other side of the mountain". [89]

The beginning of the route of perfection was to take the pilgrim through the mountain past the crypts of the Syndicates and Worker's Guilds [90] including the "Compagnons du Tour de France".[91] From the narthex of the Basilica the Route of Perfection split into three different routes, symbolic of the Trinity.[92] These then gave entry to the final room, the climax of the journey:

> ... the NARTHEX, then to an ambulatory of elliptical shape surrounding the Saint of Saints. This, still in the rock, will be built along the lines of an ancient arena. At the centre of it there will be an altar made of crystal. In it, by means of the play of refraction on non-coruscating surfaces, there the very light of the sun will be gently gathered, which, by means of technology, it will be possible to send all around the interior.[93]

3.11 – Section through Trouin's Basilica as portrayed in Le Corbusier's *Œuvre complète*

At the heart of the Basilica the initiate would follow an ambulatory in the form of an ellipse around a figure of Mary Magdalene suspended in "a shrine of crystal" bathed in a mysterious light, in doing so evoking medieval representations of the Virgin Mary as a "a crystal vase crossed by light".[94] The experience of moving through this room would be both disorienting and mysterious. It was a place for inner searching, for repentance and for pardon.

Trouin's description of this space at the heart of the Basilica provides further evidence of his fascination with the Orphic use of number. He wrote:

> There will be seven corresponding altars in the area of Forgiveness and seven entrances of Sin. The seven translucent altars will be put up at certain points, on seven crosspieces, types of bridges, "jubés", thrown out into space at varying heights and asymmetrical in relation to the monument's axis. The altars will all face different directions, in such a way that if seven priests were saying the same mass their movements could be seen simultaneously from seven different angles. The "route of perfection" will finish half way up and could be 100 metres in length. Two crossing points will make it possible to reach other higher and lower ramps leading to the gallery, synthesising with number 3, the number of the Trinity.[95]

Seven altars, each different, would float within this space, connected to each other by a helicoidal ramp at a shallow gradient.[96] Here again is the number seven, representing the union of body and spirit, amongst other things.[97]

The culmination of Trouin's route would occur at the apex of the vault where the Basilica would open "invisibly" on the mountain of Saint Pilon.[98] Here the pilgrim would be greeted by the sun on the south side of the mountain and by a dazzling view of the seawater and sun being central to Le Corbusier's iconography. Whilst the journey through the grotto would be one of penitence, the experience of the mountaintop would be one of ecstasy[99] which, like those of the Christian mystics, is described by Reau as "at first sight a paradoxical, even contradictory mixture of asceticism and sensuality"[100] expressed beautifully in Bernini's statue of Saint Teresa in Santa Maria della Vittoria in Rome (circa 1644), discussed extensively in the pages of Le Corbusier's journal *L'Esprit nouveau*.[101]

Trouin's scheme was visibly influenced by Saint Teresa's famous volume *The Interior Castle*[102] excerpts from which he hoped to include in a publication he planned to write about the project.[103] Based upon the idea of a chivalric quest, Saint Teresa described in her book a crystalline route through the subtle and complex recesses of the Soul, passing through one stage of understanding before moving on to the next.[104] The route through the Basilica was entitled the "Route of Perfection"[105] after another of Saint Teresa's works (*The Way of Perfection*), a manual providing instruction in the meaning and art of prayer.[108]

Within the *Œuvre complète* are two images of Trouin's Basilica, a large one where the spaces of the Basilica appear black against a white background and a smaller negative image in which they appear white against a background of black. This must have been done purposefully as Le Corbusier wrote that he had taken special care with the design of the section of the *Œuvre complète* pertaining to La Sainte Baume.[107] If this is the case it seems that he was implying that there were two contradictory readings of the space, readings that are associated with day and with night.

Le Corbusier's Reworking of the Basilica Scheme

Still in the form of a route, Le Corbusier's version of the Basilica, as depicted in a sketch dated July 1948 (Fig. 3.12), resembles in cross section a drawn out mandala, a representation of the cyclical form of the cosmos, derived from his symbol of the 24 hour day, discussed extensively in the last chapter (Fig. 2.5).[108] Both linear and cosmic, like the mansions of Saint Teresa's *Interior Castle*, Le Corbusier's scheme would express more effectively the subtle mysteries of the interior journey than Trouin's more literal version. At La Sainte Baume the initiate would be drawn into a physical manifestation of Le Corbusier's sign of the cosmos, "a remarkable, invisible architectural undertaking with an enormous effort dedicated to the interior, aimed solely at moving those souls which are capable of understanding."[109]

The best way to facilitate the journey to the "Lost Paradise", would be to place the initiate actually within the sign itself to experience its power at first hand.[110] This process, in the opinion of Mircea Eliade, could be likened to "initiation by entry into a labyrinth"[111] – the labyrinth being a particular preoccupation of Le Corbusier's.[112] For Moles, the modern day Compagnon, "the alchemical labyrinth is the image of life with all its uncertainties and deceptions".[113]

Le Corbusier made a note to himself in one of his sketchbooks about a "descent to the sources of sensation," evoking the first stage of the journey through his scheme.[114] Light, sound and proportion, harmony in its many forms would here act upon the visitor to the Basilica who would then experience transformation, initially through bodily response, but then through cerebral understanding. It may be that the first lower section of the Basilica, corresponding to the dark segment of the diagram of the 24 hour day, pertained to more bodily concerns and that the second segment, corresponding to the light segment of the diagram, pertained to the spiritual; the implication being as suggested by both Plato and Pico in the last chapter that the body would give access to enlightenment. The legendary transformation of Mary Magdalene from prostitute to saint would seem to exemplify this process. Evoking the siren figure in *Le poème de l'angle droit* Trouin wrote that "in the Realm of Mothers (almahae matrius, ancient divinity of Saint B[aume]) the soul was plunged again into unconsciousness in order to create itself again."[115]

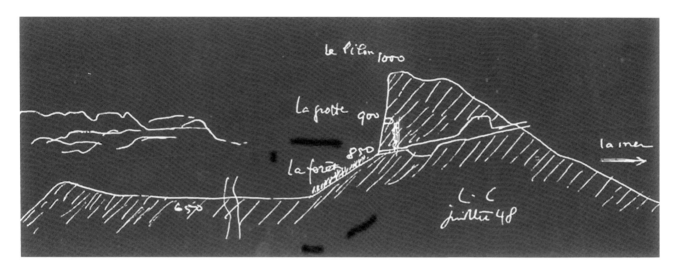

3.12 – Le Corbusier's Basilica scheme

3.13 – Sketch by Le Corbusier showing the position of the exit from the Basilica

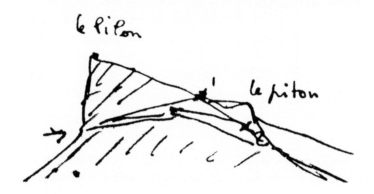

The journey through the mountain at La Sainte Baume was to take the form of "steep routes and vertical or horizontal rooms lit from the heavens by means of wells".[116] Light would penetrate the complex at the ends of the various "galleries" to draw the visitor on to the next stage of the journey in "a symphony of shadow, of half-light and of light that could be extraordinary."[117] The altar itself would, according to Le Corbusier, be "lit by the rays of the sun guided by mirrors."[118] He wrote:

> Inside, the rock would be an example of the work of architecture, movement, natural diurnal lighting, artificial lighting on one side of the rock from the entrance to the Saint Magdalene Grotto to the other side, suddenly opening on to the striking light of a never-ending horizon, towards the sea in the south.[119]

Le Corbusier carefully sited the exit of the Basilica at a point where the descending slope of the mountain Saint Pilon crossed the ascending slope of another, La Pitou (Fig. 3.13).[120] As in Trouin's scheme this threshold would be a site of maximum tension and drama manifested in the view of sun and sea. How then to present this vision of religious renewal to a skeptical and divided clergy?

The Fight to Build

The fight for the Basilica receives extensive documentation in Françoise Caussé's book on *L'Art sacré*. A central problem seems to have been internecine disagreement amongst the Dominicans.[121] Clearly there was a breakdown in communication between those on the site, most of whom held deep suspicions about Trouin's motives, and those in Paris. Indeed Father Danilo, a local, asked the prior of the St Maximin convent and the bishop of Fréjus to alert the Parisian Dominicans to the fact that they were being duped.[122] However Benoît Lavaud, one of the local Dominicans and a regular reader of *L'Art sacré*, came out in support of the project doing his best to intervene.[123]

Trouin had another powerful adversary in Canon Bouisson, a local priest and landowner in the nearby Plan d'Aups.[124] Bouisson set up a committee to protect the site which was classified for protection in 1945.[125] Further dissent would come from within the *L'Art sacré* ranks, although this was never made public. Régamey was worried that Trouin was a conman and that the project was far too expensive, using money that would best be spent elsewhere. He was also concerned about damage to the grotto itself.[126]

It is not surprising that, despite enlisting a committee of highly influential people as supporters of the project and mounting an intense press campaign in the summer of 1948, Bishop Gaudel, Head Dominican of the Provincial de Toulouse (Lavaud's superior) rejected the proposal in December of that year.[127] Trouin's reputation had been deeply damaged by an article in *Le Figaro* in which he was accused of having financial gain as his main motivation in proceeding with the project.[128]

> The ecclesiastical authorities at diocese level reacted much less favourably and it seems difficult not to agree with them. True believers do not need an underground basilica with two arcaded cities, a room for celebrations and a theatre to go and pray to Saint Mary Magdalene of La Sainte Baume if they so desire. And as for the non-believers, if they like celebration rooms, theatres and highly developed hotels, they will always find what suits them somewhere else.[129]

Couturier wrote a retort which appeared in *Le Figaro* on February 12, 1949, in which he thanked its readership for its support for the development of the Basilica, restated the "simple and pure" objectives for the scheme, made mild reference to the internecine squabbles that had caused its downfall and confirmed that the committee would continue to work for the realisation of this project, greatly angering the Provincial Head Dominican in so doing.[130] The result was a dispatch released by the Agence France Presse dated April 26, 1949 announcing that an assembly of cardinals and bishops had solemnly condemned the project.[131] Hence Le Corbusier's inclusion within the *Œuvre complète* of an extract from a newspaper headlined "Cardinals and archbishops of France condemn the project for a basilica at La Sainte Baume".[134] Trouin tried to appeal against the decision, but in vain.[135]

Evidently Le Corbusier believed that his version of Christianity, extrapolated from the ancient roots of this religion, was more "pure" (Couturier's word for the project) than that of the modern Church, "hypocritical" in his eyes. Hence his disgust that both he and Trouin were accused of sacrilege and of trying to make money out of the project when, in their opinion, nothing could be further from the case.

> Our research could only be carried out with respect ... the cardinals and archbishops of France have condemned it. They have done so with the utmost sincerity believing they are right. Ministers of souls they do not realise the humility and the grandeur that is united in undertaking this task. They wished to save the dignity of one of the most beautiful legends, that of Mary Magdalene, friend of our Lord.[134]

He remained adamant that Trouin should not give up. Indeed the Fondation Le Corbusier archives contain many letters of encouragement to his despairing client.[135]

It seems that the Church authorities were correct to be suspicious about the project for La Sainte Baume. In the Fondation Le Corbusier there is a letter marked "confidential" by Le Corbusier in which Trouin tried to enlist Picasso to the cause. It is a very significant letter so it is quoted at length:

> As you have, via Madame Jacqueline Roc, willingly given your agreement to this project, in expectation of your visit here I am sending you some photographs of the countryside, documents and some indications as to what Le Corbusier and I wanted to bring about, partly without Couturier's knowledge, under the name of the Republic of Peace and Pardon.

> The accompanying notebook, whose bombastic tone of pregnancy I am borrowing at a distance, can serve as a basis for retracing on the 16 faces of the pillars the Basilica project which was condemned for having tried to attain the spirit of religion rather than the letter of it.

> Le Corbusier said to me secretly "they don't suspect what we are going to do – not any more than the bishops of the Middle Ages suspected the symbols of the mediaeval cathedral builders". Indeed they did suspect.

> Le Corbusier, you and I, in the shadows, represent the triumphant revenge of spirit over everything. Of course we never confided in Father Couturier, whose portrait by Cocteau I sent you "a soul free and subject to laws" – with that revenge which in truth is almost esoteric, Mallarmélike,[136] Gongoresque.[137] But would he have minded so much? The day, when, in front of me, Yvonne Le Corbusier held out to him at table a fake mustard pot from under the cover of which popped a phallus on a spring, he laughed heartily. That same evening he allowed me to yell about the curators of the La Sainte Baume. "Protection,

protection, it's an argument for condoms!" These two incidents are Gaullish [risqué], he was a Celt; let's go further: he accepted, nay he promoted the grand unbelieving artists, in preference to the makers of terrible works that were sprinkled with Holy Water. He admitted you as well as Le Corbusier into the "COMMUNION OF SAINTS". Father Rzewuski, the superior of La Sainte Baume, did he not say to me: "(You are an arch-heretic), the church only advances thanks to arch heretics." He did not say HERETICS but ARCH HERETICS (arcos-chief, haireo, I choose). If in the mediaeval cathedrals as in our Basilica project, there are insurrections, it is the Church that has need of insurrections: "The Inferno sings of the glory of God", according to the psalm.

That Couturier even preferred our pious blasphemies to monkey-like piety is without doubt.

I've already written this to you: in response to the Pope of Rome who has just explicitly condemned the high thoughts of Father Couturier (who has become an arch-heretic after death), it is our business to demonstrate that what Couturier called our spirituality .... Neither Corbu or I want to create a mystification in our Basilica. Unless we use the word in the making sense of MYSTERIES, which is to say the sense of men who search the mysteries (the Orphic religion, or Pythagorician, had the mysteries). When they objected our Basilica would cost thousands of millions, I would answer: "So what? If it engenders one true man?" This pig of modern man which we wanted so desperately to seize within the forest entries of our Basilica and by means of the entrails of the soil to transform him, to lead him towards sky, to make this footed fish, this vertical digestive tube, evolve with wings of angels.[138]

Although some of the meaning is obscure, the central issues are set out with great clarity: La Sainte Baume was to be the site of a cult linked with the ancient mystery religions, notably Orphism. It was to comprise a route of initiation through a journey to the underworld and, in common with such religions, it was to be shrouded in secrecy. Of central importance would be the knowledge of mathematical harmony, a knowledge that was held by the master builders of the medieval cathedrals.

Trouin's reference to a "secret conclusion" indicates that the project did indeed have some kind of hidden agenda. It is significant that Le Corbusier did not deny that the contents of the letter were true, but simply told Trouin to take more care with such delicate information, which could prove scandalous and damaging to all those involved. As Le Corbusier put it: "The interests (of the white robe and the black cloak)," the Dominicans, "need silence and abstention in these times. All are not friends in this universe."[139] Le Corbusier urged Trouin to be more cautious in the future: "I am speaking to you in the greatest seriousness, I hope that you understand me."[140] Le Corbusier was right to be cautious as Couturier was to come close to excommunication.[141]

Aftermath – The Small Valley of Concrete

As a result of the Cardinals' decision it was no longer possible to build anywhere within a 500 metre radius of the grotto[142] so Trouin proposed an extraordinary suggestion for a new scheme for the Basilica, the small Valley of Concrete which would be built two kilometres west of the existing grotto, to the south of the planned City (Fig. 3.14).[143] In the "Trouin Report", dated April 11, 1949, he announced the dissolution of the "Association Basilique" and the transformation of this body into a new form for the realisation of the "Route of Pardon and Peace".[144] According to this plan access to Saint Pilon and the grotto would be achieved at a high level in order to protect the forest below.[145] A version of this scheme, drawn by Le Corbusier, can be seen in the *Œuvre complète*. It shows a route extending from the city past ring shaped hotels, through the park and past a museum and a theatre of Mary Magdalene and up a vast ramp to the new Basilica.[146] This time it would be built to the west of the grotto on Trouin's own land, out of Dominican territory.

3.14 – The Small Valley of Concrete scheme by Le Corbusier

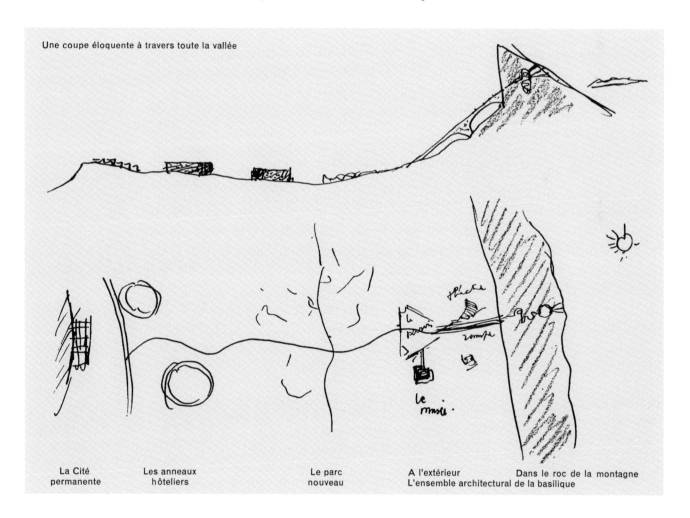

Une coupe éloquente à travers toute la vallée

| La Cité permanente | Les anneaux hôteliers | Le parc nouveau | A l'extérieur L'ensemble architectural de la basilique | Dans le roc de la montagne |

3.15 – Example of one of Trouin's paintings of an interior in the Small Valley of Concrete

In a document dated 1949 Trouin described a series of gouaches (Fig. 3.15) which he had painted of this latest scheme which would be "in the form of a square root $\sqrt{.}$"[147] Some features of his earlier scheme were retained, for example, the spiralling ramps in the central crystalline chamber which this time was to be accessed by passing along a tortuously looping tunnel. It is possible that the sinuous route was devised by Le Corbusier as it is highly evocative of what he called his "Law of the Meander", described in some length in *Precisions*.[148] A form of labyrinth, the winding route appears to represent the path to self-knowledge.[149] At the base of one of the spirals would be the figure of the Virgin Mary in a crescent moon, reminiscent of the lady of the Apocalypse in the Book of Revelation 12:1. At her feet, in submission, would be a serpent that, according to the Bestiaries, was symbolic of the devil.[150] The presence of the serpent also signposts that of Eve who could be found at the base of the second spiral. For Réau she was "the eternal seducer of man".[151] It seems likely that one spiral would symbolise the chaste, the other the sexual. As they wove their way together up through the space they would represent the union of spirit and body embodied within the Magdalene herself. It would be "LESS of a church than a votive monument for Unbelievers (and of believers) in Magdalene, Saint of Peace and Pardon."[152] This is a very significant point; Trouin's would not be an orthodox place of worship, but a place for the veneration of the Magdalene as a divinity in her own right.

Gradually Trouin and Le Corbusier turned their attention away from the Basilica in order to concentrate their efforts on the development of pilgrimage housing to be built in rammed earth, and a museum. They hoped that through building these it would be possible to persuade the authorities of the importance of building the Basilica itself but neither basilica, housing or museum were ever built. The only traces left of Trouin and Le Corbusier's collaboration at La Sainte Baume are: a bizarre concrete "garage/atelier" (recently renovated as a Trouin centre); a vaulted "temporary theatre" and an old sheepfold intended for use firstly as a chapel in memory of Couturier – who died in 1954 – all in a state of some dereliction.

Summary

Great care had to be taken with the way in which the scheme for La Sainte Baume was presented to the outside world, but Trouin was not a man for discretion. Whether he was indeed a charlatan remains unknown. There are moments, for example when he fantasises about bringing the famous French sex symbol Brigitte Bardot to act Mary Magdalene in this theatre, that his motives seem less than pure. It is possible that Le Corbusier remained loyal to him despite all his shortcomings because of his desperation to build – after all Le Corbusier had pandered to the Vichy regime with the same aim.

Whatever Trouin was doing Le Corbusier's own motives remain clear. The Basilica would encapsulate an initiation into an understanding and appreciation of the power of Orphic harmony in its many forms. The body, we refer again to Pico, would play a crucial role in all this, absorbing a sensory assault of space, sound, light and colour set within a rich and arcane terrain of Magdalenic symbolism. Through her love – Teilhard comes once more into play – we are transformed. At La Sainte Baume we begin to see the evolution of a strong agenda in Le Corbusier's work, the assertion of the role of woman – continually and perhaps problematically linked with nature – at the heart of religion and, by implication, the assertion of woman at the heart of life.

THE PILGRIMAGE CHAPEL OF NOTRE DAME DU HAUT RONCHAMP

Sited on top of a hill overlooking the quiet, ex-mining town of Ronchamp on the eastern edge of France, the chapel of Notre Dame du Haut Ronchamp (Fig. 4.1), the counterpart of Notre Dame du Bas in the village below, is framed within a complex of buildings which include accommodation for pilgrims (Fig. 4.2), a house for the curate (Fig. 4.3) and a small ziggurat shaped war memorial with seven steps (Fig. 4.4). It is characterised by the curve of its massive roof which Le Corbusier likened to a crab shell, an "object that evokes a poetic reaction", that he picked up on a beach in Long Island, admirable for its radiant geometry, its structure and, possibly, its symbolic association with Demeter. The space within the chapel and the openings into the outside world are defined by the curves of the three minor chapels, each of its four sides being very different in character. The scheme at Ronchamp was the result of "meticulous research," involving the continual adjustment of a "thousand factors … which no-one ought or would wish to speak of."[1] Its evolution, first documented by Daniele Pauly has since been subject to extensive study by others, but with minimal consideration of the liturgical and social issues that underpin its architecture, foregrounded here.[2]

4.1 – The eastern
elevation of the
Chapel at Ronchamp

4.2 – Pilgrimage
accommodation at
Ronchamp

4.4 – War memorial
at Ronchamp

4.3 – Curate's house
at Ronchamp

The Commission

The commission was proposed in April 1950 by the Besançon Diocesan Sacred Art Committee[3], the most innovative in France at that time. A new chapel was needed to replace the old one destroyed during World War II. Le Corbusier initially refused it, on the grounds that he did not want to work for "a dead institution", possibly because of the residual bitterness that he felt about La Sainte Baume.[4] Wogenscky recalled a conversation in which the architect told his friend Father Couturier that he had no right to work on the scheme and that they should find a Catholic architect instead:

> Father Couturier explained to him that the decision to ask Le Corbusier had been taken in full consciousness of the situation, in the knowledge that he was not religious. Eventually he said: "But Le Corbusier, I don't give a damn about your not being a Catholic. What we need is a great artist, and the aesthetic intensity, the beauty that you will make perceptible to those who come to the chapel ... our goal is far better than if we asked a Catholic architect: he would feel bound to make copies of an ancient church." Le Corbusier was pensive for a few seconds, then he said: "all right, I accept".[5]

Not being Catholic was clearly an issue for the scheme. When quizzed by a journalist from the *Chicago Tribune* on this subject Le Corbusier replied "Foutez-moi le camp!" (meaning roughly, "leave me alone!").[6] He did not want to get drawn into any kind of discussion on this issue.

Officially Couturier never had anything to do with the commission. Asking Le Corbusier was, in fact, the idea of Father Lucien Ledeur and François Mathey, Historical Monuments Inspector, both originally from Ronchamp (Fig. 4.5 and 4.6). Couturier kept a very low profile with regards to the project and it must be kept in mind Wogenscky's memoirs were written years after the fact. However, the tone of the story is probably quite accurate, and it is very likely that during their regular encounters Le Corbusier and Couturier discussed the chapel at Ronchamp, if very discreetly, and that Couturier had considerable influence on his decision to accept the commission that he had initially refused.[7] The only correspondence between them on this project is a very telling letter of January 20, 1951 from Le Corbusier to Couturier insisting that nothing should be published on the Chapel until the definitive plans had been agreed.[8] This was the very date the Sacred Art Commission met in Besançon and approved the pre-project.[9] When Couturier did finally dedicate an article in *L'Art sacré* to the Ronchamp project in 1953, once it was safely on site, it appeared in the back pages of an issue dedicated to Spain. Unable to curb his enthusiasm, he ended the article eulogistically:

> We are happy that the occasion has thus been offered today in this journal to pay homage to Le Corbusier: we consider him not only the greatest living architect but also the one in whom that spontaneous instinct for the sacred is the most authentic and the strongest.

4.5 – Meeting during
 construction, Lucien Ledeur,
André Maisonnier,
Le Corbusier, not dated

4.6 – Canon Lucien Ledeur
studying Le Corbusier's
Swiss Pavilion at the Cité
universitaire in Paris on one
of his trips to work with the
architect (photo taken by
François Mathey), 1949

The Ronchamp church will be his first religious edifice and we see already what it will bring.

"If you ask for Christmas long enough, it finally comes."[10]

According to Caussé La Sainte Baume had been an important case for Régamey and Couturier, a "training ground" on how to deal with this type of commission. None of them wanted to risk another disappointment like that of the Basilica.

It is worth mentioning that at this same time Le Corbusier also sought the advice of Couturier on the Delgado chapel in Venezuela, a three-sided pyramid, making it possible "to place the altar and tombs in a subtle way with effective lighting". Built on a twenty metre squared site paved in stone, it would be surrounded by a fence with "patterned openings on two sides and opaque on the third, drawing attention to the mountainous horizon beyond. There would be no flowers, only a tree "to give a lively and friendly presence to the whole thing."[11] This simple composition would be proportioned according to the Modulor, its pyramidal form an obvious reference to the architecture of ancient Egypt that he so much admired.

The importance of clerical input on the evolution of Ronchamp cannot be overstated. Indeed Father Ledeur spent much time instructing a willing Le Corbusier on the nuances of the Liturgy.[12] Beyond the resulting drawings and the chapel itself, there is little documentation of their many meetings (Ledeur wrote virtually nothing down) but clearly his lessons were in line with the *L'Art sacré* movement, leaning towards Liturgical Reform. Several pages of the small book *Texts et Dessins pour Ronchamp* published just before Le Corbusier's death in 1965 are dedicated to its liturgical set-up and function.[13]

The Ronchamp chapel was paid for with funds from the government (for war damages), bank loans, donations and subscriptions – money donated by individuals on the condition it would be later reimbursed. Apparently many refused to be reimbursed when the time finally came to do so.[14] In his book *The Cathedral Builders*, Jean Gimpel includes an image of the syndicate ticket (Fig. 4.7) sold to finance Ronchamp, noting the "proven methods", in other words the methods used by the mediaeval cathedral builders, that were "used to realise Le Corbusier's plans," a living example of what can be achieved through unified action.[15]

This support was in a way a tradition. During the Revolution the chapel was sold off by the government to a landlord in a nearby town. Seeing it fall into ruin, a group of forty local families bought it back from him, fixed it up, and re-instituted the pilgrimages. That is why, to this day, it is privately owned by what has now evolved into an association. Thus many local families have a long and proud history of supporting the chapel.

4.7 – Syndicate ticket
sold to raise funds for
construction

Christian Luxeuil, descended from one of the aforementioned families, relates that his
family defended the post World War II rebuilding campaign and contributed to it as
it could, but when Christian's mother first saw the chapel, before it was painted white
and completely finished, she was very shocked and thought it looked like a bunker.[16]
She couldn't believe she had contributed to such a thing. Like Madame Luxeuil, many
took time to accept the design. James Stirling, in his well-known and haughty essay on
the "Crisis of Rationalism" at Ronchamp was very wrong to suggest that it was easily
accepted by the locals.[17]

Not only was there concern about the look of the chapel, there was concern about its cost
when, in the early 1950s, it became apparent that the Ronchamp mines were growing
increasingly unviable, leading to their closure in 1958. The mayor at the time, Alfonse
Pheulpin, was known to complain about rebuilding the chapel, saying the money would
be better used towards aiding those out of work. It is important for this discussion to note
that the chapel took huge resources and that its simplicity came at a cost.

The Architectural Promenade

Ronchamp was designed to be experienced on the move. It is for this reason that we
have structured our description of the chapel in the form of a journey or promenade.
The *promenade architecturale* (architectural promenade) is a key term in the language
of modern architecture. It appears for the first time in Le Corbusier's description of
the Villa Savoye at Poissy (1929-31) as built where it supercedes the term "circulation",
so often used in his early work.[18]

> Architecture is a series of successive events ... events that the spirit tries to
> transmute by the creation of relations so precise and so overwhelming that deep
> physiological sensations result from them, that a real spiritual delectation is
> felt at reading the solution, that a perception of harmony comes to us from the
> clear-cut mathematical quality uniting each element of the work.[19]

4.8 – Approach to the
chapel up the hill

4.9 – The chapel
at Ronchamp seen at
a distance

Taken at a basic level the promenade refers, of course, to the experience of walking through a building. Taken at a deeper level, like most Corbusian matters, it refers to the complex web of ideas that underpins his work, most specifically his belief in architecture as a form of initiation into the delights of *savoir habiter*, at Ronchamp overlaid with an emancipatory vision of Catholicism.

Le Corbusier took a profound interest in Aristotle's rhetoric - the way in which events could be ordered to create maximal impact. In *Le Corbusier and the Architectural Promenade* Samuel has set out a framework for the discussion of route in the work of Le Corbusier.[20] It is based on the five stages of Gustav Freytag's dramatic arc – commonly used as the structure for compelling and "unified" film narrative which – in turn, evolved out of the stages of Aristotle's rhetoric. It should be noted that Roman rhetoricians built buildings in their minds, each room designed to remind them of one point of their often extremely lengthy speeches. As in Roman rhetoric, each stage in Le Corbusier's promenade prepares the visitor for the next, heightening their sense of expectation and curiosity. Samuel argues that the Jacob's ladder route from darkness to light, often in Le Corbusier's thoughts,[21] is the basic promenade type. The connection between this Biblical ladder[22] and the promenade is made clear in his description of the Maison Guiette in Antwerp (1926), the stair of which is likened by Le Corbusier to the ladder of Jacob which Charlie Chaplin climbs in *The Kid* (1921).[23] In her opinion all Le Corbusier's promenades are plays upon this original topos, a single processional route from earth to sky as exemplified by the promenade of the Villa Savoye which, like Freytag's dramatic arc, can be divided into stages: introduction, sensitisation, questioning, reorientation, and culmination. These are used to structure our discussion of the architectural promenade at Ronchamp and to facilitate comparison between this and his other religious buildings.

Introduction

The introduction or the threshold will, in many instances, occur at some distance from the building itself or will itself have a number of incremental elements strung out along the route, building up to the point of entry. Ronchamp first introduces itself as a white tower seen on a distant hilltop surrounded by trees (Fig. 4.9). From far away the radiant impact of the tower would be augmented with "electronic emissions" of sound, transmitted from above. "They will be able to make incredible music, an unbelievable sound when they have twelve thousand people outside with amplifiers."[24] The chapel is lost from sight as the pilgrim enters the village of Ronchamp where a turn into a side road, beneath a railway bridge, marks the wooded climb up towards the summit, with separate routes to be undertaken by foot or car. Ascending the path that leads up to the ceremonial south door, the way is framed above by the pilgrim's accommodation on the right (Fig. 4.8). Nothing can prepare the visitor for their first view of the chapel up close. The scale is very strange. The south wall is oddly concave. It is punctuated with windows, some with large splayed reveals set at odd angles, some deep and some not (Fig. 4.10). These serve to make the depth of the wall confusing, heightening the

4.10 – The
south door at
Ronchamp

4.11 – West elevation of Ronchamp

4.12 – Gargoyle on west elevation

4.13 – Working
drawing of cistern

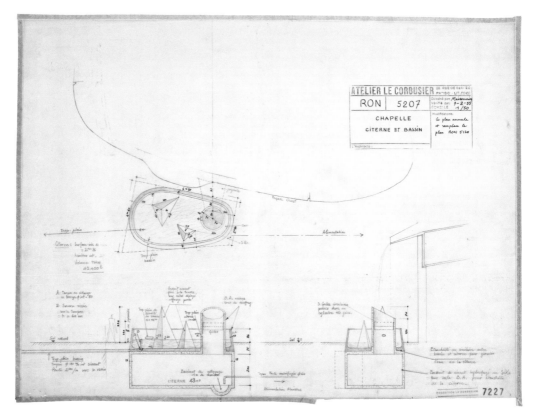

91

pilgrim's sensitivity to space. The ceremonial south door at Ronchamp (2770 mm by 2770 mm) announces itself in a variety of ways: through the extreme contrast between its colourful shiny enamel surfaces and the surrounding walls; through the way that it is set deep within the monumental wall; through the presence of its independent frame; through its dramatic and large handle; through the smooth panel of stone at its base (an enunciation of its sacred nature) and through the choreography of the elements around it, the holy water stoop inside, and the cornerstone outside. It is adorned with a range of Orphic symbols, the subject of an entire book by Mogens Krustrup.[25] The practice of ornamenting doors with talismans is ancient in the extreme, not just within Christianity. What better way to apprise the neophyte on the initiatory promenade of the meaning of the quest?

On most days the door is shut. It is only opened for major services and at the end of mass on Sundays.[26] The minor chapel that frames the south door resolutely turns its back on the visitor, its face only being revealed as you move clockwise around the building (Fig. 4.11). Here on the west facade woman is present through a carefully composed manifestation of what Le Corbusier called his "technique of grouping". Right from the beginning of his career Le Corbusier loved to make collections and groups of objects that would, in his mind, create unities at once symbolic and compositional.

> The *technique of grouping* is in some ways a manifestation of the modern sensibility in the consideration of the past, of the exotic, or of the present. To recognise the "series", to create "unities" across time and space, to render thrilling the view of things where mankind has inscribed its presence.[27]

The "technique of grouping" – italicised here by Le Corbusier to emphasise its importance – is used repeatedly in his painting and in his architecture. Here it is used in the construction of woman: the face of the minor chapel; her breasts in the form of a gargoyle (Fig. 4.12), which projects over the pregnant bulge of the wall which itself enfolds the confessionals.[28] As Albert Christ-Janer and Mary Mix Foley observed:

> … wherever one walks, on the exterior or the interior, elements, large and small, resolve themselves into perfectly proportioned compositions. This is not façade architecture to be viewed from one direction only. Nor is it solely a building contradicted by the afterthought of "applied features". Instead, everything is part of a fluid work of art which moves and changes with each change in perspective.[29]

A further belly in plan frames a "trinity" – "I love that word," wrote Le Corbusier – of enigmatic objects, a large hollow cylinder in opposition to a large pyramidical form with a small pyramidical form between them, conceivably a representation of Mary, God and Jesus their son – half immersed in water (Fig 4.13), that drains down into a large cistern below the chapel, a narrative of water that will culminate in Saint Pierre Firminy.

4.14 – North door
into Ronchamp

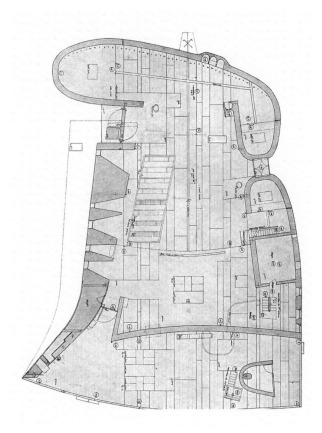

4.15 – Plan of
Ronchamp wih
north elevation
to the right

Sensitisation

The next stage in Le Corbusier's narrative arc is "Sensitisation" which usually takes
the form of a vestibule or door – "Again the little vestibule which frees your mind
from the street."[30] In grasping the door handle the visitors here meet the building
in a very palpable way, forcing them to engage, to focus and to participate. The low
key, gloomy and rather ordinary looking north entrance into the chapel (Fig. 4.14) is
universally ignored by commentators, yet we suggest that it plays a key role in the
experience of the promenade as a moment of quiet before entry. Indeed Le Corbusier
instructed his mother to enter via this door on her first visit to the chapel.[31]

The north door is flanked by two smaller chapel towers (Fig. 4.15) that appear, in plan,
to be in opposition to one another, one lined in white, the other in red (Fig. 4.16).
According to Robin Evans, Le Corbusier named the three towers at Ronchamp after
the Virgin Mary, his mother Marie and his wife Yvonne.[32] In one drawing of his mother
she is represented as a divinity, a giant sphinx flanked by the sun and the moon
(Fig. 4.17). At Ronchamp her tower/chapel, painted white inside, may represent the
maternal aspects of the feminine, while Yvonne's (in the north-east) painted red, may
represent the sexual. Together they are dominated by the larger white tower which
seems likely to represent the Virgin as eternal Feminine (Fig. 4.18). We believe that
Krustrup is correct in making the "tentative" suggestion that the Chapel is an homage
to Le Corbusier's mother as well as the mother of God.[33] In addition, we argue that it
also encompasses a tribute to his wife – his Messianic aspirations have already been

mentioned in Chapter 2. As Le Corbusier wrote in *Towards an Architecture*: "All great works of art are based on one or other of the great standards of the heart: *Oedipus, Phaedra*, the *Enfant Prodigue*, the Madonnas, *Paul et Virginie*, Philemon and Baucis."[34] He was fascinated by the " great stories", Jesus and Mary, Theseus and Ariadne, archetypes that he believed to repeat across time so it came naturally to him to see his own life in these epic terms. As Le Corbusier wrote of Ronchamp, "for me it is a personal, intimate affair."[35]

Significantly the arrangement of the chapels is similar to a drawing in *Le poème de l'angle droit* – roughly contemporary with the chapel – accompanied by these words (Fig. 4.19):

Between the poles reigns the tension
of fluids the scores
of opposites are settled an
end to the hatred of irreconcilables is
proposed union ripens
the fruit of confrontation[36]

If seen in terms of the Ronchamp north entry, the charged zone in the middle encompasses some kind of union. Like a funnel or ear, here two sets of timber doors – warm and pleasant to touch – form a constricted space of entry lined in yellow – sun and spirit in Le Corbusier's theogony – that propel the pilgrim into the splayed funnel that is the chapel itself. The intense light penetrating the interior of the south facade and the scale of the interior feel all the more spectacular when experienced in contrast with the mute and gloomy proscenium of the north facade (Fig. 4.20). This idea is endorsed by Louis Mauvais, formerly priest at Ronchamp, who writes of the "initiatory" itinerary of

4.16 – Interior
of red chapel

à 91 ans, Marie charlotte
amélie
Jeanneret Perret
règne sur le soleil, la lune,
les monts. Le lac et le
foyer, entourée de l'admiration
affectueuse de ses enfants 10 Septembre 1957

4.18 – View upwards
in white chapel

4.19 – Detail from
Le poème de l'angle droit

95

visiting the chapel that is possible when you enter through the north door: "I've often had the experience with groups. You go in slowly into what Corbu wanted to be 'a space of silence and prayer'."[37] The entire journey up the hill, past a series of enigmatic clues, both symbolic and spatial, sensitise the visitor in preparation for this moment of return.

Questioning

Entry by the north door is a dazzling experience. Robert Maguire and Keith Murray wrote disapprovingly of Ronchamp: "The forms and materials are perverse enhancing the dreamlike unreality of the whole." Similar sentiments were expressed by James Stirling.[38] This, we would argue, was precisely the intention of the Chapel which was designed to elicit curiosity and questioning.

> The shell will rest on walls of old, salvaged stones ... The shell was laid on walls foolishly but usefully thick. Inside the walls, however, are reinforced concrete columns. The shell will rest at intervals on top of these columns, but will not touch the wall; a horizontal beam of light ten centimeters wide will cause surprise ... [39]

The concrete floor roughly follows the slope of the hill, leaving it intact, and is marked out in what Le Corbusier called *opus optimum*, a Modulor pattern, that causes a distortion in the sensation of space (to be discussed in more detail in the next chapter). Le Corbusier laid down the following challenge – "Modulor everywhere. I defy a visitor to give, offhand, the dimensions of the different parts of the building,"[40] – one that has resulted in several agonisingly meticulous geometrical studies over the years. This game of scale, we argue, was designed more to inspire meditation on the meaning of ineffable space than on the literal mechanics of laying out the building.

In terms of Le Corbusier's narrative arc this is the point at which various options are examined and questions are asked. In his domestic architecture it usually constitutes the main living spaces, each offering a different possibility for dwelling. Very often it provides a distraction from the main promenade: an exploration of the pleasures of *savoir habiter*. Sometimes playful, it offers "up the anticipation or surprise of doors which reveal unexpected space."[41] It contains within it numerous sub-routes and sub-destinations, places for rituals such as eating or contemplating the fire, and places for making decisions. Though, as by Ariadne's golden thread, the reader is always drawn back to the main promenade generally expressed through a crescendo in light.

Similarly, at Ronchamp, a variety of routes are available. It is however likely that the pilgrim will continue the looping journey, swooping in a clockwise spiral past the ceremonial door, the three chapels, and then back to the altar – such spiral journeys are common in Le Corbusier's work, for example in the Maison du Bresil.[42] It is less likely that he or she will immediately make a hard left turn to view the interior elevation of the east wall which, either way, is the focus of discussion here (Fig. 4.21), framed on the left by the pulpit.

In her book *Le Corbusier in Detail* Samuel has identified a category of staircase in the work of Le Corbusier which she calls "precarious".[43] It is designed to be frightening, to focus the mind on the importance of what is at hand. The stair up to the pulpit at Ronchamp is particularly unnerving, especially if negotiated under the eyes of an entire congregation (Fig. 4.22). Here the space between the ground and the first tread seems to symbolise a separation between earthly and spiritual realms, acting as a reminder of the responsibilities of the priest (Fig. 4.23). Significantly the priest must enter into the red bodily chapel before he can rise up and address the congregation. Beneath the pulpit on the south side is seating for two hundred – the sculptural pews designed with the aid of the sculptor Joseph Savina. The rear and north side of the church are left free for processions and overflow. Apparently Le Corbusier did not want seating at all, but was persuaded to include benches for those at prayer by Ledeur.[44] Allusion is made here back to the early church which was designed for worship on foot. Similar aspirations would underpin Firminy.

4.22 – Detail of steps up to the main pulpit

4.23 – Main pulpit

4.21 – Interior view of east elevation as portrayed in the *Œuvre complète*

By his own admission, Le Corbusier found the organisation of the altar at Ronchamp very difficult, perhaps because it was here that he had to reconcile the needs of the Liturgy with his own beliefs. The problem was to balance the altar with the rest of the "elements of the interior choir ... that testify to the Christian drama," the Virgin and the cross.

> The cross, but human cross in all the cruelty of a reality devoid of emphasis,
> of discourse. Cross of agony.
> The Mother present because the son is implicated, virtual, at the level of man,
> on earth with graspable materiality, breathing without triumph.
> The objects of the rite, the elements of the drama.
> The drama is designed, installed.
> For you living men, to live the drama as well.
> But in the elevation of who has taken hold of the things brought together here:
> signs and material proportions totally loyal and noble.[45]

The drama is at "human scale". Here Le Corbusier could be alluding to the fact that the chapel is proportioned in accordance with the Modulor or he could be alluding to his belief that we, at a small scale, are living out the archetypal dramas of the gods – probably both. While the cross of the crucifixion is the most visible and important sign in Christianity it also refers to Le Corbusier's right angle and the very human need to balance spiritual and bodily concerns in order to live life well. Simultaneously it makes reference to "the God within", the belief that each of us contains a spark of the divine mentioned in chapter 2.

Although Le Corbusier was a great lover of concrete, although he saw concrete as reconstituted stone, the stone for the altar had to be real stone. Nothing else would do.

> ... the stone for saying Mass, consecrated and which is brought, which is fitted
> into 1 cavity (otherwise filled with a dead stone) although marked with 1 or with
> 5 crosses and which will receive the Host and ?[sic] two materializations of the
> highest sacrifice. The stone will be carried out by the officiant at the end of Mass
> ... The altar is the most maximum block of solid stone with proportions cubit
> [Egyptian] and Modulor.[46]

Le Corbusier may well be drawing an analogy between the stone of the altar and the philosopher's stone or *lapis*. This seems all the more likely given that the altar is proportioned according to the Modulor, which had links to the mathematical systems of the alchemists and back to the Egyptians. The altar at La Tourette would be a similarly charged focus of geometrical force (Fig. 4.24).

Two years after the dedication ceremony of Ronchamp, Le Corbusier wrote that he was beginning to feel an "increasing uneasiness" about the position of the wooden cross, "the latter occupying a position on the axis of the high altar, produces a mutual lessening in importance of these two opposing elements." [47] This is an intriguing passage. Why do the cross and the altar oppose each other? The altar is traditionally symbolic of Christ, as is the cross, so there should not have been a problem. It is possible that the vertical cross and horizontal altar form an opposition – a right angle, but this again would reinforce, not lessen, their message. He then made further sketches of a further "technique of grouping" which would bring "order, hierarchy and dignity" to the "protagonists", the altar, the Tree (wooden cross), and the Virgin (Fig. 4.25).

4.24 – Detail of the tabernacle
on the altar

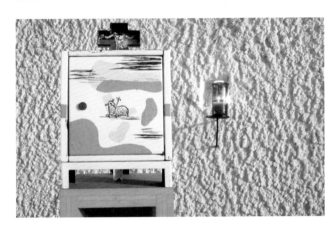

4.25 – Sketch of altar
from Le Corbusier's
Chapel at Ronchamp

4.26 – Marriage of
heaven and earth
from Michael Maier's
Atalanta Fugiens

Hierarchy.
1. The sign of the cross on the axis.
2. The witness (the Tree).
3. The presence of the Virgin Mary.
Side by side happily in the scheme.

> The consecration of the host is performed on the altar
> under the sign of the cross placed on the tabernacle
> dominating the axis which commands
> the architectural arrangement of the building.
> But close by and obliquely sited, upright and full sized is the witness,
> the tree, upright standing alone and embedded in the ground.

In the new version, the tree is set apart, in some way special, centred between the altar and the Virgin. "The protagonists are apparent, clearly visible, they are not confused on an opposing axis," noted the architect.[48]

Perhaps the ultimate symbol of Le Corbusier's cosmos, the tree, simultaneously refers back to nature, the tree of life, the Teilhardian tree of evolution and the tree of the iconostasis in his *Le poème de l'angle droit*. Just why they are considered to be protagonists is unclear, unless Le Corbusier conceived of the altar as the masculine Jesus, the counterpart to the feminine Virgin and the cross as symbolic of their union. The set up is highly reminiscent of a common image in alchemical texts, where the tree is flanked on one side by the sun (symbolised by Christ) and on the other by the moon (symbol of Mary) – another example of the *coniunctio*, the union of opposites, both spiritual and bodily (Fig. 4.26).

In his book *Christocentric Church Art* of 1922 Johannes Van Acken set out the principles of a Christocentric church architecture, one that emphasised our relationship with the Son, usually in a penitential context.[49] Christocentric architecture emphasises the centrality of Christ's sacrifice through strong expression of the altar which is set free standing in a simple space with minimal side chapels, no esoteric symbols or Latin inscriptions. It is elevated, well lit and often expressed on the exterior. Rudolf Schwarz and Romano Guardini developed such ideas into a more "theocentric" view of architecture, emphasising a father not manifest, the God beyond human experience and our "play" before him. Mies was a supporter of Guardini, the mute forms of his chapel at IIT, expressing an apophatic view of that which we cannot speak (Fig. 4.27). Whether Le Corbusier himself was party to these debates is not known though it seems very likely that he was familiar with the widely publicised work of Dominikus Böhm, strongly influenced by Van Acken, perhaps through the pages of *L'Architecture d'aujourd'hui* or through conversation with the enlightened clergy that he counted amongst his friends.[50] A special edition of *L'Art sacré*, featuring the work of Böhm, Schwarz and others appeared late in December 1950, perfectly timed to influence the thinking of both Le Corbusier and his colleagues within the Church (Fig. 4.28).[51]

The Canon of the Council of Carthage that took place in the year 397 made clear the importance of not confusing the Son with the Father.[52] What then is the role of the Mother in all this? Wolfgang Jean Stock has observed that at Ronchamp: "Architecturally the Virgin is allocated to a precise liturgical position. For Mary

101

4.27 – Mies van der Rohe,
Carr Memorial Chapel at Illinois
Institute of Technology, 1952

4.29 – A service
at Ronchamp,
FLC L3 (2) 270

4.28 – Cover of *L'Art sacré*, December 1950

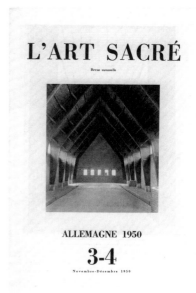

is the intercessor, she is not the centre but the mediator between God and man.
The prayers are addressed to her and she passes them on; and the architecture
replicates this sequence."[53] Such ideas are echoed in *L'Art sacré*. Here Cocagnac
quotes from the Book of Wisdom to explain the nature of the Virgin's mystery which,
for him, is characterised by the "grace and freedom" of the architecture of Ronchamp:

> When the Lord set the earth's foundations
> I was working near him, happy each day
> Playing continually in his presence, playing on the globe
> of the earth and finding my delights among the children of men.[54]

There is an echo here of the "play" before God discussed above with regard to the
theocentric church. Could it be that the Chapel at Ronchamp is the Other of Acken's
Christocentric churches, that Le Corbusier is reversing Acken's rules to create an
architecture of Mary? Certainly the altar is not elevated, it is not strongly lit, it is not
expressed on the exterior, it is not framed and it is not the focus of the composition.
Knowingly or unknowingly, Le Corbusier uses liturgical means to decrease the
importance of Christ in the reading of the space. (Fig. 4.29)

4.30 – Interior of east door

4.32 – Piero Della Francesca, (1410/1420- 1492) *Flagellation* (1447), Panel held at the National Gallery of Le Marche in the Palazzo Ducale, Urbino, CAL-F-008159-0000. Reproduced with the permission of Ministero per I Beni e le Attività Culturali

4.31 – Re-enacting the story of Jesus through the carrying of the cross

4.33 – Photograph of fireplace in Le Corbusier's penthouse 24 Rue Nungesser et Coli showing the split screen of the Annunciation

We know from Le Corbusier's journey to the East and from *Le poème de l'angle droit* that he took a keen interest in the iconostasis which, in the Eastern Church, is a screen prioritising images of the Virgin, representing the transition between this world and the next, an ancient exemplar of a more Marian architecture. The suggestion here is that the wall behind the altar at Ronchamp, the wall into which the figure of Mary is set, may in Le Corbusier's mind have been an iconostasis, a threshold into another world.

A further clue as to the meaning of the altar at Ronchamp lies within the *Œuvre complète*. Le Corbusier worked closely with his photographers to create highly contrived images of his buildings. Here in the photograph of the east end of the chapel interior (Fig. 4.21), our view is on axis with the Virgin in her glass box, emphasising her importance within the overall composition. If the photograph is divided in two horizontally, the inner corner of the seating platform is at its exact centre. At this point, we are immediately aware of two very different geometries at work: one leading us to the altar (via lines in the concrete of the floor), and one leading out of the east door into nature (via the seating platform).

> The main altar is situated in the nave (the axis of which is delineated in the flooring by a simple concrete band) where the ceiling is the highest, being 10 m high at the mid-point of the altar wall and only 4.78 high at its lowest point.[55]

wrote Le Corbusier in his usual cryptic fashion, although what we are supposed to make of it is not clear. The ceiling is not highest above the altar: it is at its highest and most well-lit above the east door. Le Corbusier identifies a tendency for human beings to be "attracted towards the centre of gravity" of a site,[56] which in his buildings nearly always takes the form of the stair or ramp, often highly contained, combined with the distant prospect of light. The same is the case at Ronchamp. Here altitude and luminosity draw attention to the east door's pivotal role as point of reorientation within the Chapel (Fig. 4.30).

Reorientation

Screened from the main altar, the east door at Ronchamp is a site of great importance. Formed in concrete, a perverse but highly intentional choice of material, and icy cold to touch, it is more than just reminiscent of the stone that the angel rolled away from the entrance of Jesus' tomb on the third day, the day of his resurrection. Although not customary any more, the cross used to be carried through it from within to without on rare and specific days of celebration in a small scale re-enactment of the story of Jesus (Fig. 4.31). It is not for general use.

Le Corbusier was fascinated by Piero della Francesca. The structure of such paintings as the *Flagellation*, or the *Annunciation* – encompassing contrasting views both near and far – is used repeatedly in his architecture and its representation (Fig. 4.32).[57] Thomas Schumacher notes that:

4.34 – Section F3,
*Le poème de l'angle
droit*, 1955

4.35 – Detail of
east door

... the genre [of the annunciation] ... almost invariably uses a split screen;
the angel is on the left and the Virgin is on the right. And while the figures of
these compositions consistently oppose each other, creating a binary tension,
the frame often holds the same tension. Left/right, inside and outside, then/
now, near/far, all are in opposition, expressing the hinge of History that Christian
doctrine attaches to this event.[58]

In his belief Le Corbusier used this format so frequently in his architecture and its
representation that it is likely that it held some kind of significance for him (Fig. 4.33).
If so it is repeated here in the iconostasis east door of Ronchamp, representing the push
and pull between "immanence", God approaching us through his incarnation Jesus and
"transcendence", our moving up from terrestrial life towards God.[59] As Le Corbusier
himself wrote, "there is a tide ceaselessly rising towards the spiritual and ebbing
towards the substantial realities of life."[60] Further, "sometimes there is a door: one
opens it – enters – one is in another realm, the realm of the gods, the room which holds
the key to the great systems. These doors are the doors of the miracles."[61] (Fig. 4.34)

The handle of the east door appears to take the abstract form of a woman's body
(Fig. 4.35). It is juxtaposed with an imprint of a cockle primarily symbolic of St
James and the pilgrimage to Santiago da Compostela in Spain, and thus to Catholic
pilgrimage in general, however, the shell could equally well signify Venus and the realm
of Eros. The feminine iconography of the east door is reinforced by the symbolism
of water, Mary and the moon in the painted glass of the south wall with which it is
juxtaposed (Fig. 4.36). This reading fits with the ideas of Teilhard who believed that
woman played an important role in bringing man closer to God. What this means if the
pilgrim is a woman herself is another matter.

4.36 – Detail of window
in south façade

Culmination

To go through the door, to enter nature, one must grasp the handle and push, encounter the goddess in a physical sense. Working drawings showing it in plan reveal its uncanny likeness to a pair of breasts (Fig. 4.37), a fact that could not have escaped Le Corbusier, who wrote "try to look at the picture upside down or sideways. You will discover the game."[62] A similar handle is used on the main door of the Zurich Pavilion where it is juxtaposed with a huge enamel illustration of the union of Icône and Taureau (Fig. 4.38). At Ronchamp the male visitor to the church is in union with the goddess. As Le Corbusier himself stated: "This church increases in value when there are people inside and around it."[63] The figure of Venus, goddess of birth, love and death, has long been associated with that of Mary Magdalene, who also has a place in the symbolism of this door. She anointed Jesus' feet, prefiguring her role in his burial, and left her previous life to join him as a disciple. She came to the tomb on the third day, and was the first witness to his resurrection, carrying away with her his message to which she gave new life. Orientated to the rising of the sun, the east door, the culminating point in Ronchamp's promenade, appears to symbolise the death and resurrection of Jesus. Simultaneously, in an alchemical sense, it evokes the *petite morte* of union, the relinquishing of the body and subsequent spiritual rebirth. There is a poetic irony in the fact that the door is so rarely used.

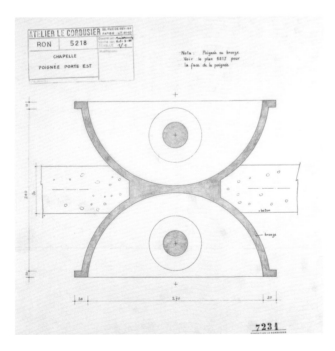

4.37 – Working drawing showing section across door handle

4.38 – Enamel door in Le Corbusier's Zurich Pavilion

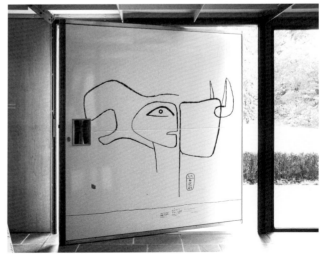

The Eternal Feminine

Having established that Mary played an extremely important role in the initiatory experience of Ronchamp – the chapel was after all in her name – we will now explore her significance, firstly within the Church and secondly within the work of Le Corbusier. The "woman question" as it came to be known attracted wide public interest between the wars and would become still more urgent after World War II as French women fought for suffrage.[64] Such ideas would prove influential on Le Corbusier who developed a rather different take on Mary to that of traditional Catholicism.[65]

The Ascendancy of Mary within the Church

The nineteenth century saw a renewed interest in Mary mother of Jesus, considered by Catholics to be Mary Mother of God, leading to what Duffy calls "a more emotional and colourful religion of the heart."[66] Mary has, since the very beginning of the Christian Church, been venerated through feast days and churches in her name. Supposed apparitions of the Virgin prompted the founding of extremely popular Marian shrines in France such as at La Salette (1846) and at Lourdes (1858) and added immensely to her esteem.[67] As with Mary Magdalene, her image has been exploited by artists, writers and others to further an agenda about woman's role in society. She was used, as Marina Warner has noted, "as the instrument of a dynamic argument from the Catholic Church about the structure of society, presented as a God-given code."[68] This explains why "this blossoming of the cult of Mary" is said by Duffy to be "intimately linked to a growing loyalty to the papacy."[69]

In 1854 Pius IX promulgated the dogma of the Immaculate Conception in a papal bull, an open letter from the pope of great solemnity, *Ineffabilis Deus*, in which Mary was declared to have been conceived without the stain of original sin (sexual intercourse). A hundred years later, in 1950, Pius XII promulgated the dogma of the Assumption of the Virgin Mary – the taking of Mary's body and soul up to Heaven at the end of her life – in his apostolic constitution, *Munificentissimus Deus*. It is the only papal statement to be officially qualified as "infallible" since the declaration of Papal Infallibility of 1870.[70] In tandem with this, the pope declared Mary as Queen of Heaven, and dedicated the year 1954, shortly before the completion of Ronchamp, to her. As Warner has observed, "the historical process that changes the character of the Virgin is seen merely as a gradual discovery of a great and eternal mystery, progressively revealed."[71]

The Vatican II Council pronounced the importance of Mary in the dogmatic constitution *On the Church*, dedicating a chapter to her, "The Role of the Blessed Virgin Mary, Mother of God, in the Mystery of Christ and the Church".[72] Further, in 1966, Paul VI proclaimed her "Mother of God and of the Church".[73] In *On the Church*, Catholics are reminded the Church is also "our Mother" (mother of the faithful).[74] This renewal of interest in Mary may have built upon the canonisation of Joan of Arc by Rome in 1920; in France she was consecrated as the country's (secondary) patron saint in 1922, in some ways mirroring the figure of the revolutionary Marianne. The promulgation of these important female figures within the doctrines of the Church was arguably more about the pacification of women than their emancipation.

Mary in the Work of Le Corbusier

Le Corbusier took a keen interest in the pilgrim's manual written for the chapel that had once stood on the site, destroyed during the War. Of particular note was the fact that it was the site of a pagan temple which had been replaced by a chapel dedicated to the Virgin.[75] Mary is of central importance to the conception of Ronchamp, so important that Le Corbusier wrote the word "Attention!" next to a reference to "the good mother" in the pilgrim handbook.[76] Further, and most importantly, he wrote the word "feminism" next to a reference to the "cult of Mary" at Ronchamp[77] underlining references to "Annunciation, the Presentation, the Visitation and Crowning of Mary in heaven".[78] It seems almost uncanny that, in defending the decision to give Le Corbusier the commission for Ronchamp, Dubourg, the Archbishop of Besançon, asked the earnest question: "What if the Virgin is waiting for Le Corbusier at Ronchamp?"[79]

An illustration in *The Chapel of Ronchamp* makes the connection between Mary and some more primal feminine deity very clear (Fig. 4.39). A circle of people sit in the dark around a fire in front of the exterior chapel, as if re-enacting some ancient ritual, while Mary looks on from the shadows. The Virgin, and her counterpart the Magdalene, continue the tradition of the Great Mother, whose fertility was less primly portrayed in archaic times. Her symbolism can be seen most clearly in the painted glass of the south wall, in close proximity to the east door. Traditionally swathed in a cloak of blue[80] she is the water, the sea and the moon. Her name, Marie, painted on to the glass, also evokes that of his own mother.

Mary appears in *Le poème de l'angle droit* – published in 1955, the same year as Ronchamp's dedication – cementing her role in Le Corbusier's cosmos (Fig. 4.40). Oddly enough she is surrounded by red, Le Corbusier's colour for "Fusion" or physicality, red being the traditional colour for the cloak of Mary Magdalene. In a developmental sketch for the poem Le Corbusier's Mary is depicted with a halo (Fig. 4.41), as she is in a Crucifixion scene at Santa Maria Antigua in Rome which, as Mogens Krustrup has illustrated, is the most likely source of the image,[81] but in the poem itself she appears on the beach, her halo gone. Close inspection of the Mary figure reveals that she is not one, but two draped women, one facing towards us and one facing away: a two-sided Mary, at once Magdalene and Virgin. Overleaf, next to a full colour image of Icône (Fig. 4.42), appear the words:

> who made her thus where does she come from?
> She is rightness child of
> limpid heart present on earth
> close to me, daily acts of
> humility vouch for
> her greatness [82]

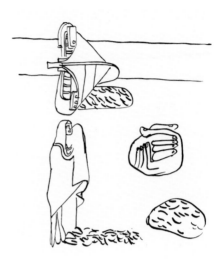

4.39 – Illustration of
the exterior chapel from
Le Corbusier's *The Chapel
at Ronchamp*

4.40 – Mary in *Le poème
de l'angle droit*

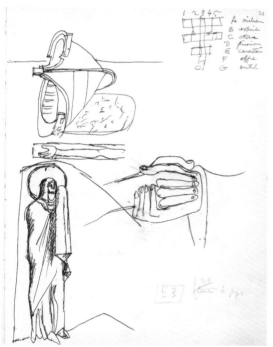

4.41 – Sketch study for Mary
from *Le poème de l'angle droit*

4.42 – Icône from
Le poème de l'angle droit

Whilst obviously referring to his wife Yvonne, these words link back the Mary on the beach with the humble Mary Magdalene who washed Christ's feet with her hair. Charles Jencks writes that "several French acquaintances" have said that Yvonne "was more than a woman of easy virtue," another possible reason for her association with this Biblical sinner.[83]

One aspect of Marian symbolism in which Le Corbusier took a particularly strong interest was the Catholic topos of the "three Marys". Significantly, a reproduction of a medieval painting showing the dead Christ surrounded by a trinity of Marys appears on the wall of the Pilgrim house at Ronchamp, one of several Marian images (Fig. 4.43). The same subject appears in the *Radiant City* in the form of a statue from Chartres Cathedral of Jesus with his arms around three women. The caption reads, "eternally permissible product: the work of art, final end of human nature," suggesting the enduring significance of this story.[84] According to the Gnostic Gospel of Mary, all three Marys of the canonical books were interchangeable.[85] That Le Corbusier appears to have been fully aware of the multiplicity of possibilities embodied in this one name has already been indicated by his use of the word "Marys" in his account of the life of the Magdalene in the *Œuvre complète*.[86] Given what we know of Le Corbusier it seems highly unlikely that he would have taken much interest in the standard virtuous Mary – so virtuous that she managed to conceive without losing her virginity – unless she is considered the "spiritual" counterpart to her corporeal sister Mary Magdalene.

In the *Œuvre complète* there is an image of the exterior chapel at Ronchamp where the figure of the Madonna framed within her niche can be seen half in sun and half in shade (Fig. 4.44). Attention is drawn to her by the spike of an open umbrella. "Observe the play of shadows," writes Le Corbusier with specific regard to Ronchamp.[87] Working drawings indicate that it was his specific intention that she should be bisected into zones of light and shadow (Fig. 4.45). By representing her like this Le Corbusier is suggesting that she has a dual aspect, an idea that is given further substance when we consider that the statue of the Virgin is fixed on a pivot so that she can be turned around to reveal either of her two sides - outwards to face exterior congregations or into the interior (Fig. 4.46). Yet again she is framed in red, Le Corbusier's colour for "Fusion" or physicality, juxtaposed with the green of nature.

The role of the Virgin Mary in Catholicism is well known, but what is perhaps less well known is her paramount role in alchemy. In fact, the invention of alchemy itself has been attributed to "Mary the Jewess".[88] Described as the "siren of the philosophers, born of our deep sea (Maria)", she is depicted pouring milk and blood from her breast. White and red appear in the flower of the alchemists, sometimes called the womb of the *Filius Philosophorum,* or glorious child.[89] Apollinaire took advantage of this symbolism to compare his lover Marie Laurencin with the mystical rose, another symbol of the Virgin with alchemical connotation.[90] Comparisons should be made with Le Corbusier's own treatment of the theme of the Mystical Rose when deliberating over designs for the chapel (Fig. 4.47).[91]

4.43 – Interior of Pilgrim
House at Ronchamp in 1950s

4.44 – Mary half in sun half in
shade from *Œuvre complète*

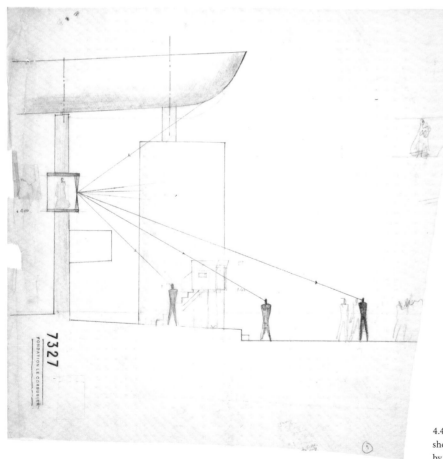

4.45 – Working drawing
showing Mary bisected
by shadow

4.46 – Mary in her niche at Ronchamp

4.48 – The Chapel at Ronchamp as depicted in Giedion's *Space Time and Architecture*

4.47 – Sketch by Le Corbusier on the theme of the Mystical Rose for Ronchamp

Le Corbusier describes Ronchamp as "a vessel of intense concentration and meditation."[92] Both Mary and Mary Magdalene are represented through vessel symbolism, the Virgin through her womb and the Magdalene through the Myrrophore, the jar of funerary oil that she carries with her – it is worth mentioning here that Le Corbusier's friend Sigfried Giedion identified the chapel with Neolithic funerary monuments in his book *Space Time and Architecture* (Fig. 4.48). Together they preside over the realms of birth, death and love. As vessels, they are embodied in the form of the chapel described in curiously erotic terms by Le Corbusier as "a vase of silence, of sweetness. A desire."[93]

Lucien Hervé, a photographer who worked closely with Le Corbusier, made the connection between building and body perfectly clear by juxtaposing Le Corbusier's statement, "I believe in the skin of things, as in that of women,"[94] with an image of the southeast wall of Ronchamp, which looks uncannily like skin seen at close range.

> Tenderness!
> Seashell the Sea in us has never
> ceased to wash its wrecks of
> laughing harmony upon the shore
> Hand kneading hand caressing
> hand brushing. The hand and the
> seashell love each other [95]

The imprint of Le Corbusier's own fingers can apparently be seen in the plaster of the wall by the figure of the Virgin Mary.[96] In touching the building he has touched her. When we enter into the body of the church, through its highly physical curves we enter the womb of the Eternal Feminine in her guise as Mary – again ambiguously chaste and sexual.

Le Corbusier went so far as to observe that "In my drawings and paintings I have always shown only women, or pictures, symbols and genealogies of women."[97] Given that his paintings were for Le Corbusier a source of architectural form, it follows that his buildings too would retain echoes of the body from which they were conceived.

Christopher Pearson has made the point that, within Le Corbusier's domestic architecture, a work of art was intended, amongst other things, to act as a "carefully sited human presence within the building, which could dramatise … the visitor's relationship to and participation in the architectural space by the creation of a sympathetic bond between visitor and sculpture."[98] The statue of Mary above the altar at Ronchamp provides a clear example of this. Le Corbusier would similarly adopt anthropomorphic forms into his architecture in order to maximise its psychological impact on the visitor.

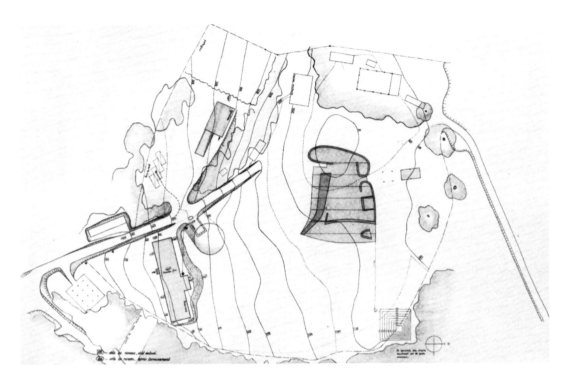

4.49 – Plan of the Ronchamp chapel complex

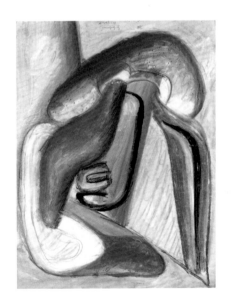

4.50 – Le Corbusier, Acoustic forms, pastel on paper, New York 1946 (rotated 180 degrees)

4.51 – Le Corbusier, *Portrait de femme à la cathédrale de Sens* (l'ange gardien du foyer II), 1944

4.52 – Le Corbusier Ozon, Opus 1, 1947 Sculpture FLC 4

Jaime Coll has convincingly linked Le Corbusier's painted representations of Yvonne to the figure of Ariadne as she appears in André Gide's version of *Theseus,* which Le Corbusier read in 1951.[99] Gide's Ariadne is a lunar deity symbolised by the moon and sea with two aspects, one positive and one negative. In the opinion of Jaime Coll the plan of the chapel (Fig. 4.49) was derived from an "acoustic" sketch (Fig. 4.50).[100] Certainly the similarities are striking. Indeed the whole building retains elements of the *Icône* series of paintings, further endorsement of the suggestion that certain parts of the building might be compared with elements of a woman's body. Reference should also be made to a series of paintings entitled the "Cathedrale de Sens" (Fig. 4.51). Sens here could equally refer to the town of Sens where there is a cathedral and to the woman's body – a cathedral of senses. Julia Kristeva writes in a different context:

> … of the virginal body we are entitled only to the ear, the tears, and the breasts. That the female sexual organ has been transformed into an innocent shell which serves only to receive sound may ultimately contribute to an eroticization of hearing and the voice, not to say of understanding. But by the same token sexuality is reduced to a mere implication. The female sexual experience is therefore anchored in the universality of sound, since the spirit is equally given to all men, to all women.[101]

In doing so she unknowingly draws together a number of Corbusian themes. The shape of Ronchamp's towers owe much to the earlike forms of Le Corbusier's acoustic sculptures (Fig. 4.52). In 1928, according to Richard Moore, Le Corbusier started to symbolise "aesthetic matters of vision through a representation of the water balance in the inner ear which, combined with the open hand, represented the giving and receiving of sound." The use of realistic anatomical detail of the inner ear dissolved into a representation of the womb of the "archetypal woman", her fertility tied to the tides, and thus to the moon.[102]

Le Corbusier described the lighting in the towers as "very special", we would suggest because of a link between light and sound, erotic and spiritual revelation.[103] Gregory of Nyssa (d. 394) posited the idea that Mary conceived Jesus on hearing the words of the angel.[104] This idea quickly gained a "literal stamp" and was celebrated by many medieval poets resulting in the notion that the Virgin was impregnated through her ear. Le Corbusier may be alluding to this belief. Through its earlike form the tower acts as a receiver of sound. The word of God enters Mary's body in the form of light. The tower is simultaneously ear and vagina, open to spiritual or erotic connotations.

On April 3, 1954, whilst working on the Chapel, Le Corbusier started a new sketchbook, entitled H32. He copied into it, though not word for word, several pages of Book Five of *Gargantua and Pantagruel*, those pages in which Panurge seeks advice from the Oracle of the Holy Bottle on whether or not to marry.[105] Echoes of this journey permeate the scheme for Ronchamp, particularly through the symbolism of the bottle, sound, the body, nature and woman.

It is Le Corbusier's consideration of the issue of proportion and harmony both in music and in art that leads him directly on to Rabelais' description of Panurge's arrival at the sanctuary of the Holy Bottle and a complex analysis of the route in terms of number. Le Corbusier's transcription begins:

> ... arrived in the longed for isle ...
> At the end of this fatal number you will find the Temple door ...
> = true psychogony of Plato so celebrated by the
> Academicians and so little understood, of which half is
> composed of unity, the first two whole numbers, of two
> squares and of two cubes (1=2 and 3= squared 8 and 27 Total 54=Plato)
> they descend 108 steps ...[106]

The presence of these numbers filled Panurge with fear, such import do they carry. Scribbled calculations suggest that Le Corbusier cogitated over the meaning of these figures for some time searching for their inner significance. The journey which describes Panurge's initiation in tender detail is discussed at length in Samuel's book *Le Corbusier and the Architectural Promenade*. Weighty emphasis is placed on listening hard to what the Oracle has to say – hence the earlike, "acoustic", quality of Le Corbusier's representations of Panurge in his art. The Oracle's extraordinarily anticlimactic pronouncement of the word "trink" does not disappoint Le Corbusier who responds ecstatically:

> This sybilline quotation [Trink] merely anticipates the conclusion I mean to give this work by giving the last word to an author who is forever formidable, forever clear-sighted.
>
> Patience, reader, you shall read the oracle in good time.[107]

Summary

Such was the importance of the message to be delivered by Ronchamp that it was worth very considerable expense in Le Corbusier's eyes. The curved forms and innovative roof structure added greatly to its cost. The original building estimate in 1950 was for 50,000,000 old francs. It was finally paid for in 1974 at a cost of 80,000,000 old francs which included Le Corbusier's own fee of 15%. Apparently 600 tree trunks were used to support the coque during its construction, "a veritable forest" in the words of Jean-François Mathey.[108] In being so lavish it completely went against the grain of what was happening in church construction at that time.[109]

Stock observes that "In the initial post-war period the approach was deliberately unassuming, unmonumental, and not just because of limited funds."[110] In an article entitled "The Magnificence of Poverty" in *L'Art sacré* Father Couturier set out his vision for what a church might be. "Today, in order for a church to be a 'real' church, it should be nothing other than a flat ceiling supported by four walls. However, inside there would be such pure and intense use of correlative proportions, spatial volumes and distribution of light and shadow that one would be instantly struck by its solemnity and spiritual dignity." [111]

Richard Keickhefer writes grudgingly that "if any one church is generally recognised as a model of mid-twentieth century ecclesiastical innovation it is surely … Ronchamp," ascribing its status to its "unconventionality". [112] Le Corbusier knew that in building what Nikolaus Pevsner described as "the most discussed monument of a new irrationalism" [113] he was risking his professional reputation amongst an established fan base that admired him for the "functionalism" of his offerings. The Chapel at Ronchamp is loud. Whilst not being kitsch, it goes against the 1947 Principles of the German Liturgical Commission in "trying to catch the attention of the passer-by with the architectural equivalent of the market place." [114] It is perhaps for this reason that Rudolph Schwarz described it as "trash". [115] Indeed it seems positively decadent – lavish and wasteful in the extreme – when compared with another contemporary chapel, Saint André near Nice built in 1955 by the architect Reiner Senn, built for the Companions of Emmaus, one of Abbé Pierre's homeless communities (Fig. 4.53). Clad on the exterior in vertical unsquared offcuts of logs with a roof covered in bituminised paper, and a floor of loose pebbles, the chapel is twelve metres square constructed with four massive beams in the form of a pyramid [116] and was apparently built by the architect with one of his friends using a scaffold of old bed springs. [117] Le Corbusier was himself very fond of building with simple local materials and took a strong interest in the plight of the homeless; many of the fallow years of the War were spent exploring such themes. [118] In his own copy of *La Vie de Jesus* Le Corbusier underlined Ernest Renan's words, "the founders of the kingdom of God are the humble." [119] He could have used the most "humble" techniques at Ronchamp, but he chose not to.

4.53 – Saint André near Nice built in 1955 by the architect Reiner Senn, built for the Companions of Emmaus

It is our suggestion that it all comes back to Mary. If Le Corbusier had built an achingly simple shrine he would have lost the opportunity to use his full toolkit of architectural techniques on winning people over to her cause. It has been seen that Le Corbusier favoured Catholicism over Protestantism because of its sensuality, a sensuality that he felt was embodied in the figure of the Virgin. To celebrate the role of woman in the experience of the divine was, for Le Corbusier, to celebrate the body and its responses. This was something that an ostensibly simple, intellectual, theocentric church such as Mies' chapel at IIT simply could not do. "I have a body like everyone else," wrote Le Corbusier, "and what I'm interested in is contact with my body, with my eyes, my mind."[120]

That Le Corbusier was a manipulative man should by now be evident. The recoding of building types was a long-term interest of his. The houses of the 1920s and 1930s reused the language of industrial architecture to make homes equally well suited for an industrial magnate or his employees. Similarly he worked with Charlotte Perriand to recode the meaning of furniture, for example using "masculine" steel and leather in "feminine" curves in the design of his famous chaise longue (Fig. 4.54).[121] He took the same approach with his church architecture, recombining the curves, geometry, colour, theatricality and sheer populist appeal of the Baroque in an entirely new way.

4.54 – Charlotte Perriand, Le Corbusier and Pierre Jeanneret, Chaise Longue, 1928

James Stirling railed against Ronchamp for its "entirely visual appeal" and for the fact that it demanded no "intellectual participation".[122] It is notable that Couturier believed that visual sensibilities of the public had not only been perverted, but had been imprisoned by conformism and pretentiousness.[123] Stirling's words are perhaps a case in point. Le Corbusier's architecture, like that of the great Gothic cathedrals, was designed to be read like a book, experienced at different levels of intellect and education.[124]

I give you this chapel of dear, faithful concrete, shaped perhaps with temerity but certainly with courage in the hope that it will seek out in you (as in those who will climb the hill) an echo of what we have drawn into it.[125]

Significantly Le Corbusier wrote that "the requirements of religion have little effect on the design" of Ronchamp. Instead "the form was an answer to the psycho-physiology of the feelings."[126] Further "The key is light and light illuminates the shapes and shapes have an emotional power."[127] Firstly the chapel would impact on the visitor through the "emotional" effects of its sober yet deeply sensual form and materials. A second set of more intellectual messages would then be available to "those with eyes to see", an alchemical aphorism utilised by Le Corbusier in *Towards an Architecture* and adopted by Couturier in the pages of *L'Art sacré*.[128] André Vigneau, in an article on "Light and the Liturgy" in that journal, emphasise the importance of light for the "psychological plan" of a church suggesting that Le Corbusier's rhetoric was not at all at odds with *L'Art sacré's* thinking.[129] It seems therefore that when Le Corbusier wrote that "the requirements of religion have little effect on the design" of Ronchamp he was actually talking about the dictats of the Vatican, not the "free" religion of his Dominican friends.[130]

> The situation was very delicate. It is the most revolutionary work of architecture made for a long time. And this on religious grounds, on Catholic grounds. On the grounds of rites. The rites are by my architecture raised to the highest, purified, returned to the Gospels. This is said by the priests – the good and true ones – a gesture perhaps carrying with it unexpectedly unpredictable effects, good or bad.

> All was joy and enthusiasm. BUT the devil must snigger in a corner and he is in the habit of not staying inactive. Rome has its eye on Ronchamp. I expect storms. And watch out, wickedness, low blows."[131]

The architecture of the chapel at Ronchamp, like that of La Sainte Baume, is an expression of the modernising agenda of *L'Art sacré* underpinned with the arcane. At the same time Le Corbusier twisted renewed Vatican interest in Mary into something more politicised, a reassertion of the role of women both in religion and in life. In the words of Cocagnac, "Le Corbusier has reunited sacred space with the profane world which turns its hopes towards the Virgin."[132] When asked to produce a design for another church Le Corbusier wrote in his sketchbook:

> I did one taking 1[sic] risk the big risk. It's done. I possess a sense of the unknown, of the immense space left to man before his imagination, his possible choice between good and evil. Define the one and the other? A single light: discern and opt.[133]

THE MONASTERY OF SAINTE MARIE DE LA TOURETTE

Penance through "regular observance" is central to the Dominican way of life and is for this reason central to the Monastery of Sainte Marie de La Tourette, built for this order in 1953 and located at L'Arbresle, some twenty-five kilometres from Lyons. Standing proud on the slope on which it is built and framed in woodland, it is fortresslike in character, protecting the sensitive life within (Fig. 5.1). The four sides of La Tourette form an uneasy cloister, a reinterpretation of a typical Dominican monastery plan, illustrated in the *Œuvre complète*, but open to the landscape (Fig. 5.2).[1] This paradisiacal garden would traditionally be enclosed and protected by the ecclesiastical buildings within which it sits. At La Tourette it is occupied by a system of enclosed ramped walkways open to the rough hillside that comes tumbling through the building (Fig. 5.3). "The monastery is posed in the savage nature of the forest and grasslands which is independent of the architecture itself,"[2] wrote Le Corbusier underlining its defensive fragility.

Built out of painfully rough *béton brut* the building is carefully proportioned to the Modulor. The top floors are dedicated to two layers of cellular accommodation for the monks (ninety-four in total), linked by three flights of stairs. Entry to the communal spaces – the Church, the Refectory and so on – is below this.

5.1 – The monastery
of Sainte Marie de
La Tourette

5.3 – Centre of cloister
showing exterior of Oratory

5.2 – Plan of a traditional
Dominican monastery
included in *Œuvre complète*

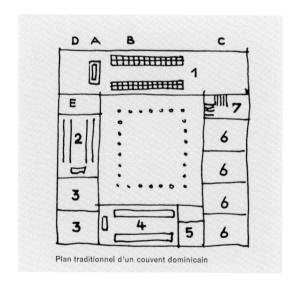

Plan traditionnel d'un couvent dominicain

5.4 – Miracle box for
Tokyo, FLC 29936B

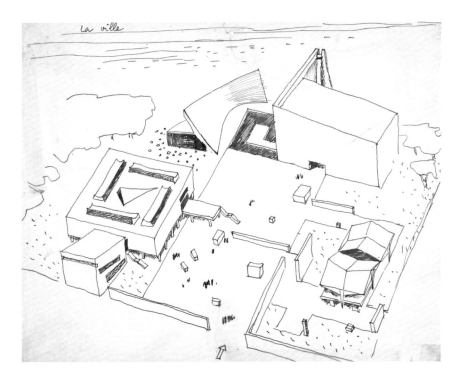

5.5 – Church at
La Tourette

5.6 – 15 Rue de Sevres

5.7 – Sketch of Pere Corbu and Pere
Claude from letter to the young
monk Claude Ducret, stepson of his
associate Paul Ducret, 1963

The monastery was designated as a *studium*, a school, complete with classrooms and a library. Correspondingly, there were three groups of monks forming the community that lived there: professor fathers, student brothers, and lay, convert brothers (called "convers" in French) who performed domestic tasks – the students being the largest group. Each group had separate living quarters and came together for class, meals and worship. The community is rather different now.

The church, accessible to the local community, is essentially a rectangular box with free form appendages that house the sacristy and more private chapels (Fig. 5.5). Philippe Potié describes it as a "miracle box", a theme conceived for the Pavillon des Temps Nouveau (1937) and included in his museum designs for Tokyo and Chandigarh (Fig. 5.4). Here at La Tourette, writes Potié, the miracle box is "endowed with its primary meaning."[3]

The project offered him the opportunity to explore a subject close to his heart – monastic life. "I have something of a monk's soul," wrote Le Corbusier to Father Levesque in 1963.[4] It should not be forgotten that his own atelier in Rue de Sèvres was within part of a Jesuit complex and that music trickled in through the windows from the nearby church on a regular basis (Fig. 5.6).[5] Le Corbusier thought of himself as a monk, Père Corbu[6] (Fig. 5.7), living with the spiritual torment and anguish that he believed to be the key elements of monastic existence, but without the intolerable constraints of celibacy: "... my life is more or less exactly that of a Trappist or any other kind of monk of your choosing (except for the vow of chastity)."[7] Herein we find the crux of the matter. Couturier and the Dominicans had made a vow of chastity something, seemingly, that Le Corbusier could never do. Whilst he was very much in accord with *L'Art sacré* thinking on most things, he remained passionate about the importance of love between a man and a woman. Having celebrated Mary with such enthusiasm at Ronchamp he could not relinquish her now. As a young man Le Corbusier wrote with regret of the absence of women at the monastery of Mount Athos: "Not a single woman is to be seen; thus everything is missing here in the East where only for the sight of her woman is the primordial ingredient."[8] La Tourette and Mount Athos are clearly linked in a 1954 sketch.[9] The absence of women was a theme he would return to, much later in life, in a jocular letter to one of the fathers on the amount of visitors that the monastery was starting to attract.

> Fortunately for you, your door is closed to ladies, which diminishes by half the invasion into the place. Still, had they been allowed in, they might have learnt it is not essential to have decorated interiors and silks, and that the love one should give to one's neighbour can be manifested just as well in a sober architecture on the slenderest budget.[10]

This statement directly contradicts his many pronouncements on women and the pioneering way that they had changed their fashion for the modern world.[11] One can only assume it was written to please his rather traditional correspondent. Either way it shows a continued interest in the absence of women in the building.

Rabelais' description of the Abbey at Thélème in Le Corbusier's beloved *Gargantua and Pantagruel* provides a parody of monastic life in which the comingling of the sexes was an absolute priority. To be in a room solely with members of the same sex would incur severe punishment. It seems likely that Le Corbusier would not have taken Rabelais' frequent allusions to the gross sexual appetites of monks and nuns literally. He would have taken them as a critique of the Church and its inability to recognise the important role that love between man and woman plays in the attainment of the higher soul. La Tourette encapsulates the hardships of his vision of monastic life, forcing those within to look deep inside to make this spiritual connection, just as Saint Teresa did within the confines of her *Interior Castle* discussed in chapter 3.

Phyllis Zagano writes that "A Dominican man or woman chooses to live a celibate life within a community of contemplative preachers in order to share the family life of the Gospel community formed by the Holy Spirit through the proclamation and hearing of the word of God."[12] It was seen in the discussion of La Sainte Baume that Saint Teresa had experienced a powerful spiritual relationship with Christ within the interior castle of her imagination. By the same token, if Le Corbusier's rather dualistic view of gender is to be taken into account, the monks of La Tourette would be in dialogue with their inner feminine, Mary, to whom the building is dedicated.[13] Only in this way could the "fusion" of gender, so central to Le Corbusier's *Le poème de l'angle droit* and to his cosmos, be attained. In the words of Le Corbusier's colleague Iannis Xenakis: "The drama had to remain internal and luminous."[14]

La Tourette largely exemplifies "the strong objectivity of forms under a Mediterranean sky" that, in Le Corbusier's opinion, characterises "male" architecture.[15] It is radically different from the "infinitely subjective" free forms of Ronchamp, perhaps because of the gendered nature of its narrative. If all this sounds too much we refer to Colin Rowe's trenchant observation of La Tourette: those "sceptical of the degree of contrivance" and "temperamentally predisposed to consider the game of hunt-the-symbol as an overindulgence in literature" really need to look at the architecture once more.[16]

The Commission and the Development of the Project

It was Couturier's idea to press for the commission of Le Corbusier to "create a silent dwelling place for one hundred bodies and one hundred hearts."[17] His first advice to the architect was to visit La Thoronet, a monastery in southern France (in fact, not far from La Sainte Baume, Fig. 5.8).[18] Le Corbusier found the twelfth-century Cistercian architecture so moving that he wrote a preface to a book about it published in 1956, *La plus grande aventure du monde, l'architecture mystique de Cîteaux*, translated into English as *An Architecture of Truth*, featuring the chiaroscuro photography of Lucien Hervé.[19] Significantly Le Corbusier dwelt upon the quality of the stonework – stone and concrete being intimately connected in his mind. He also commented on the "male and female ... population of [roof] tiles" – possibly a comment on the absence of women in the community beneath them. Le Corbusier ended the preface with, "In the hour of 'raw concrete' as blessed, welcome and hailed as it is, along my route, such an admirable encounter."[20] The "greatest adventure on earth" refers here to the quest for the Holy Grail (with which the Magdalene is sometimes conflated, echoing the vessel symbolism of Ronchamp) and is appropriate for a locality with such strong Templar connections. The second half of the book is filled with citations from the Bible (mostly Psalms) and writers from the medieval period having affinities with Cistercian theology. "I cannot consider in this light neither height, nor length, nor width; for me, this light is named the shadow of the living light," wrote Saint Hildegarde (1098-1188).[21] One can imagine this speaking to Le Corbusier in his research on ineffable space, indeed a great number of the passages inspire a correlation between the two.

On 4 May 1953 Le Corbusier visited the site for La Tourette where, as was his custom, he made a series of sketches of the landscape (Fig. 5.9), the prominence of the site being an important consideration for his church designs. He also began to enter into a close dialogue with the monks (Fig. 5.10). At the same time he wrote to Couturier, who had just been hospitalised, to reassure him about the progress on the project.[22]

5.8 – The Cistercian abbey Le Thoronet as photographed by Lucien Hervé, 1951

5.9 – Le Corbusier's initial sketches of the site for La Tourette, FLC K3 19 179

5.10 – Le Corbusier and the Dominicans from Le Corbusier's *Œuvre complète*

Ideas that were present in Le Corbusier's very first sketches were the quadrangular form of the building, a ramped promenade (later to be rejected by the monks), the pilotis and the retention of the terrain beneath, as at Ronchamp (Fig. 5.11). In July, from his hospital bed, Couturier sent the architect a long letter full of instructions and drawings, which Le Corbusier only partially took into account.[23]

On February 3, 1953, the commission was passed by Father A. Belaud in the name of the Dominicans of the Province of Lyons for a monastic study centre, later dubbed Sainte Marie de la Tourette.[24] It must have been a period of expansion for the Dominicans who, at roughly the same time, commissioned Pinsard and Hutchinson to build a very simple priory in Lille (Fig. 5.12, 1954-58), echoing in form and materials the factories in the local neighbourhood.[25] At the end of January 1954, no longer able to write himself, Couturier dictated his final article for *L'Art sacré* which, significantly, was about Le Corbusier. It was at once a eulogy and a warning: an homage to Ronchamp and La Tourette and a warning about the bad copies that were inevitably on their way (we will return to this in Chapter 7). The article also served as an homage to Couturier, who died on February 9, 1954, before the article was published in March. A photograph of him on his deathbed appears on the first page of his article about Le Corbusier, showing just how close Le Corbusier had come to the Dominican order[26] and indeed to Couturier (Fig. 5.13). A farewell message to Couturier from Le Corbusier (written from Chandigarh) also featured in the issue along with messages by Rouault, Braque, Léger, Bazaine and Manessier. Le Corbusier stated:

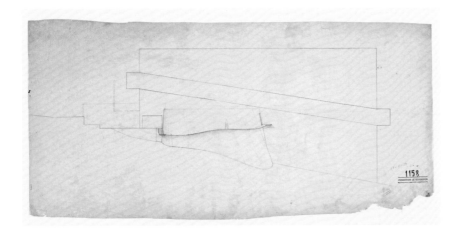

5.11 – Early sketch showing proposal for ramp, FLC 00158

5.12 – Pinsard and Hutchinson, Dominican Priory Lille, 1954-58

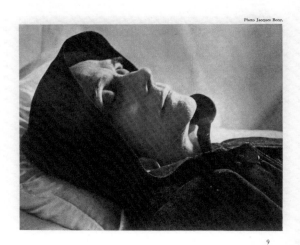

Son dernier article

Le Corbusier

CERTAINS se sont étonnés de l'hommage sans réserve que nous avions rendu à Le Corbusier, lors du commencement des travaux pour l'église de Ronchamp. Nous disions que « non seulement nous tenions Le Corbusier pour le plus grand architecte vivant, mais encore pour celui en qui le sens spontané du sacré est le plus authentique et le plus fort... » Nous le redirons et nous insisterons. Et nous ajouterons qu'il y a plaisir à dire de telles choses, face à la conjuration des médiocres (et, hélas, on a la tristesse de voir s'y mêler parfois d'assez grands noms) qui ne cessent de le calomnier, de l'épier et de le piller : « Ils nous fusillent, mais ils retournent nos pochès », disait Degas, il y a cinquante ans. Ainsi la même histoire se répète sans fin : on enferme les créateurs dans un isolement où leur génie s'exaspère et se durcit, on leur refuse (et on s'adjuge à soi-même) les amples travaux où ce génie se serait épanoui et apaisé — quitte, plus tard, à revendiquer ces grands hommes pour maîtres et pour pontifes, quand, la décrépitude et la vieillesse étant venue, toute puissance créatrice est décidément éteinte

Photo Jacques Bony.

9

We feel an intense sadness. Around his idea, his dream, his mission, he had gathered the adhesion, devotion and activity of well-known people: the long-standing "hard" ones, people who, adding to his own life-long self-invoked youth, brought their "youth" into their mature years conquered the hard way, through perseverance, courage and invention.

Father Couturier was our friend, friend of that which is the most sacred to us: faith in our art. But he was also the friend of our homes. His company was agreeable, alert, and we were at total ease in our remarks. For me he was a man of history, who in great strides traversed certain books in which "men" find in themselves the alert action, the lively word, the unshakable trajectory – come hail or high water.[27]

The citation says as much about Le Corbusier, speaking of himself in the plural (or as the spokesman of a community), as it does about his friend. One could speculate that he would have liked to have heard or seen himself described as he had described Couturier. Indeed, the architect seemed to have identified with his friend. This loss occurred concurrently with the final building stage of Ronchamp and the first stage of La Tourette, neither of which would have happened without Couturier, as Le Corbusier was quick to acknowledge.[28]

In 1953, the young engineer Iannis Xenakis was charged with the job of interpreting the sketches Le Corbusier made for La Tourette (Fig. 5.14).[29] Le Corbusier would spend several hours each week with him developing the design.[30] "At the time the monastery was being designed, there was a large degree of complicity between the five or six of us working with Le Corbusier. We clicked, and from then on Le Corbusier was open to all sorts of suggestions."[31] When compared with other accounts of the project that of Xenakis seems slightly too rosy.[32] Again slightly implausibly Xenakis wrote that "the religious or ideological side" was never brought up by Le Corbusier."[33] Perhaps he had learned by now to keep this to himself.

The project was conceived in anticipation of receiving state reconstruction funding which was then diverted to the cause of housing. Finding the money to fund the scheme, which initially came in way over budget, was a constant struggle forcing Le Corbusier to make major changes to his original conception. The result was a 1:50 model, representing the monastery largely as built, which was eventually approved by the Council of Dominicans in 1954 (Fig. 5.15).

Construction

It was the contractors (Sud-Est Travaux et Construction SETC) who came up with the most innovative way of saving costs. As Philippe Potié points out, concrete was, at that time perceived to be more of a civil engineering material than a building material. Fortunately the contractors who were assigned to the project (Favre, Burdin and Vallade) all had experience in this area.[34] Their expertise and contacts impacted upon the project in two ways, firstly through the quality of the concrete formwork and secondly through the highly innovative use of prestressing techniques. If a beam is prestressed with tension wires it does not deflect so much when under pressure. This means that a shallower beam can be constructed which, in turn, uses less concrete. This technique was applied to the long spans across the wings of the building – the top two storeys are post and beam construction – and to the church itself. In the opinion of Potié Le Corbusier gave the engineers of Sud-Est Travaux and Xenakis a free hand with his building because he saw their rationalism as a foil for his own more poetic approach.[35]

The details of the monastery belie the sophistication of its structure, a reworking of themes developed over serial projects. The simple timber latches of the aerateurs in the cells of La Tourette (Fig. 5.16)[36], the concrete logs that protrude from the side of the saddlebag crypts (Fig. 5.17) and the sacristy at La Tourette all hark back to earlier forms of construction.[37] Robert Rebutato, who was responsible for the prestressed concrete used at La Tourette, has noted that the logs were entirely decorative – a reminder of some more ancient architecture.[38] This self-conscious use of "primitive" detail is something that we shall return to as it is debatable whether it is really expressive of "poverty".

5.14 – Le Corbusier's atelier
with Xenakis on the
extreme left

5.15 – 1954 model
of La Tourette

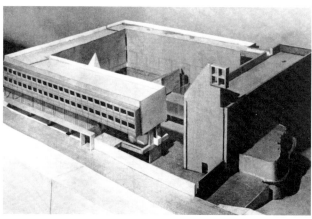

5.16 – Timber latches of the
aerateurs in the cells

5.17 – "Logs" protruding
from the saddlebag crypt of
the church

Communal Living

Le Corbusier's visit to the fifteenth-century Monastery at Ema near Florence (in reality the Galluzzo monastery[39]) has now become the stuff of architectural legend. He first visited this "radiant vision" in 1907.

> The noblest silhouette in the landscape, an uninterrupted crown of monks' cells; each cell has a view on the plain, and opens on a lower level on an entirely closed garden. I thought that I had never seen such a happy interpretation of a dwelling. The back of each cell opens by a door and a wicket on a circular street. This street is covered by an arcade: the cloister. Through this way the monastery services operate – prayer, visits, food, funerals.[40]

He enthused to Couturier about the "humanity"[41] of the scheme. "I would like to spend my life living in what they call their cells."[42] These were to become a repeated trope within his architecture.

The Unité

Any consideration of La Tourette would not be complete without a discussion of the Unité schemes, most particularly the first Unité "prototype" (foundation stone laid 1947) on the Boulevard Michelet in Marseilles which Le Corbusier described as the fruit of twenty-five years of study, beginning with the monastic architecture of the Middle Ages – in other words Ema (Fig. 5.18).[43]

Le Corbusier believed that the construction of domestic architecture was a sacred activity. "One preoccupation has concerned me compulsively: to introduce into the home a sense of the sacred; to make the home the temple of the family."[44] Significantly there are a number of images of the Unité in *L'Art sacré* suggesting that the Dominicans concurred with this view. Indeed they made links between it, La Sainte Baume and the chapel of Notre Dame du Haut at Ronchamp.[45] Father Couturier visited it as soon as it was inaugurated in 1952 and wrote to Le Corbusier singing its praise, saying he thought it looked like it was made for monks.[46] It is important to note the way that it is depicted in *L'Homme et L'architecture*, a publication over which Le Corbusier had much influence (Fig. 5.19).[47] In one image the vast pilotis that support the structure of the block frame images of mysterious gods in a darkened underground world. Le Corbusier referred to the space beneath the pilotis as the "main hall" and the "place of honour" indicating that it was for him very special (Fig. 5.20).[48] Here he placed a large block of stone, very much like an altar, at the entrance to the Unité at the level of the pilotis (Fig. 5.21). "Symbolically the entire construction rests upon it," he wrote.[49] Designed to help the visitor understand the central issues at stake in the building, one side of the block is adorned with his symbol of the twenty-four-hour day, the other with an image of Modulor man. Ostensibly a utilitarian housing block, the Unité embodies a complex spiritual programme that builds upon the scheme for the pilgrim housing at La Sainte Baume and would feed

5.18 – Unité Marseilles,
Boulevard Michelet

5.19 – Photograph of
a model of the under-
croft of the Unité as
portrayed in *L'Homme
et L'Architecture*

5.20 – Signs at the
entry to the Unité

into the project for La Tourette with one significant difference; the Unité was designed to accommodate men and women in a loving family cell (Fig. 5.22), while La Tourette was designed for men alone.[50]

The Architectural Promenade

Despite, or perhaps because Dominicans as a group are not processional, Le Corbusier's first instinct was to create, as was his wont, a dramatic denouement to the promenade upon the dazzling rooftop of La Tourette. A sketch of the monastery drawn on site on May 4, 1953 makes this explicit. However, he soon started to have second thoughts: "I think you've all been on the roof and you've seen how beautiful it is. It is beautiful because you don't see it. You know, with me there will always be paradoxes ... The pleasures of sky and clouds are perhaps too easy."[51] Instead Le Corbusier created sub-routes expressive of the inner turmoil and darkness (his Romantic roots emerge here with full force) of monastic existence. It is just possible for the monks to go upon the grass covered roof and use it as a cloister for meditative walking and contemplation, however, it is not easy to get there (Fig. 5.23). At La Tourette there is no toplit orientating stair. As they reach the top of the narrow and precarious stairs and negotiate the small doorway that opens out onto the vast landscape, the monks encounter a strange window cut into the side of the box that covers the stairwell. In form it is reminiscent of the plan of the monastery, flipped up onto the wall like an orientating map – a reminder of where the monks should be, instead of enjoying the deceptive beauty on the roof (Fig. 5.24).[52] Views of the outside world are carefully revealed or suppressed as you move around the building, most notably in the Sacristy where even a view of the clouds is hard to attain through the skewed rooflights (Fig. 5.25).

5.21 – Stone at the entry to the Unité

5.22 – Family cell enjoying supper in the Unité as portrayed in Le Corbusier's book *Les Maternelles*

5.23 – Rooftop garden as it looked in 2011

5.25 – Skewed rooflights in the sacristy

5.24 – Stairwell at rooftop level

135

"The composition of the convent starts at the summit and descends to the hollows of the valley in functional stages," wrote Le Corbusier.[53] It is traditional in architecture, including Le Corbusier's architecture, to progress upwards in pursuit of revelation, the vertical of the "right angle". The opposite is the case in the early Christian catacombs, in churches such as San Clemente in Rome which were hidden away underground. Significantly this is also the case at La Tourette. The vertical journey excavated down into the most sacred parts of this building seems to echo Le Corbusier's own researches through the layers of Catholic doctrine to something altogether more pure. Given Le Corbusier's fondness for creating Jacob's Ladders, connections between earth and sky, and his association with the vertical with the spiritual, it is odd that the culmination of the route in the church happens in relative darkness at almost the lowest possible level (Fig. 5.26) suggesting that he felt it important for the monks to gain contact with the earth. Le Corbusier spoke of his initial concept on a return visit to the monastery ten years after its conception:

> I said: I won't place the base on the ground because it will be hidden. Instead let's place it up high, along the top line of the building, blending it with the horizon. And we will use this horizontal top line as our point of departure reaching the ground as and when.[54]

This is a very significant statement as it points to the downward trajectory of the promenade. La Tourette is the product of two contradictory journeys. One is painful and complex leading out of life and down into the recesses of the earth, the final destination, the other – prohibited – a more natural and enjoyable progress up to the delights of the roofspace. It is the first journey that is captured in the following analysis of the stages of its promenade.

Threshold or Introduction

The first stage of Le Corbusier's narrative was planned to begin far beyond the confines of the building itself with sounds emanating from a vast "acoustic conch" on the church roof that would send liturgical chants down the valley advertising the presence of the monastery.[55] Although the monks eventually had to make do with a simple belfry, the principle remains the same (Fig. 5.27).[56]

The young friars who were to enter the Monastery would arrive on foot at the local train station and climb the steep slope to the monastery above. Approaching along the leafy lane from the car park, the blank wall of the church, flanked by a much lower ear-shaped extrusion,[57] is the first part of the monastery to become visible in what Rowe describes as "some very private commentary upon Acropolitan material" (Fig. 5.28).[58]

The church itself has two sides and two entrances: one for the monks from within, and one for the public from without. As you round the corner of the church, the angular

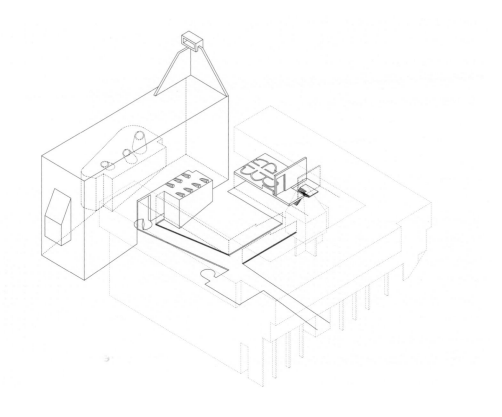

5.26 – Diagram showing
the downward circulation
of the promenade

5.28 – Approach to La Tourette
as portrayed in Le Corbusier's
Œuvre complète

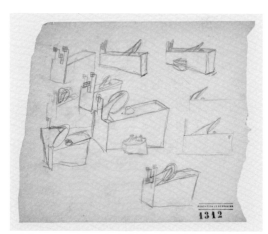

5.27 – Sketch of the 'acoustic conch'
to be situated on the roof of the
church at La Tourette, FLC 001312

thrust of the belfry comes into view. With his usual fondness for anthropomorphism Le Corbusier evokes woman – Mary to whom the whole project is dedicated – here in the gable of the church where she extends her cape over the gathered flock as in Piero della Francesca's *Madonna della Misericordia* (1462, Fig. 5.29) as well as the veiled woman that appears in the "labyrinth" section of *Le poème de l'angle droit* (Fig. 5.30). Significantly the etymology of the word "chapel" derives from "cape" or cloak – Le Corbusier was always one for wordplay. Her body forms the gable end of the public end of the building and is directed outwards, disappearing from view as you approach the entrance. She holds the church in her embrace.

The 1954 model of the monastery shows a wall along the alley, on the east side of the building blocking views of the internal cloister (Fig. 5.15). The visitor would have to walk a good way without much to look at before arriving at the portal that marks entry into the complex, in this way heightening expectation of what is to come (Fig. 5.31). It is likely that budgetary constraints prevented the wall being built, its absence causing what Rowe calls the lack of "preface" to the composition. If built as originally intended, the open portal would be set, like the doors in so many of Le Corbusier's buildings, within a taut horizontal band of wall protecting the space within. As it is, the composition does feel unsatisfactory.

Sensitising Vestibule

The second, sensitising, stage of the promenade begins with a freestanding portal that gives onto a space that is, in essence, a bridge spanning between two very different forms of existence. The portal is built to Modulor proportions – 2.26 × 2.26 metres – meaning that it acts like the modulor block at the entrance to the Unité, setting the scale of what is to come. In the floor a grating for the cleaning of shoes spans only half the width of the frame, as if waiting for a single file procession of monks to enter in. It is this – like so many of the spaces of monastic existence – both open to the air and under cover, that marks the vestibule of the building. Le Corbusier called this floor of the monastery level 3 (Fig. 5.31).

The area protruding beyond the shade of the block of cells above is in essence a square, the pure form conferring a greater authority on the space than something more irregular. The undercroft hinterland is occupied by a range of five extraordinary biomorphic pavilions that house what was the porter's lodge and the parlours, the opulent curves of which are finished in a deep mottled gunnite plaster, similar to that of Ronchamp, the number five in Christian art referring to the five senses. As Wolfgang Jean Stock notes, "these are the only 'corporeal' forms in the monastery, for this is where the monks meet with relatives and come into contact with worldly life."[59] Lighting is brought into these bulbous forms through slots of red, for Le Corbusier the colour of the body and of fusion. This then seems to be the issue in the sensitising curves of the forecourt vestibule of La Tourette, the relinquishing of the sensual pleasure in favour of something more profound.

5.29 – Piero della Francesca, *Madonna della Misericordia* (central detail), tempera on panel (c. 1462), Pinacoteca Communale, Sansepolcro, BEN-F-001167-0000

5.30 – Le Corbusier 'Labyrinth' from *Le poème de L'angle droit*

5.31 – Portal over bridge into the monastery complex

5.33 – Sculptural mounds on
the roof of the Unité Marseilles
echoing the mountains
of La Sainte Baume beyond

5.32 – Sculptural mounds
by porters lodge

5.34 – Red door into monastery

5.35 – View of precipitous
seat from inside cloister

Le Corbusier flanked the biomorphic lodge with two *informe* sculptural mounds sitting one in front and one behind the pavilions (Fig. 5.32). These are similar to those on the roof of Marseille Unité's echoing the mountains of La Sainte Baume behind (Fig. 5.33).[60] Similar rocks appear in the floor of the existing grotto at La Sainte Baume. It is very curious that they should be evoked here.

The bodily curves of the entry space lead the initiate to the shockingly physical red door that gives entry into the monastery itself. Just next to the door is a moment for pause, possibly for regret, in the form of a concrete seat (Fig. 5.34) which turns its back on the vertiginous space of the cloister and the deprivations within (Fig. 5.35, Fig. 5.38). Rowe observed that:

> The visitor is so placed that he is without the means of making coherent his own experience. He is made the subject of diametric excitations; his consciousness is divided; and, being both deprived of and also offered an architectural support, in order to resolve his predicament, he is anxious, indeed obliged – and without choice – to enter the building.[61]

The highly utilitarian stairwell within offers no clue to the complexities within.

The three groups of monks living in La Tourette had somewhat separate lives as required by Dominican rule. While cells were all gathered on the top two floors (called levels 4 and 5 by Le Corbusier Fig. 5.36),[62] these were, in turn, separated into three distinct groups: the "converts", or servant brothers, whose cells were on the east side; the student brothers whose cells were on the south side (this was the biggest group and their cells "spilled" out onto the east side); and the teacher fathers whose cells were gathered on the west side. Between the student cell section and the teaching cell section there was a double cell with an entrance door from each side, allowing a student and professor to meet and confer in private on an individual basis.

Each group had their own stairwell to go from floor to floor, hence their own promenade. Each section was delineated – the hallways were literally blocked by grated metal screens in the corridors that were only taken down in 1968. Traces of these can be seen in the walls. For the students and converts, their stairwells went all the way down to the second level, to the "conduits" that led each group to the atrium. The teachers had an internal stairwell for the top two floors (levels 4 and 5) like the other groups and would use the round exterior stairwell to go down to the atrium. It is typical of Le Corbusier that he made them go outside for part of the journey, stirring the senses through contact with the environment – the spiral-shaped stair an echo of the route to higher knowledge in his mind.[63] The atrium was and is considered a gathering place like a public square. From there all the monks have equal and direct access onto the chapter house room, the refectory and the hall leading down to the doors of the church and the sacristy.

5.36 – Plans of
levels 2, 3 and 1

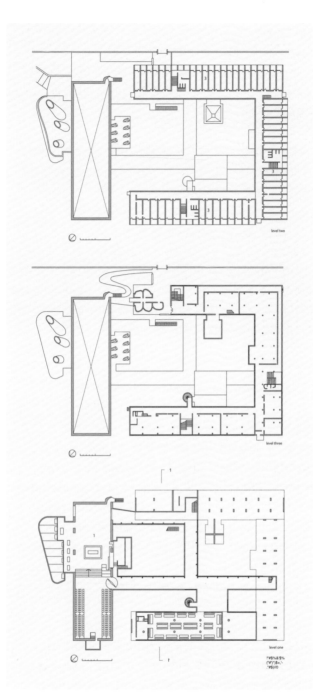

5.37 – Corridor to monks' cells as
portrayed in *Œuvre complète*

5.38 – Section across
monastery showing
drop behind seat

5.40 – Baffles as seen on the exterior

5.39 – Baffle at the end of the corridor from interior

Questioning Space

There is no obvious pomp and ceremony in the architecture of La Tourette, just constant incitement to thought and reflection through the questioning of spaces that characterise the third stage of the narrative. The main circulation corridor at the level of the alley (level 3, Fig. 5.36) provides access to the oratory, the library, and a variety of other communal rooms arranged according to the convert, student and teacher promenades. The circulation corridor at alley level, like that in the levels of monk's cells above (Fig. 5.37), finishes in a dead end where a window, presumably in position for air and light, is baffled, preventing the view outwards and forcing the visitor to retrace their steps (Fig. 5.39 and 5.40).

The vertical dissection of space continues on level 3. Here the converts had a small recreational room just under their cells (so next to their stairwell). Just beyond this was a much larger recreational room for the student brothers. In this room is a stairwell leading up to the next floor, level 4, to the corridor where their cells were located. So if you were a student brother who had gone outside and returned into the priory and wanted to go up to your room you would take this path. If you lived in the upper level of cells, you would then take the south-side stairwell up to level 5. On level 3 on the south side is the library. The student brothers had direct access to this from their stairwell. Beyond the library, on the other side of their stairwell, the series of classrooms began and wrapped around to the south side – the teacher side. Here were the rest of the classrooms. One room was reserved as a recreational room for the professor fathers. They could come down to this level from their own stairwell (or come up to it from the atrium via the spiral stairwell).

Within the main stairwell the finishes are rough and, as in much of the building, repulsive to the hand. Nicholas Fox Weber writes of the "challenging" nature of the stairs that link between the levels of the building.[64] These long flights are of an unusually sharp incline; the spacing of the treads and risers is uncomfortable and physically demanding, precisely, we argue, because Le Corbusier wanted to draw attention to the bodily effort of descent. The centre wall of the dogleg is eroded at the lower level to make space for a vertical fluorescent light bulb resulting in an odd sensation that the stair is somehow supported on this flimsy column of light (Fig. 5.41). Here the extremely low levels of artificial illumination produce a distinctly crepuscular atmosphere at night.

There is a distinct lack of colour in the living quarters of La Tourette, making its presence in the church all the more vivid. Le Corbusier asked Father Vincent de Couesnongle his opinion on the use of colour, as in the Unités: "It fits secular houses quite well. But for a religious house, no. There is silence, an introspection … that does not easily fit a vivid colour scheme."[65] Given that the use of colour was for Le Corbusier about life, the body and the senses it would only cause temptation.

Mention should be made of the rough finishes of the building. The exterior of the monks' cells bristle with the large flinty pebbles of the bush hammered concrete panels (Fig. 5.42). The interior of the cells are not much better. The walls next to the beds are so rough that you need to take care not to injure yourself as you turn over in bed at night. "That some monks read the surfaces achieved by means of quasi-industrial techniques as 'stigmata of suffering' is only one of the building's many paradoxes," writes Réjean Legault.[66] The rough surface so reminiscent of the gunnite "skin" of Ronchamp is highly corporeal – yet it feels vaguely oppressive within the limits of the monks' cells. It should be remembered that Le Corbusier wrote with pride of the surface defects left in the concrete of the pilotis of the Unité Marseilles – the flaws of the building acted as a reminder of what it is to be "human".[67] There is surely a message of hardship hidden within the brutal materials of the monastery.

Le Corbusier wrote that La Tourette "involves the presence of fundamentally human elements in the ritual as well as in the dimensioning of the spaces (rooms and circulation)."[68] The monks' cells are dimensioned to the Modulor, 2.26 metres in cross section and 5.92 metres long (Fig. 5.43). The corridor outside is another 2.26 metres. The word "human" crops up again and again in Le Corbusier's descriptions of the building, carrying with it the importance of questioning, of *savoir habiter* – acute sensitivity to the important things in life set against the limited span of our lives.

As the brother ventures down to the refectory level, the primary entrance stair shifts over a bay for no obvious reason other than marking the point of arrival at ground level. The main stair feeds onto a conduit at base level which itself seemingly lines up with nothing in particular.[69] It cuts into the walkway that leads down to the church, extending roughly north-south, but it does not line up with the atrium as it could. A further corridor leads on to the refectory, chapter house room and atrium, secondary to the north-south

5.41 – Lighting detail
on stairway

5.42 – Detail showing bris-
tling texture of walls

5.43 – Interior of cell showing view
away from window toward door

route which slopes down to the church. The corridor is framed in ondulatoire glazing devised by Iannis Xenakis, its Modulor proportions based on complex musicological theory (Fig. 5.44).[70] This gives a peculiar fluctuating rhythm to the experience of space as it expands downwards towards the entrance to the church. (Fig. 5.45)

Here entry is barred by a forbidding bronze door. It is facetted outwards like a jewel – its convex surface rebuffing entry. The riveted surface, tarnished with time, resembles nothing so much as the side of a submarine – a modern translation of Jonah's whale (or "great fish" as it is actually called in the Bible)? The handles of Le Corbusier's doors are a delight to touch, but not so in this case. Here a vertical slot frames a facetted back plate (Fig. 5.46). To pull the door shut is to gain a precarious hold on the sharp rim of its opening. Abstract form and hard geometry afford nothing to the softness of the hand. To open the little wicket gate within the door is difficult because of its extreme weight and because of the high threshold that must be negotiated on entry. It clangs shut behind the reader with all the finality of a prison cell (Fig. 5.47).

Once within the burst of vertical space that is the church it becomes apparent that there is no immediate dramatic conclusion to the vista. The north-south corridor lines up with nothing other than the side of the glistening watery slate steps (Fig. 5.48) leading up to the low pyramidical platform for the altar which subdivides the monks from the "lay faithful" (Fig. 5.49).[71] Xenakis wrote of the altar: "I had conceived it a little like a place for terrible sacrifices. It was too dramatic, too Aztec, Christ sacrificed himself, as did Dionysos."[72] That Xenakis refers to Dionysos, an incarnation of Orpheus, is unlikely to have been accidental. Both are, of course, implicated in the propagation of harmony. The vaguely heretical nature of the altar did not escape critics such as Father Belaud who argued for its removal.[73] Mary looks benevolently over this adventure, her effigy a statue on a low key shelf designed by Le Corbusier for the red (bodily) south wall of the church, focus of the *salve regina* ceremony that takes place there every Saturday evening (Fig. 5.50)

5.45 – Route down to the door of the church showing ondulatoire glasing

5.44 Exterior view of ondulatoire glasing

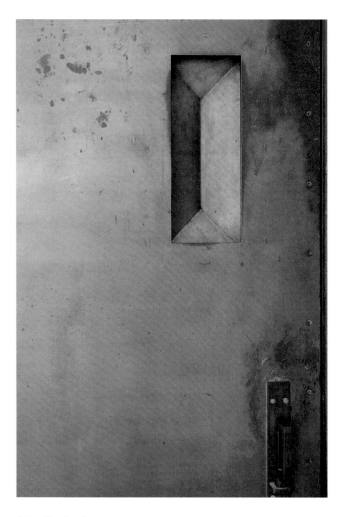

5.46 – Handle of
door into church

5.47 – Door as seen from
within the church

5.48 – Detail of watery
steps up to altar

5.49 – Steps leading
up to the altar

5.50 – Statue of Mary
against red 'bodily' background in the church

5.51 – View of main
altar showing
opus optimum floor

Luis Burriel Bielza notes Father Couesnongle's instructions regarding the altar for the monastery of La Tourette: "The altar does not have to be formed by a slab on columns, but to make block with the ground, a solid mass."[74] The importance of the connection with the ground will be developed in the next chapter. Like the stone blocks at the entrance of each Unité, the altar is the tuning fork of the whole space. When interviewed by the Dominicans in 1960 Le Corbusier said of La Tourette:

> The altars mark the centre of gravity as well as the value and hierarchy of everything. In music there are keys, ranges and chords. An altar is "par excellence" the hallowed place that sets the tone, that has to trigger the radiance of the work. This is made possible by proportions. Proportion is an ineffable thing. I invented the term "ineffable space": places start to radiate and they generate an "ineffable space" – a shock.[75]

Altars, "high" altars, also designate, like the "high" seas, the depths and profoundness of their *raison d'être*. Once again the experience of religion is firmly allied to the experience of space. The floor is finished in Le Corbusier's *opus optimum*, meaning that the steps of the reader are continually mapped against the sequence of the Modulor (Fig. 5.51).[76] The walls similarly were conceived in Modulor panels. Prostration forms an important part of the Dominican liturgy but it only happens at the key stage of initiation into the order. When a Dominican monk lies flat on the Modulor floor of La Tourette its lines are imprinted on his body and he is absorbed into the radiant web of mathematical relationships that govern both the building and its environment. Le Corbusier and Trouin discussed the possibility of a "Radiant Order" to be created at La Sainte Baume – something similar appears to be happening here.[77] The voices of the monks would add to the overall effect, amplified by the extraordinary acoustic, a reverberation time of seven seconds, sounds bouncing back from the deepest recesses of space, stimulating questions about its meaning.[78]

Particularly intriguing is the dark void that holds the organ pipes at the end of the monks' side of the church (Fig. 5.52). Le Corbusier wanted it to be circular in form but it was built square as a cost cutting measure.[79] Set into the wall, it is a geometric echo of the square in the ceiling above, this time releasing a blaze of light. What appears to be at stake is the x-axis of the body set perpendicular to the y-axis of the spirit emanating from the hole in the roof above. All our movements are mapped within this grid.

There are three key light sources in the church that let in light at different times of day: "Thus the church was joined to the cosmos like the pyramids and other sacred edifices," wrote Xenakis, something that should be borne in mind for the discussion in the next chapter.[80] There is a vertical slot in the wall in the more public east end of the building, a square hole in the ceiling at the other end, and the coloured circles set within the single height space of the ear-shaped crypt that protrudes beyond the northern boundaries of the church. In order to reach this space it is necessary either to step laboriously up and over the corner of the main altar platform or go past the

main altar itself. This more intimate area is pleasantly lit by the rooflights that spill tantalisingly into the crypt below. Yet, frustratingly, the lower altars are inaccessible from the church itself, unless via the sacristy behind the red south wall of Mary.

The sacristy is lit by a series of light canons that, in the opinion of Trouin, were originally conceived for La Sainte Baume (Fig. 5.53 and Fig. 5.54).

> I was touched by the fact that the canons of light took on a theme dear to the underground Basilica. The thin shadow of Father Couturier, a shadow itself, the great shadow you made reign through the light, a dualism that your so-called Cathar ascendants led me to suspect is a bit Manichean. But can art be Manichean or Albigensian, or what? Still, in your blood and spiritual family origins there are definitely all the temple builders, religiously atheistic and atheistically religious.[81]

5.53 – Light canons down into sacristy

5.54 – Light canons as seen within church under reconstruction, 2012

From here a diminutive and highly compressed stairway leads into the bowels of the church into another chapel space and along a subterranean corridor beneath the church to the northern chapel which bears an uncanny resemblance, both in its form and in its relationship to the main church, to the side chapel within the grotto at La Sainte Baume as it must have existed in Le Corbusier's time and still exists today.

5.57 – View down crypt containing seven altars

There are within the ear-shaped crypt seven private altars (Fig. 5.55 and Fig. 5.57). As was seen in the discussion of *Le poème de l'angle droit* in chapter 2, the number seven signifies the union of the spirit with the body. Seven is the number of years it takes to train as a Dominican father and the number of prayers that take place during the course of the day. It also refers to the notes in a musical scale. Altars, as stated above, were for Le Corbusier tuning forks of proportion. Those at La Tourette are stacked in steps up the slope yet, as one might expect, there is no hierarchical climax to the space. The topmost altars may be higher and wider but they receive no more light. Indeed it could be that the lowermost altar at the narrowest point in the piano-shaped space,[82] just to the left of the doorway, is more important than those at the top. In this highly constrained space of dynamic equilibrium it is only the orbs of coloured light from the periscope rooflights above that offer the possibility of release (Fig. 5.56). Here the final two stages of Le Corbusier's dramatic arc, reorientation and climax are conspicuous by their very absence. The culmination of this journey is in the spaces of the soul, and then back to share their knowledge of God with others.

5.56 – Detail of roof-light above altar

5.55 – View of the seven altars in crypt looking upwards

The public would never have access to these hidden spaces which were designed for the required individual mass that the fathers were obliged to complete, with the aid of one of the student brothers, before Vatican II. When the church was built there were about 20 fathers, each of whom should have had an individual altar.[83] After Vatican II co-celebration became permissible allowing the fathers to do a daily mass together – this currently takes place in the room used as a chapter house before an elegant table designed by Charlotte Perriand serving as the altar (indeed, the set-up is quite Guardinian, see Chapter 1). The corollary of this is that the crypt, so lovingly designed by Le Corbusier, is now redundant.

Responses to La Tourette

La Tourette caused intense excitement amongst architects across the globe. "In contrast to his chapel at Ronchamp," wrote Robert Maguire and Keith Murray, Le Corbusier "has been able, without being personally involved in the life, to make a building in which it can flourish."[84] The building that is most clearly indebted to the monastery is the Roman Catholic Seminary of St Peter's near Cardross in Scotland, designed by Gillespie, Kidd and Coia and built between 1961 and 1966 (Fig. 5.58 and 5.59). St Peter's never reached its proposed population of hundred monks and quickly fell into disrepair. Patrick Hodgkinson makes the connections between the two monasteries, both of which "stand fortress like against the land," very clear. He describes what he calls its "Janus section", the lower levels being about "introspection for religious formality," the upper floors for the students' rooms "as they prospect the earth and look up into the heavens."[85] The Cardross monastery is however slightly less ascetic with pine used for all the "touchable parts". The church itself shares in the atmosphere of that of La Tourette, with a similar *opus optimum* floor, but is barrel-vaulted in the manner of the Jaoul houses.

Acknowledging the arcane mythological roots of Le Corbusier's architecture, Patrick Hodgkinson makes the significant point that "the line dividing paraphrase from plagiarism may often be finely drawn, but the spatial/constructional concept that

5.58 – Cell block in the Roman Catholic Seminary of St Peter's near Cardross in Scotland, designed by Gillespie, Kidd and Coia, 1961-66, now derelict

5.59 – Detail of St Peter's, Cardross

is related by family association to the master architect's way of thinking is an aeon apart from some figurative agglomeration of his forms without the spirit."[86] In doing so he sets the scene for chapter 7 in which we discuss the way in which the forms of Le Corbusier's religious schemes have taken priority over the thinking behind them.

Summary

To be a Dominican monk requires the rigorous discipline of unruly desires for pleasure and comfort, and a concentration on the mission of the Order – spreading the word within a communal setting.[87] The narrative at La Tourette is in sympathy with this cause. The needs of monastic life are expressed through its punishing materials, through its promenade – a relinquishing of the body and of woman in favour of a spiritual engagement with an internal Mary – and through a sensitive balance of individual and community facilities. All of this is framed in a carapace of geometry and light, acting on those within and radiating out to the world beyond.

Like La Sainte Baume and Ronchamp the building has two interpretations, one in keeping with the Church and one more heretical that talks of the impossibility of separating woman from man. In designing the scheme Le Corbusier observed, "I was performing either a criminal or worthy act. The first step is to choose".[88] It should be noted that he had made a similar statement about Ronchamp. Here, for Rowe, "An architectural dialectician, the greatest, was to service the requirements of the archsophisticates of dialectic," the Dominicans, hence the extraordinary tensions that are built into its programme.[89]

On receipt of the much overdue final payment from the Dominican provincial receiver Father Levesque, Le Corbusier wrote, "let me state, very seriously, that I felt great joy in building La Tourette, in going there, in seeing you, and I thank you for this joy you gave me."[90] When he died in 1965 Le Corbusier's body rested for forty-eight hours in the church of La Tourette on its way from his Cabanon in Cap Martin to the Cour Carré of the Louvre in Paris where André Malraux officiated over his funeral rites.[91] The silent vigil of the monks over the body of their dead friend would bring to an end their close association. "I am rather attached to your priory and consider myself, a little bit, amongst your friends."[92]

"The tighter the credit, the more the architect is challenged, and the smaller is his fee. This will teach some architects to be more detached from worldly goods," wrote Le Corbusier reverting perhaps to his Cathar ancestors' dislike of the material world. He publicly wrote of La Tourette that "the interior displays a total poverty,"[93] yet behind the scenes he was of the opinion that: "At 68 years old I do not have to prove that I can make inexpensive architecture."[94] The irony is that it is expensive and difficult to achieve an acceptable finish in exposed concrete – it requires very careful advance planning on the positioning of services and a skilled builder. What is achieved here is an artful degree of poverty, a tectonic conceit.

THE PARISH CHURCH SAINT PIERRE, FIRMINY-VERT

In his *Œuvre complète* Le Corbusier stated enigmatically that Saint Pierre "after Ronchamp and La Tourette, represents a third, new type of church" (Fig. 6.1).[1] Whether he meant in terms of function or meaning remains unclear, but Father Cocagnac of *L'Art sacré* had his own theory on the matter:

> With Ronchamp, Le Corbusier already knew how to offer a chapel that would open us up to the mystery of pilgrimage sites. With La Tourette, he knew how to create a perfectly coherent religious ensemble for our time. With the parish church of Firminy, he dilates its spiritual space to the dimensions of the city and in this way demonstrates that the church, in its very architecture, in its relation to the urban setting, is a place of influence and radiance."[2]

Cocagnac saw Saint Pierre as the logical evolution of Le Corbusier's religious architecture translated to an urban scale, spreading the word of the *Athens Charter* and the *Radiant City*. In his latter years Le Corbusier resolved to spend what little time he had left building dwellings. Despite this resolution he was persuaded to accept the commission for Saint Pierre by his friend Eugène Claudius-Petit (Fig. 6.2). Saint Pierre we argue is an extension of the home, built this time in service of the community. As Le Corbusier wrote at the end of his life, "today you can build a temple to meet family needs beside the very cathedrals ..."[3] (Fig. 6.3).

6.1 – Saint Pierre Firminy

6.3 – Stained glass window in the chapel of Le Corbusier's Maison Jaoul A in Paris, 1954-1956

6.2 – Eugène Claudius-Petit, Le Corbusier and Father Cocagnac

The lower two floors of Saint Pierre remained an abandoned bunker for twenty-five years, a forgotten corner at the edge of the Firminy-Vert area, where Le Corbusier built the largest complex of his work in Europe encompassing a Youth and Cultural Centre, now called the *Maison de la Culture Le Corbusier* (Fig. 6.4); an *Unité* located further away on another hill (Fig. 6.5); as well as a sports stadium finished posthumously (Fig. 6.6).[4] Construction on the church had begun in 1973 but stalled, mostly because of lack of funding. It commenced again in 2003 when sufficient funding was raised so it could be completed by José Oubrerie who had worked with Le Corbusier on the church in the 1960s.[5] The church was finally consecrated in 2006.

Saint Pierre was to take the form of a "squared prism"[6], with sides twenty-four metres in length, surmounted by a parabolic cone made of reinforced concrete, thirty-six metres high and held up by pilasters, the gap between the two negotiated by undulatory glass.[7] Two light canons in the inclined oval roof would provide overhead light to the sanctuary, with a third skylight on the west face of the cone, not quite half way up.[8] The entire structure would be made of reinforced concrete, left untreated on the exterior. Many interior walls, ceilings, doors and "accessories" would be painted in various, bright (though unspecified) colours.[9] Final decisions on these matters would have been made by Le Corbusier during the building process itself, hence their omission on the drawings. The recently constructed Oubrerie church has been built on speculations as to what they might have been.

Firminy-Vert

Firminy-Vert was a new (post-war) low-income residential area of Firminy, a working-class industrial town near Saint-Étienne not far from Lyons where the number of practising Catholics was estimated at about twenty per cent of the population – high compared to national figures (Fig. 6.7).[10] Like Ronchamp it was a coal-mining town but, unlike Ronchamp, here the industry was booming with the current population of four thousand inhabitants projected to double in the near future. In 1954 the architects Charles Delfante, André Sive, Marcel Roux and Jean Kling were asked to develop plans for the new area. By 1957 over one thousand dwellings had been built to house some four thousand inhabitants providing, for the first time, many of Firminy's population with drinking water, as well as other modern facilities such as the nation's first laundrette. The project represented an opportunity for these architects, loyal to the terms of Le Corbusier's *Athens Charter*, to finally put this social experiment into action, initially with such positive results that, in 1961, it was awarded the national *Grand Prix d'Urbanisme*.

The Commission

Le Corbusier was already involved in the sports, culture and housing projects of Firminy-Vert when he was offered the church commission, following the unexpected death of André Sive in 1960.[11] According to Eugène Claudius-Petit Le Corbusier agreed to the project only after studying and sketching the site.[12] In a letter of 1961

6.4 – Acoustic signs on the
side wall of the Maison
de la Culture

6.5 – Unité Firminy

6.6 – Sports stadium
at Firminy

6.7 – Saint Pierre
in context

to Father Cocagnac at *L'Art sacré,* with whom Le Corbusier had already worked on the La Tourette project, he explained his decision, saying that "the geographical and topographical conditions were favourable."[13] It is of note that he had recently rejected a commission in his home town of La Chaux-de-Fonds on the basis of the way in which the site was described: "Had you said, 'Will you create a place open all the year, situated on the hilltops in the calm and the dignity, in the nobleness of the beautiful Jura site?' the problem could have been considered. It would have been a problem of psychic nature and, for me, of decisive value."[14] It is our suggestion that Le Corbusier was attracted by sites that gave his buildings monumental presence, enabling them to act as radiant beacons like his beloved Parthenon.

Le Corbusier's rhetoric was that church building was a form of social action, not an excuse to fly from reality. "I'll do it because it is for workers, for working people and their families," he stated.[15] At the same time he wanted to demonstrate his loyalty to his old friend Claudius-Petit,[16] an active member of the Resistance during World War II, former Minister of Reconstruction (1948–1953) and mayor of Firminy from 1953 to 1971, to whom he owed the commission for the Unité Marseilles. "It is for you, Claudius, that I am doing this job and I will do it with my conscience serving as referee."[17] It should be mentioned that, after his brief flirtation with the Vichy regime, Le Corbusier was not entirely a popular figure in France and that he was in need of friends in high places (Perret too had been burnt by Vichy, but he cleared his name by being active in the Resistance thus giving him the edge when it came to the commissions for reconstruction projects). Claudius-Petit was only able to engage Le Corbusier for Firminy-Vert when the project was already under way and its citizens had been convinced of the benefits of modernism.

The Parish Association and the Diocese of Lyons

In his capacity as mayor Claudius-Petit sold the land for the church to the Church for a symbolic fee of one franc. A Parish Association was then set up to be the official client led by Jean-François Baud (Fig. 6.8), a member of Claudius-Petit's city government, including several other allies[18] such as Father Roger Tardy, named the priest-to-be of Saint Pierre (Fig. 6.9). A charismatic and respected figure, he managed to rally local support,[19] for example, by inviting the Dominicans from nearby La Tourette to talk to the people of Firminy about their monastery.[20] Saint Pierre was chosen as patron saint of the new church in memory of a local church of the same name demolished earlier that century.

The town, now in the Diocese of Saint-Étienne, was at that time in the Diocese of Lyons. The Church as an institution follows a strict hierarchy as shall become evident in this account of the intricacies of building a parish church. The Parish Association and Father Tardy had to answer to Father Joannès Mazioux, the head of the Diocesan Office for New Parishes, based in Saint-Étienne, which had decision-making powers in accepting architectural projects for new churches. Oddly enough he held the symbolic

6.8 –Le Corbusier walking on site with Paul Parayre, secretary of the parish association, Jean-François Baud, its president, and Father Roger Tardy, 1960

6.9 – Le Corbusier on site studying topography map with Paul Parayre, secretary of the parish association, Jean-François Baud, its president, and Father Roger Tardy, 1960

title of Monseigneur, usually reserved for bishops (a source of some confusion in understanding this aspect of the commission) and was considered a "technicien", a logistical thinker, by the Church. Monseigneur Marius Maziers, the auxiliary bishop of the Lyons Diocese based in Saint-Étienne, was above him. Above Maziers was the archbishop of Lyons who, during Le Corbusier's lifetime, was Monseigneur Pierre-Marie Gerlier, involved in the *Action catholique* movement and in promoting the "new Church – new churches" – not just making new church buildings, but in imagining them as part of modern society. [21] Gerlier knew Le Corbusier because he had consecrated La Tourette. Considering this configuration it may come as a surprise that Mazioux did most of the decision-making Church-side in this high-profile case. Anthony Eardley notes that the project "was looked upon with thinly concealed distrust by the conservative hierarchy of the diocese of Lyons," notably Mazioux, "who correctly anticipated that it would represent the Mother Church in too obdurately antique and incarnate a form." Simultaneously, in keeping with current thinking at that time "its fate" had become "a matter of indifference to the new left in the Church, for whom the separation of the sacred from the profane by means of ecclesiastical monuments would seem quite peripheral to the critically pressing crusade for a new world social conscience and political morality." [22] One could surmise that Gerlier was the embodiment of this latter stance. Claudius-Petit cited a message from the Parish Association's president written early on in March 1960 in the pages of the *Œuvre complète*: "We have made it clear to our Bishop that we are determined to have our church built by Le Corbusier. His Lordship is not opposed to the idea *a priori* if Le Corbusier creates a fitting church ... He is a prelate who knows what's what and who has in mind a church that is simple in design but beautiful and representative, for the future, of our contemporary architecture ..."[23]

It should be borne in mind that Claudius-Petit was a right wing Gaullist who defeated a Communist city government while the majority of Catholics in Firminy, including clergy, were left-leaning *Action catholique* sympathisers. Claudius-Petit, as an active Catholic lay-person, was part of a growing phenomenon in France in which high-profile professionals in the private sector and elite civil servants became more involved with the Church, something new for the Church hierarchy to get used to. It proved to be a source of tension for the project in its early stages.[24]

The Parish Association's Brief

The Parish Association was ahead of its time in steering Le Corbusier in the direction of Liturgical Reform. Its list of requirements, produced in early 1961, predates the opening of the Vatican II Council by a year.[25] What was needed was a church to seat six hundred, with a week-day chapel capable of seating fifty to sixty, a mortuary chapel, and a large sacristy with a small adjoining office. The Association also wanted a large interior entrance hall, four rooms for catechism classes, two meeting rooms, and an additional, large room for gatherings, capable of holding three hundred persons. As for the presbytery, it was to be planned with room for two priests, one extra lodging, and three small offices. The terrain was meant to be pleasantly landscaped with the sun's orientation taken into account. They did not request a traditional bell tower, but a more modest architectural "signal" containing one or two bells. As for the church, the six hundred were to be seated on pews, not chairs, and these were to be arranged not to create a long, narrow – in other words traditional – church, but to be gathered around the altar (anticipating Liturgical Reform). The floor of the nave was meant to slant slightly downwards, with the choir slightly raised, and the altar large and visible. The ambo was to be highly visible as well. The Association asked that the altar be lit from the sides so that the priest would not appear as a silhouette, presumably to increase intimacy between him and the congregation. Confessionals were to be discreet, their entrances on the sides rather than at the back, with direct access to the church at the entrance level to avoid making people "climb up" to the church.[26] In comparing this report with what Le Corbusier finally designed, one could imagine the Parish Association quite satisfied. Le Corbusier was in the mood to listen.

Saint Pierre was to be a large endeavour on a restricted budget. In 1961 the Parish Association report specifically declared that the spirit of the church had to be "simplicity, poverty, truth" adding "Do not sacrifice the interior to the exterior." This approach would be in keeping with the general move towards simplicity mentioned in Chapter 1, *L'Art sacré's* dislike of excess, as well as Le Corbusier's own penchant for asceticism. Further requests included the characteristic of sobriety, the absence of pretence and harmony with the city.[27] These loose terms were ripe for reinterpretation by Le Corbusier who had received the best possible instruction on the Liturgy from his friends at *L'Art sacré*. Indeed he wrote "Pour Eglise Firminy" on the cover of the 1-2 September-October 1960 issue of the journal entitled "The place of celebration"

(Fig. 6.10). In 1962 *L'Art sacré* published its May-June issue, strategically entitled "Rome", which encouraged those involved in contemporary church architecture to take a good look at the ancient Roman churches for inspiration. It featured a two-page excerpt of Le Corbusier's 1923 adulatory text from *Towards an Architecture* on the Roman church Santa Maria in Cosmedin (Fig. 6.11), called here "Rome byzantine".[28] This passage cleverly reminded the reader of Le Corbusier's long-time interest in liturgical space. One can also pause and compare Santa Maria in Cosmedin's pulpit with that designed for Saint Pierre and remark on their similarities. The Dominicans had also advised Le Corbusier to read *La Maison-Dieu* issue number 63, December of 1960, containing a transcription of the proceedings of a meeting on August 31, and September 1, 1960, at the School of Santa Genoveva, in Versailles concerning the Liturgy. Luis Burriel Bielza has demonstrated the impact of this document on the project.[29]

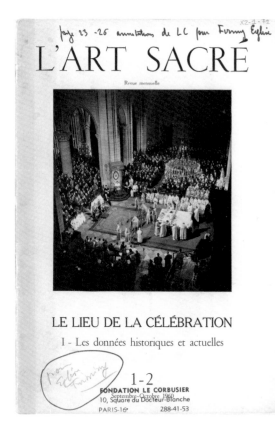

6.10 – 'Pour Eglise Firminy' written by Le Corbusier on the cover of the 1-2 September–October 1960 issue of *L'Art sacré*

6.11 – Image of Santa Maria in Cosmedin, Rome from Le Corbusier's *Towards an Architecture*, 1923

6.12 – Le Musée
Mondial, 1929

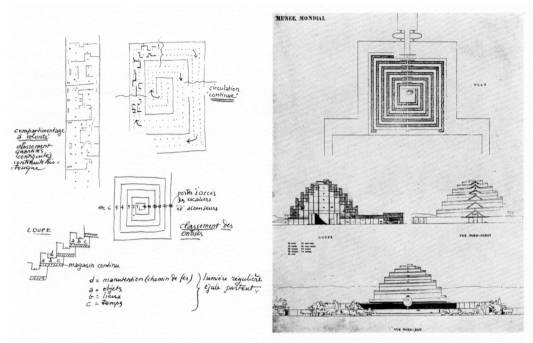

Le Musée Mondial: Le visiteur pénètre dans le musée par le haut. Trois nefs se déroulent parallèlement, côte à côte, sans cloison pour les séparer.
20) Entrée, 21) Centrum, 26) Ascenseurs, 27) Musée, 28) Rampe spirale, 30) Espace centrum, 43) Magasins, 44) Belvédère et entrée dans le musée.

6.14 – Detail, Section A1, *Le poème de l'angle droit*, 1955

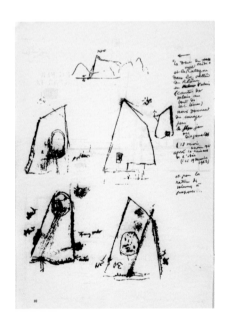

6.13 – Sketch of Saint Pierre included in "Un projet d'église paroissiale de Le Corbusier" (A Parish Church Project), *L'Art sacré*, issue 3-4, November-December 1964

6.15 – Le Corbusier, *Les îles sont des corps des femmes*, 1945

Design Development

In 1961 Le Corbusier declared to Claudius-Petit, "I have gone ahead and invented a church for Firminy – it is born."[30] The 1964 issue of *L'Art sacré* entitled "A Parish Church Project", devoted to the church at Firminy, featured twenty-four pages of notes, commentary, sketches and photographs showing its evolution across four years of work.[31] Two notable references for the church's silhouette are given. The first is his Le Tremblay church designed in 1929 (see chapter 1) with its tall rectangular structure and spiralling (straight-edged) exterior ramp that wraps around its bottom third, though its name is not mentioned, nor is its date of 1929; instead Le Corbusier gives the approximate dates 1925-30 meaning that it could also allude to the Musée Mondial schemes (Fig. 6.12).[32] One can speculate that Le Tremblay was designed with Perret's Raincy church (1922-23) in mind, with its tall, skyscraper-like bell tower, as well as his rival's rejected designs for the Parisian Sainte-Jeanne-d'Arc church (1925) with its 200-meter-high spire. Perret had completed his last church project, for Le Havre – Saint Joseph (1954), a rectangular tower, reaching 106 meters high during the construction of Ronchamp. Le Corbusier would not want to appear to be following in the footsteps of his former employer by building a similar tower.

Second in the *L'Art sacré* article is a sketch of what looks at first to be the silhouette of La Sainte Baume, floating above four profile sketches of Firminy's lopped-off cone (Fig. 6.13). Clearly Le Corbusier had something else in mind as he annotated the drawing with the words: "la Dent du Midi and the Mont Catogne in the Rhone Valley in Valais (the canton of Valais at the end of Lake Geneva) gives us courage for the game of the diagonals ... and for the nature of the volumes to propose." It is possible that the "game of diagonals" links to the diagonal shaft of light that was to become so central to his conception of the interior.

Peter, the patron saint of the church, is often referred to in Christian symbolism as "the rock" because of being called the rock upon which Jesus would build his church (Matthew 16:18). "Pierre", of course, means rock in French. According to Catholic dogma Peter is considered as the first pope and judge at the gates of heaven – roles which Le Corbusier was unlikely to find endearing. Further Peter could be seen to have usurped the Magdalene in the role of foremost apostle. The rock emerging from water (Fig. 6.14) is a repeated topos in Le Corbusier's work.[33] It is associated with the vertical axis of the spirit as opposed to the horizontal of the body. It is however based on the body of woman, as is made evident by the painting *Les îles sont des corps des femmes* (Fig. 6.15, 1945). It is our suggestion that the form of Saint Pierre was intended to represent a "fusion" of elements, as befits a church for a radiant and harmonious community of men and women.

Saint Pierre embodies a lifetime of thought on the meaning of sacred space as is amply illustrated by Eardley. Le Corbusier himself acknowledged the influence of light studies made in Istanbul's Hagia Sofia in 1910.[34] The top lit spaces of Hadrian's villa, so influential on La Sainte Baume, are likely to be implicated here. Of course there are parallels with the Assembly at Chandigarh[35] the roof of which is populated with a cluster of signs and symbols mediating between the gods and man described by Eardley as "a flamboyantly attired dress rehearsal for Firminy" (Fig. 6.16).[36]

Progress on the Firminy church project was slow. Initial drawings and architectural plans from 1961 were considered unacceptable and Le Corbusier was asked to rework them.[37] For more than three years, plans, information, requests and rejections went back and forth between the parties involved.[38] Cost was a major concern. Dominique Claudius-Petit, son of Eugène Claudius-Petit, reflected in retrospect, "He [Le Corbusier] had to deal with the obstinacy of the adverse forces belonging to the clergy and fiercely opposed to the project. To gain time, they procrastinated, protesting about problems concerning the site and money. The terrain was decided on, but he had to find ways to save, cut, shrink, but without 'undressing' the work."[39]

The Architectural Promenade

Not only is Saint Pierre a third type of church, it also represents a third type of promenade, the spiral route to knowledge, manifested in the Mundaneum (1929) and Le Corbusier's spiral museum schemes (Fig. 6.12).[40] It also has much in common with the Jacob's ladder route manifested in such early domestic schemes as the Villa Savoye (Fig. 6.19). Le Corbusier had a strong antipathy to seating:[41] "the faithful or others (six hundred) / are standing up / or are seated / in front of the liturgical drama / they are standing up or they get on the knees (if they have the taste)."[42] Saint Pierre was designed for worship on the move.

From its conception in 1961, Saint Pierre went through several phases of development.[43] The description that follows is based largely on the plans for the church completed in late 1963 and the official written description drawn up in early 1964.[44] Like Le Corbusier's own scheme our description of the promenade remains unfinished as we will never really know what the culmination, manifested in the detail of the project, might have been.

Introduction

The church was "by virtue of the terrain, located at the bottom of a valley."[45] It would announce its presence from afar, easily visible from the housing built in its vicinity and fulfilling the requirements of the clergy who wanted the parishioners to go "down" to church like one went "down" to market.[46] As at La Tourette, there would be electronic emissions of sound to call people to the church, exercising a radiant force on the surrounding countryside.

The building itself would occupy the west half of its site, with the "Place de l'église", or church square, on the east half. As at Ronchamp it would form an enigmatic composition with a series of other sculptural objects. In the end these included the 1970 cornerstone (designed by Le Corbusier and executed by Oubrerie, Fig. 6.17), and, built after 2003 as well as an inverted pyramid (inspired by a design Le Corbusier originally

6.16 – The assembly building at Chandigarh, 1953-1963

6.17 – Cornerstone of Saint Pierre showing diagonal beam of light

6.18 – Gutter spiralling around Saint Pierre

6.19 – 'The Architectural Promenade' of the Villa Savoye as presented in Le Corbusier's *Œuvre complète*

made for Chandigarh) with a lectern-sculpture at one end.[47] From the square one could either enter the building on the ground level into the spacious reception hall, leading to a large parish meeting room and other amenities or take an exterior ramp and spiral up to the third level, to the entrance of the sanctuary on the building's west side.

Water is evoked at the entrance to Firminy as it is at Ronchamp. Here a series of clues hint at the elemental nature of the interior (Fig. 6.20). The gutter-ark on the church's east facade is described by Le Corbusier as necessary to protect and keep rain from troubling the "constellation" of openings below it, just as the circling gutter system on the other facades is meant to protect and fend water off the glass-covered opening between the squared prism and the cone (Fig. 6.18). It can be no accident that the prismatic form of the church is an extruded blend of circle and square, a three-dimensional union of opposites. In form the church is that of the *Cathédrale des Sens* and *Labyrinthe* of Le Corbusier's paintings – Icône reduced to a geometric form – her cape protecting the space within, just as it does at La Tourette.

Threshold

The earliest plans for the church (Fig. 6.21) feature a long, spiralling covered ramp leading up to the sanctuary,[48] encompassing the fourteen Stations of the Cross (featuring the preparation for, crucifixion and resurrection of Jesus). This initiatic feature was eliminated in favour of a shorter open air ramp, but an echo of it remains mapped onto the facades in the form of the spiralling gutter system. As William

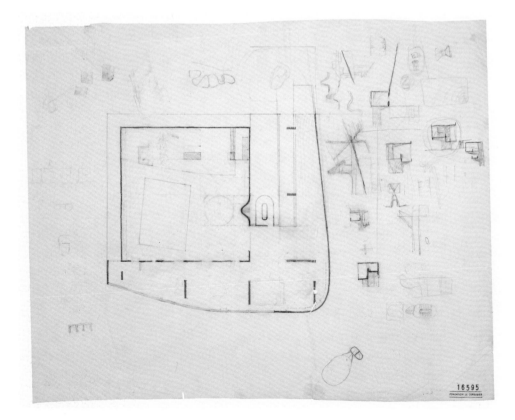

6.21 – Early plan showing long spiralling ramp up to the sanctuary of Saint Pierre, 1960. FLC 16595

Curtis wrote of the ramp of the Carpenter Centre (1963) at Harvard, "to experience the 'promenade architecturale', with the ramp grooves, intervals and ratios of pilotis and other elements slipping by was also directly to perceive the kinaesthetic spatial rhythms of an architectural music – the bars and notes of Le Corbusier's 'architecture acoustic'." [49] At the Carpenter Centre, roughly contemporaneous with Firminy, and as in several of Le Corbusier's later buildings, entry is negotiated via a tight box, modulor in proportion. [50] A similar square zone was planned for Saint Pierre, a place of restraint before the explosion of space beyond.

The baptistery is positioned here on the threshold, in keeping with its traditional role as rite of entry into membership of the church community and an echo of the prominent sinks that occur at the entrance of several of Le Corbusier's domestic schemes, notably the Villa Savoye. [51] These have sometimes been referred to as secular fonts or holy water stoops, and justly so in light of the idea that he wanted domestic space to harbour sacred meaning with ritual potential. [52] Thwarted in his desire to build for the church a baptismal font large enough for total adult immersion which featured on the early plans, Le Corbusier instead seems to have conceived of the entire building as a baptismal font of aqueous light (Fig. 6.22) surrounded by the spiralling system of rainwater gutters that channel water round and round the exterior of the building with the small font located at the entrance. [53] As he stated emphatically in *Towards an Architecture* nearly forty years before conceiving the Firminy church, "we need to wash ourselves". [54]

Questioning and Reorientation

In the December 1962 scheme the route leading from the ramp and into the church dips down and then moves up to the altar. This is quite peculiar as it requires the exterior ramp to go higher than necessary in order to allow the worshipper to travel down. The journey is a much flattened version of that through the Basilica at La Sainte Baume, down into darkness and up into light (Fig. 6.23). Bielza quotes from *La Maison-Dieu*: "The altar must be heightened by means of steps to remind us that it brings us closer to God, that is a place of encounter, a threshold – Jacob's ladder – which connects us to the sky." [55] At the same time the raising of the altar elevates the primacy of Christ's sacrifice, possibly explaining the very minimal raising of the altar at Firminy. As at Ronchamp, the altar at Saint Pierre is not quite centrally placed, again reducing the primacy of Christ's sacrifice and promoting other possibilities in the reading of the space (Fig. 6.24). It is simultaneously a place of questioning and reorientation.

In the main sanctuary the principal liturgical furnishings, about which Le Corbusier had consulted with Father Cocagnac, would be permanent fixtures, very sculptural in nature. [56] It is unsurprising that Le Corbusier referred to liturgical furnishings as instruments as he believed base matter to be in some sense alive, working on us through the power of radiance. [57] A good example is the simple steel cross,

6.22 – Interior
of church showing
watery light

6.23 – December
1962 section across
Saint Pierre

6.24 – The altar within Saint Pierre

6.25 – Le Corbusier's sketch for the Bologna church, 1962

FONDATION LE CORBUSIER

32269

proportioned to the modulor[58] (183 x 140 cm like the wooden cross at Ronchamp) which would be placed behind and south of the altar, again as at Ronchamp. The plans feature an unidentified liturgical/sculptural object on the south side of the choir, just before the wall separating the choir from the daily chapel. Oubrerie has – quite appropriately we think – interpreted this as a niche of blue glass, an echo of the niche of Mary at Ronchamp, completing the altar complex. Above and behind the altar, the eastern facade, as at Ronchamp, would be pierced by small variously coloured glass-filled openings, forming a kind of constellation, which Le Corbusier referred to as a "rosace", or rose window, borrowing the terminology from the stained glass realm of cathedral architecture and making further connection to the mystical rose and the alchemical Mary discussed in Chapter 4.[59]

The light canons in the roof not only bring in light but also represent the moon and the sun, making further links between the building and the cosmos. The moon and sun could also have for Le Corbusier the Christian/alchemical connotations of Christ (sun) and Mary (moon) – there are uncanny similarities between Saint Pierre and the alchemical alembic celebrated in so many historical prints. Eardley had shown that the Chandigarh Assembly, based on Le Corbusier's love for the form of power station cooling towers was toned down for Firminy as such an overt celebration of the sun would be considered "an intolerably offensive pagan gesture by a Catholic congregation."[60] The strong cruciform incision that can be seen in the earliest scheme was replaced by two light canons designed to spotlight the altar on Good Friday and Easter Mornings, a reworking of a similar idea for the Assembly which itself builds on ideas generated for La Sainte Baume. The diagonal beam of light is celebrated on the cornerstone of the church and was based on light studies developed by Le Corbusier, see for example the drawing dated December 19, 1962.[61] For Burriel Bielza the connection between earth and sky is vital for an understanding of Saint Pierre, the church a marker of the passing of the seasons and the days.[62] It should be noted that Le Corbusier's sketches for the abortive Bologna church were similarly cosmic. Here a vast ramp, similar to the "Vallon du Beton" conceived for La Sainte Baume, would lead directly up to a vast steeple-like structure, a ladder between earth and sky (Fig. 6.25).[63]

We argue that, as Le Corbusier discovered Teilhard late in life, the impact of his ideas (set out in chapter 2) on Saint Pierre is particularly strong. At Firminy the parish community is lifted above the hum drum reality of quotidian existence and projected into mythic time and space. Saint Pierre is a power house, an incubator of planetisation, drawing on the spark of energy at the core of people and of things and reflecting Le Corbusier's (and Teilhard's) belief that as people grow closer in community they will grow closer to the divine.

It is here that we need to mention the lower, alternative route into the church. In the June 1962 version of the drawings the second level plan shows an entrance at the level of the Place de l'Église past three biomorphic spaces, very much like those at the

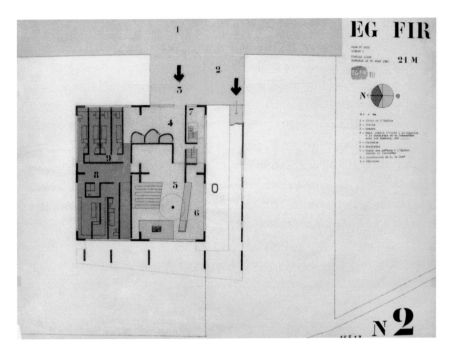

6.26 – Ground plan of Saint Pierre,
June 1962, FLC 16513A

6.27 – Fireplace of Le Corbusier's
Maison Jaoul B, 1954–56

6.28 – Plan of Level 1,
Saint Pierre, December
1962, FLC 16517

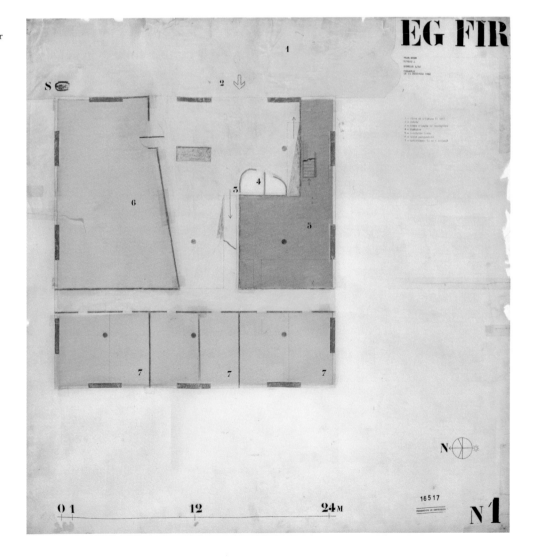

entrance of La Tourette (Fig. 6.26). On entry into the church sanctuary, the way is barred by the column that carries the mushroom-like suspended choir loft. This barring of the way by a column is characteristic of Le Corbusier's work, for example in the ground floor entrance hall of his own home at 24 Rue Nungesser et Coli. It also happens in Maision Jaoul B where the column is the chimneystack leading up from the freestanding fireplace at ground level. Here the movement of the inhabitants is governed by this fulcrum point (Fig. 6.27). In the December 1962 version the church's suspended choir loft has gone. The life of the building would then revolve quietly around the altar whose own base-column projects down from the church into the parish spaces below (Fig. 6.28 and 6.29). Apparently Cocagnac was most insistent that this vertical connection should be maintained, it being a requirement of Catholic churches.[64]

Entry from the Place l'Église brings the parishioner straight into dialogue with the lower level of the altar at ground level. Burriel Bielza makes the point that the column that pierces down through the parish spaces is evocative of the hearth at the centre of the home. A Victorian print in Le Corbusier's book *The Marseilles Block* illustrates the primacy of this space in his thinking.[65] Indeed he spoke of the kitchen of the Unité

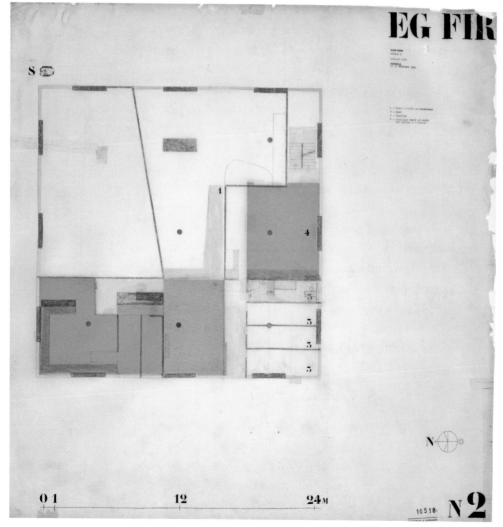

6.29 – Plan of Level 2, Saint Pierre, December 1962, FLC 16518A

apartment as "the fire, the hearth, that is to say something ancestral, that eternal thing which is the very key to everything."[66] Such ideas chime with Todd Wilmert's writings on the inspirational power of smoke in Le Corbusier's early work.[67] If we were to follow this chain of association the conclusion would have to be that the altar relates to "foyer" or hearth that Le Corbusier identified with his wife Yvonne,[68] represented by Icône holding the flame of divine inspiration at the centre of *Le poème de l'angle droit*. This leads to a further Teilhardian concept – the central role of woman in the spiritual life of man and the importance of love in the creation of community. It was pointed out in chapter 2 that Icône's flame is also strongly evocative of Christ represented through the *vesica piscis*, illumination, crystal, or philosopher's stone – take your pick. This circle of association brings us back to Christ's sacrifice traditionally present at the altar, or potentially, the table at the heart of the home.

"Simplicity, poverty, truth"

The Parish Associations' requirement of "simplicity, poverty and truth" like the Liturgy, sits within an overall framework of theological ideas. It was essential in defining the type of pastoral message the Church wanted to send to both its members and the world at large via the architecture of Saint Pierre. One could argue that the church's reinforced concrete structure gave the appearance of simplicity, poverty and truth, providing for the practical and spiritual needs of the parish without extravagance or ornamentation. The debatable nature of this claim was a real area of concern for the Diocesan Office for New Parishes who represented the Bishop of Lyons who used logistical problems of finance and land to block the project. Beyond the question of literal cost, the ethical issue of a kind of faux-poverty, so central to the culture of modernist architecture, was perhaps at last being challenged.

One telling example of how Mazioux manipulated these issues occured in 1962 when he presented Le Corbusier with the ultimatum of removing the choir loft-balcony or changing the site of the church, in an effort to economise on land and money.[69] Probably betting that Le Corbusier would concede to neither (an indication, in fact, that he understood the project and the architect quite well), Le Corbusier must have surprised him by agreeing to his former demand. This was one of the many concessions he made at the request of the Church. It was a particularly significant one, because the elimination of the balcony also prompted the adding of the spiral seating and the modification of the baptistery, as well as the elimination of the bell tower initially planned on the exterior of the church. Ironically, Mazioùx' ultimatum enabled Le Corbusier's atelier to further embrace the Parish Association's initial requests.

Le Corbusier claimed that truth lay in the clear unambiguous expression of the concrete itself. Claudius-Petit defended this general line, describing Saint Pierre as a "rough church, modest, poor in spirit."[70] Le Corbusier probably thought he was in tune with what the Parish Association was requesting (and he probably was – the Parish Association was not adverse to his proposals) because he was driving his creative decisions according to the understanding of these terms as they were promoted by the Dominicans of *L'Art sacré*. One can surmise that Le Corbusier certainly thought he was aligning himself with this movement through the act of building the Firminy church, and that his church design would be welcomed by the hierarchy of the Lyons diocese. However this was not to be the case.

The title of Eardley's landmark essay on the Firminy church spells out the problem very clearly: "Grandeur is the Intention".[71] Perhaps not as tall as Perret's church in Le Havre, nor as lavish as the pilgrimage basilica Sainte Thérèse de Lisieux (1929-1954), nor as obviously monumental as Guillaume Gillet's Notre Dame de Royan (1958), nor as vast as Pierre Vago's (along with Eugène Freyssinet, Pierre Pinsard, André Le Donné) underground Saint Pius basilica at Lourdes (1958) for 20,000 pilgrims, the Firminy project was indeed nevertheless grand in intention. It was meant to crown an ambitious civic project, led by an ambitious civil servant, Claudius-Petit. The architecture itself was problematic in its audacity, but so too was the audacity of the mayor in his determination to build a church of his own choosing.[72] The problem was that the Diocesan Office of New Parishes perceived this audacity as a fundamental disregard for the workings of the institution of the Church.[73] Just how lay people are expected to engage within such a process remains unclear, even today. Regardless of the fact he was an active member of the Church, Claudius-Petit had gone too far.

In 1963, due to poor soil conditions, it was estimated that major, expensive, foundation work would have to be done to support the structure, apparently more than doubling the cost of the church.[74] Despite the many difficulties a contract between the Parish Association and the architect was signed with a clause about budget and honorarium limits.[75] As mentioned earlier, plans for the church were completed in late 1963 by Le Corbusier's office, and the official description written in early 1964 but, when final cost estimates were revealed shortly thereafter, the Parish Association gave Le Corbusier three months to redesign the church – this time for an entirely different site.[76]

Le Corbusier, at his wits' end with his client, wrote to Claudius-Petit, stating heroically: "It is too easy to wash one's hands egotistically! The church planned for Firminy-Vert is a remarkable creation. Moreover, it brought to your initiative for Firminy-Vert an architectural element of capital importance which would have had great repercussions."[77] Although, with much effort, he was able to persuade the Parish Association to continue the project, providing it could find the funds, there was no sign of any action.[78] Seen in this light, the *L'Art sacré* issue devoted to the church published in November-December 1964 can only be read as an attempt – a last attempt? – to drum up support. By recording within it all the different versions of the scheme the priests of *L'Art sacré* underscored just how much work had gone into the project and how much Le Corbusier had to concede to the Parish Association.[79] The same issue also showed on its cover Le Corbusier standing next to the 1962 model of the church, pointing his finger in the air, words caught on his lips. Continuing the dialogue? Explaining yet again his project? Pointing the blame on an unseen antagonist across from him? How must this image be read?

Despite the Dominicans' efforts with the special issue, Claudius-Petit's and Father Tardy's unceasing efforts, attempts by the Minister of Culture André Malraux and Ronchamp's priest Bolle-Reddat to intervene as well as the support of many others, the situation dragged on unresolved. Finally, a letter from Tardy in January 1965 brought the project to an end.[80] Le Corbusier felt compelled to reply with the following:

> A job was entrusted to me, I did it conscientiously ... I struggled with materials, forms, and the trades. I carried out all the conditions of the contract. I did my work, and I feel more bound than ever to this work of ours ... I cannot conceive of anything else at this point than the beginning of construction, for the great spiritual joy of all.[81]

He would build his church only on the original site where it would complete the vision of unity that he planned for Firminy. Le Corbusier died on August 27, 1965, before anything further was achieved. Father Tardy died accidentally shortly thereafter, and in 1971, Claudius-Petit lost the municipal elections and was no longer mayor, losing much of his leverage with the local political and ecclesiastic authorities.

The push to build continued throughout the 1970s, funded by local people, industrialists, artists (including Sonia Delaunay and Jean Dubuffet) and members of the architectural community (including the Fondation Le Corbusier).[82] Activity finally picked up again in 2003. The Claudius-Petit family, first Eugène, then his son Dominique were central to the cause. Oubrerie continued to play an important role in the realisation of the scheme.

6.30 – Relief image of man and woman from the base of the Unité, Firminy

Saint Pierre as it stands is not a parish church. Mass is held there once a month on a revolving schedule with other churches in its parish of Saint-Martin. It is also held at Christmas and Easter, a typical reality for churches in France in the twenty-first century. Thus the parish and Diocese of Saint-Étienne have an active role in its usage. The parish facilities planned for the first two levels of the building house a space run by Saint-Étienne's Museum of Modern Art dedicated to Le Corbusier and the modernist milieu. The potential of cultural tourism guided much of the decision-making behind the impetus to build, a principle the church-builders were constrained to embrace if they wanted – finally – to see the edifice completed.

Summary

If, in Le Corbusier's gendered world, Ronchamp is about woman in the spiritual life of man and La Tourette is about the woman deep within man, Saint Pierre is about men and women in community (Fig. 6.30). Like all his built space it is a lesson in *savoir habiter*, knowing how to live, drawing attention to the connections between people and their environment at a cosmic scale. "We have made a house, where, I think, up and down, Earth and Sky join together."[83] The domestic hearth, a place of exchange, food, conversation and love is taken to the scale of the city, in a natural gathering place within the wider landscape.

A section (Fig. 6.23) through the scheme is dotted with printed figures of Modulor man. Oddly enough the two "men" at each entrance, below and above, have been given skirts rendering them women. Who transformed them in this way, perhaps unprecedented in Le Corbusier's work? We suggested, in chapter 4, building on the ideas of Teilhard, that it was necessary to negotiate with woman to pass through the east door of revelation at Ronchamp. Woman is keeper of the door. In the Saint Pierre section a woman is present at each of the two entries to the church, the lower parish business route and the upper more spiritual circuit. They seem to us to evoke the Biblical story of Martha and Mary with whom the Magdalene has often been associated, one that exercised a strong pull on Le Corbusier. In Luke's version of the story[84] an exhausted Christ takes refuge in the house of "a certain woman named Martha" whose sister Mary sits at his feet and listens to him talk. According to the account in the Bible Martha is annoyed because Mary does not help her prepare the house for their guest. Jesus reminds Martha that, although her own role is important, Mary's "good part" is equally necessary. Le Corbusier seems to have taken a particular interest in this story as, within his copy of Ernest Renan's *La Vie de Jesus*, he underlined Jesus' words "Martha, Martha you worry about many things when it is only necessary to worry about one thing."[85] The story of Martha and Mary tells of the tensions between the life of the body and the life of the spirit, social action (made possible through the parish community) and spiritual action (to be fulfilled in the sanctuary), the resolution of the two being of central importance to Le Corbusier's work, seemingly embodied in the designs for Saint Pierre.

THE LEGACY OF LE CORBUSIER'S CHURCHES

What then is the nature of Le Corbusier's influence on modern church architecture? Is it more than a complex asymmetric plan, oddly shaped windows and the use of brutalist materials? Having discussed the furore caused by Le Corbusier's churches, particularly Ronchamp, we will explore his influence via the work of seven recent architects. We begin with the bunker church Sainte Bernadette by Claude Parent and Paul Virilio, and the critical manipulation of architectural meaning, before moving on to its antithesis, the porous, light, and festive spaces of Richard Meier's Jubilee Church. Meier's church is deeply unhierarchical unlike Stephen Holl's Saint Ignatius which is framed around the Corbusian promenade. Holl, like Alvaro Siza, has clearly learnt much from Le Corbusier's treatment of the Liturgy. In Siza's Santa Maria, Porto, views of nature also play a strong role in the work of narrative, as they do in Ando's churches where geometry comes into play. We then move to Estudio Sancho-Madridejos' chapel at Valleaceron which takes Le Corbusier's preoccupation with concrete, geometry and light, so skilfully worked by Ando, to new monumental extremes. The studied perfection and isolation of their chapel is contrasted with Rudolf Reitermann and Peter Sassenroth's Chapel of Reconciliation in Berlin which, we argue, is the natural successor to Le Corbusier's vision of a politicised, site-specific, community church. While illustrating a range of subtle shifts in architectural emphasis, these examples will highlight through contrast the very singular character of what Le Corbusier set out to achieve. Free from many practical constraints church architecture reveals the ethics of architecture in its purest form.

That Le Corbusier's churches received a mixed reception should by now be clear. Ronchamp was seen as problematic by some architects, particularly in Britain, as can be seen from the writings of James Stirling who seems to have seen the chapel as some form of betrayal. Nikolaus Pevsner was similarly disturbed and was clearly reluctant to include it within his famous history of modernism. Their basic gripe was with Le Corbusier's romantic attachment to symbolism, lack of constructional truth, his subjectivity and general lack of apparent rigour. Peter Hammond wrote damningly that:

> Particularly in church design, Ronchamp has provided a justification for architects to ignore any discipline, to pursue private whimsy without concern for function. Ronchamp does not diminish one's respect for Le Corbusier as an architect, because seen as a folly it is outstanding; but in the development of church building, it is a blind alley.[1]

Such sentiments were echoed by Peter Smithson who thought, in line with Vatican II, that "we should be heading towards rather plain brick boxes with no tricks".[2] Some modernists, like Smithson, took the side of Mies van der Rohe (the simple box – Fig. 4.27), some Alvar Aalto (organic and informal – Fig. 7.1) and some Le Corbusier (atmospheric, symbolic and ordered). Their three very different takes on sacred space are implicated in this discussion.

7.1 – Church of the Three Crosses, Alvar Aalto

Despite criticisms from the upper echelons of architecture Le Corbusier was solicited for the construction of "nine chapels, a convent, two monasteries and seventeen churches, coming mostly from Switzerland, Germany, Belgium and France, but also from Italy, the Netherlands, the United States, Venezuela and Rwanda."[3] Clearly his architecture had struck a chord with those who wanted more than the minimum.

It is perhaps useful to reflect on Charles Jenck's often ignored proposal that the Ronchamp chapel should be read not as treason from within modernism but as the first Post-Modern building.[4] This changes the place of Le Corbusier in architectural history; he ceases to be considered the inspiration behind countless Post-Modern projects, becoming instead a key instigator.

Very briefly, Jencks grants Post-Modern status to Ronchamp for several reasons: because the "pantheist" Le Corbusier built a monument to nature; because of the synaesthetic metaphor of "acoustic sounds" that Jencks qualifies as a "deep metaphor" – the quintessence of Post-Modernism and because of what Jencks classifies as the first-time use of fractal geometry to create Ronchamp's many basic curves. Further, Jencks emphasises the sculptural aspect of the building when seen from afar in the landscape, qualifying the building itself as one of Le Corbusier's "Ubu" sculptures. Dual readings are encouraged (grid versus curve, light and shadow) and the individual subjectivity of the visitor embraced. All these characteristics make Ronchamp Post-Modern. This evaluation is especially useful for us in the case studies that follow as they all embrace the experience of the individual to a greater or lesser extent, revealing no singular route to God, but a range of different possibilities each inspired by an aspect of Le Corbusier's work in this area.

Bunker Architecture: Sainte Bernadette du Banlay, Nevers, France, by Paul Virilio and Claude Parent (architecture principe), 1966

If Ronchamp is taken to be Post-Modern it logically displaces what has been considered for years by architectural historians and theorists as the first post-modern building in France, Sainte Bernadette du Banlay in Nevers, 1966, our first case study. This "fractured monolith",[5] expressive of rupture – physical, social, historical – announced the beginning of "critical" architecture in France (Fig 7.2).[6] In the article "L'Architecture sacrée, architecture de transfert" ("Sacred Architecture, Architecture of Transference") appearing in a 1966 edition of *L'Architecture d'Aujourd'hui*, the young Claude Parent and Paul Virilio praised Le Corbusier's sacred architecture – and the enlightened fold within the Church who had commissioned it – declaring:

> The Church still remains the only constituted body – parallel to autonomous individuals, enlightened by architecture – capable of exalting in the creative freedom of its buildings and, hence, the genesis of a future. In the domain of construction, this is its permanent mission. And it very clearly manifested this in the period of Ronchamp and La Tourette."[7]

They wrote disapprovingly of the use of past styles and praised poverty of
materials and the concepts of modesty and simplicity, but warned prophetically
that a misunderstanding of these terms could lead to churches of poor design
and construction.

The 8th December that same year saw the consecration of their parish church of Sainte
Bernadette, situated in the sprawling, immigrant Banlay neighbourhood of Nevers,
the town in the centre of France where Saint Bernadette, the girl-saint to whom the
Virgin was said to have appeared in Lourdes in 1858, is buried. The church in Nevers
had been commissioned three years earlier by the local bishop, a daring engineer-
turned priest, Michel-Louis Vial, who defended the difficult project through thick and
thin, as did its parish priest, Father Robert Bourgoin.[8]

Parent and Virilio were at the time the main members of a young, short-lived (1963-
1968) experimental group called *architecture principe*. Parent was a trained architect,
Virilio had been a master-glassman working in sacred art circles. He knew Father
Couturier and had worked with Braque and Matisse. He had also acted as advisor to
Le Corbusier at one time.[9] Having been converted by worker-priests after the war, Virilio
became an urbanist and theoretician especially known for his critical texts on speed
and technology.[10] *Architecture principe's* main aim was to promote critical architecture
and Sainte Bernadette was its only built project. Conceived during the Cold War,
as fear about the "atomic age" reached its height, Sainte Bernadette's aesthetic owes
something to the World War II military bunkers, objects of fascination for Virilio, that
in the 1960s still populated the Atlantic coast.[11] The church also embodied the, rather
hopeful, idea that oblique angles and what Parent called "the slant" would provoke
much needed change in society, an obvious, if slightly literal, nod to Le Corbusier's
"right angle". "Having traversed the eras of the horizontal, and then the vertical, the
latter's possibilities having been exhausted ... *architecture principe* believed it was time
to turn to the slant as an alternative, as the solution for saving civilisation" (Fig. 7.3).[12]

Parent had been mentored by André Bloc, founder of the group *Espace* (and of the magazine *L'Architecture d'Aujourd'hui*), together evolving a series of possible church designs. Parent was working in Le Corbusier's studio in 1953, the point when Ronchamp was under way and La Tourette was in its beginnings.[13] He also worked with Pierre Vago on the colossal (capacity 20,000) underground Saint Pius X Basilica in Lourdes that was built in the 1950s and consecrated in 1958. Bloc's work, like Le Corbusier's, remained anchored in utopian ideals, which the young Parent felt compelled to reject while retaining the belief that employing the slant would prevent crisis and re-dynamise society. Fusion was the answer.

A surprisingly strong connection can be established between Sainte Bernadette and Ronchamp via the physical elements they share: slanted flooring; one large more or less squared nave space instead of an elongated rectangular traditional nave; seating and liturgical furnishings as permanent, unmovable fixtures designed by the architects[14]; "periscope" elements that create indirect and diffuse lighting, and the use of reinforced concrete. Curved walls, a grotto-like interior, and asymmetry are also shared (Fig. 7.4). As at Firminy, parish rooms were planned on the ground floor, and the sanctuaries elevated to upper floors. Both churches were planned to seat about 600 and were to serve new communities founded as a result of immigration and a predicted expansion of industry (Fig. 7.5). Both provided the basic needs of the parishioners with little decoration; they were stripped fairly bare.[15]

The architectural promenade at Nevers is also significant. The church is set back far on its plot, at some distance from the street and is clearly conceived as a promenade.[16] Once inside, it is necessary to negotiate with the ground floor narthex and baptistery, before climbing the stairs in the core of the church and being propelled up into the midst of the wooden-bench pews of the obliquely raised nave, the sanctuary's choir displayed opposite, rising before the approaching parishioner. Indeed, the floor of the nave hits its low-point at the juncture. It rises towards the front and the choir, and behind, the seating rises towards the back to the last, elevated row of pews, creating a sort of elongated V-angled floor, highly reminiscent of Firminy (Fig. 7.3).

The bunker was a complex sign; its primary association was with the enemy and the Nazi regime, but it could be read more universally as a "survival machine".[17] According to Virilio, the Nevers church demanded the visitor-parishioner to accept the more universal reading, a warning of the threat of atomic war.[18] "We wanted to Christianize the Bunker, the anti-atomic refuges!!! (sic) Putting the hope of Faith just there where the anxiety of the period lay," stated Virilio.[19] The bunker became an ark – place of refuge – the ark connoting both crypt and nave, the spaces making up churches.[20] He thus transformed a "place of war into a place of worship."[21] Both Le Corbusier and Virilio saw the church as a defensive structure, protecting the faithful from the material world. At the same time the Church itself needed defence being "one of the last programmes that allows architecture to obtain spirituality through the transcendence of forms." "In a world in which men suffer the evolution of ugliness

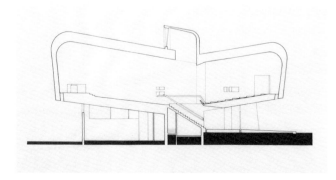

7.3 – Sainte Bernadette du Banlay, elevation showing slant, drawing, 74 x 91.2 cm

7.4 – Sainte Bernadette du Banlay, sanctuary interior

7.5 – Sainte Bernadette du Banlay, church under construction and surrounding neighborhood

complacently, architects must defend the cult of beauty, of spirituality, above all and even more so when it concerns a religious edifice."[22]

Virilio, Parent and Vial created an ambiguous and perhaps troublesome sign, especially for the French Catholic Church. It cannot be forgotten that many French were forced to participate in the construction of the Atlantic Wall Bunkers in the STO "Forced Worker Service".[23] It is imperative to ask why the Church, in this case, was able to accept such a blatant reminder of the War and why it, unlike the bunker of Firminy, came to be built. Could it be read as an unconscious "mea culpa", a way of acknowledging the problematic role of the French Church during the War? Were Parent and Virilio, much like Le Corbusier, employing a sort of double language, using Vatican II and church-building requirements to create an acceptable liturgical programme to cover up their more radical intentions? Both churches engage with major social issues; Le Corbusier with the place of women in society, *architecture principe* with the dangers of Cold War culture. Unlike Firminy, which was perhaps too uncritical, the "fractured monolith" of Sainte Bernadette clearly chimed with something in public consciousness. However the bunker church of Nevers would never have been built, but for Le Corbusier's pioneering effort.

Although Sainte Bernadette triggered a search for new forms in the field of secular architecture, it was perceived as problematic as a precedent for church architecture in France.[24] The Church, an organism meant to inspire hope, security, faith and assurance, suddenly found itself resembling a cultural signifier of disaster. What could be the pastoral message sent out by "the Bunker", which was deeply demanding and above all bellicose in spite of its architects' discourse? One example was quite enough.[25]

Porosity and Play: Chiesa del Dio Padre Misericoridoso or the "Jubilee Church" for a Suburb of Rome by Richard Meier, 2003

The Chiesa del Dio Padre Misericoridoso is in many ways the antithesis of the critical, bunker architecture of Sainte Bernadette. Richard Meier stated in the 2003 press release announcing the consecration of his church in the suburbs of Rome, "… the coalescence of aesthetic and spiritual inspiration that one sees in the great modern churches of the 20th century, from Le Corbusier's Notre Dame du Haut in France to Alvar Aalto's church of the Three Crosses in Finland, has informed my own work for some time."[26] Meier's concern with whiteness, route, light and layering are clearly early Corbusian in origin. It is however arguable that the Jubilee church has more in common with the shell forms and organicism of Le Corbusier's friend Aalto's Three Crosses (Fig. 7.1). We include it here as it represents a more informal, open and possibly more personal route to God, less critical than Sainte Bernadette which is so serious and so angry.

Meier was chosen for the competition to build the Chiesa del Dio Padre Misericoridoso, God Our Merciful Father, called *The Jubilee Church* by the architect, to mark the new millennium of the Christian era and crown the Diocese of Rome's ambitious plan for re-investment in its suburbs. It was the programme's fiftieth church, commission awarded in 1996.[27] The project aimed to provide much needed coherence and "social and cultural focus" for Rome's To Tre Teste area (25,000 inhabitants) where a third of the population live in the nondescript 1970s block-towers that surround the church.[28]

Stretched out in front of the church is the stone *sagrato*, or open plaza, designed to give breathing space for the neighbourhood (Fig. 7.6) it allows the church visibility and invites engagement with an architectural promenade that culminates in the church's interior. Apparently the triangular-shaped site determined the non-traditional orientation of the church with its west-end choir and east-end entrance preceded by its inviting portico, flanked by a bell tower, but one cannot help thinking that such a skilful planner as Meier could have got around this problem had he so wished. The non-traditional orientation suggests that it was a priority for Meier that the church sat at ground level, thus maximising fluidity of movement between inside and outside. It seems less likely that he was wilfully challenging what a church might be, but this is also possible.

The complex is deceivingly compact. Its design is based on a geometric drawing that combines a series of gathered squares, intersected by sections of three same-radius circles, governed by a 45-degree angle extending into space. The result is a trinity of curved, closely-aligned white concrete "shells" that form the distinctive south side of the church. The squares, circles and shells could all be Corbusian in origin, but here seem so deconstructed that they become all Meier. Glass employed as roofing and walling connects them (and provides discrete entrances to the daily chapel, reconciliation rooms – confessionals – and baptistery housed within their spaces). Inside, the walls are cut away, their presence on the open space of the nave being minimal (Fig. 7.7). They seem to be more about the exterior look of the building than the experience of space within. The sanctuary is covered by a glass roof that connects the south side's innermost curve to the north wall of the church. On the other side this wall, in turn, connects a glass atrium to the four-storey L-shaped white concrete community centre (class rooms, recreational rooms, auditorium, offices) that occupies the north side of the plot, opening out onto exterior terraces, courtyards and playgrounds. The building is open at every level. Clear glass on all sides ensures maximum connection with the site.

The liturgical set-up of the church's sanctuary is handsome, if fairly conservative. An elongated nave with wooden pews is punctuated on the west end behind the choir by a sacristy "tower" and on the east end – above the entrance – by the choir loft and organ. The altar wall is asymmetrical in composition. Behind the crucifix, to the right

7.6 – Chiesa del Dio Padre Misericoridoso or the "Jubilee Church", plaza and surrounding area from above

7.7 – Chiesa del Dio Padre Misericordoso or the "Jubilee Church", interior showing cut-away wall and nave

7.8 – Chiesa del Dio Padre Misericoridoso or the "Jubilee Church", detail of niche above choir

7.9 – Chiesa del Dio Padre Misericoridoso or the "Jubilee Church", exterior showing curves and low horizontal window

of the altar, is a curious perspective box, a geometric echo across architectural history of Mary's niche at Ronchamp (Fig. 7.8). The liturgical furniture and choir floor are made of stone, which also lines the lower section of the nave's north wall.

Of primary interest here is light, its manipulation and movement in the spaces, and how this light has determined the use of space. The sphere segments rising one higher than the next on the south side provide shade for the church's interior, which would otherwise bake in the Roman sun. As "sun breakers" or brises soleil, they constitute a poetic environmental solution; the control of natural light being at once a spiritual and technical issue in Le Corbusier's mind. Light nevertheless enters from above and through the east and west glass walls, providing the majority of the church's lighting in daytime. Along the floor level of the outer sphere, a long low horizontal opening like a slit also provides diffuse light into the church via the daily chapel (Fig. 7.9). All of the church's glass surfaces mean that, when artificially lit in the evening, the building glows, or radiates, to use Corbusian vocabulary.

In Meier's preparatory text for the church, written in 1997, he wrote of being influenced by Hans-Georg Gadamer's ideas about the role of play and ritual in human culture, the whole building encompassing the play of light and movement:

> We have thus conceived of this entire complex as a site for both formal and informal festive celebration wherein the act of symbolic remembrance is to be enacted through prayer and the orchestration of human movement.[29]

The development of the architectural promenade dissipates once inside the church. Here there seems to be a myriad of choices for ambling and taking it all in – possibly a rebellion against the structured routes of Le Corbusier. But this freedom, just as the light is free, this possibility of play (before God), seems to be what it is all about – the opposite to the 1960s bunker church – a subtle shift towards the democratic free play of Aalto's architecture, so reliant on sensitive response to issues of site, material and community, but with the concomitant danger of messy, undesigned space and experience. Meier's architecture – unremittingly immaculate, white and textureless – draws attention to conditions of light but what it affords to human inhabitation is debatable.

Promenade Architecturale: the Chapel of Saint Ignatius, Seattle, by Stephen Holl, 1997

Stephen Holl's Saint Ignatius Chapel, in the heart of the University of Seattle Jesuit learning centre, was consecrated in 1997. Its commission was part of a campus development plan and its form and deployment in space were conceived within this specific site and situation. Unlike Meier's church it was clearly designed with a highly structured promenade in mind. Holl never cites Ronchamp as an influence, though he admits in an interview on general influences in his work: "How could you practice in

7.11 – Chapel of Saint Ignatius,
Bottles of light watercolor

7.10 – Chapel of Saint Ignatius,
exterior side facade

7.12 – Chapel of Saint Ignatius,
exterior main facade with pool

the 20th century and not be influenced by Le Corbusier" (Fig. 7.10).[30] Holl, well known as a theoretician, has observed that: "As soon as you make a statement, you want to transcend it. You actually have the desire to transcend any kind of definitive frame because in the unknown is joy."[31] This statement, pure Le Corbusier, is what seems to be at the "Heart of the Matter" regarding the chapel of Saint Ignatius: ever shifting light as ever shifting theory, Saint Ignatius' "Spiritual Exercises" – no same route for two different people – on the road to faith.

The point of departure for the chapel is a drawing of "seven bottles of light emerging from a stone box," each one representing a key point in the building's liturgical programme, and each designated a particular colour, moving from blue to red to yellow (Fig. 7.11). These can be read symbolically as a neatly Corbusian sequence of water, fusion and sun (spirit and enlightenment) and can be seen at a distance after dark projecting, in the sensitising stage of the promenade, glowing coloured light out into the Seattle night-scape. Like Ronchamp, Holl's chapel introduces itself via distant views (Fig. 7.12). Le Corbusier's concern, born of Rabelais, with the "holy bottle" and indeed the number seven are uncannily echoed here. Is it chance that led Holl to open his text on the chapel in his book *Urbanisms, Working with Doubt*, with a quote from *The Heart of the Matter* by Teilhard de Chardin:

> Within every being and every
> event there is a progressive
> expansion of a mysterious inner
> clarity which transfigures them.[32]

Concerned with the order of things at a microscopic level, Holl here appears to allude to that divine spark perceived by both Teilhard and Le Corbusier at our core.[33]

The visitor approaches the chapel from the south. The sensitising stage of the promenade takes the form of a reflective pool and a lawn named a "thinking field" by Holl. As in Le Corbusier's promenades this is clearly a place for questioning. Between lawn and pool stands the bell tower; the pool and tower signifying one of the "bottles". The main entrance is a big wood and bronze door on a pivot for ceremonial use, inscribed with seven oval shapes (again evoking the bottles, this time in plan – a highly Corbusian geometric twist), juxtaposed by a smaller door for everyday use. Just inside, a carpet designed by the architect evokes an important moment in Saint Ignatius' life which took place by a river. Is it chance that the undulating blue line – highly reminiscent of the "Law of the Meander" ("the sign of the 24 hour day" rotated by ninety degrees) painted on the south ceremonial door at Ronchamp – was for Le Corbusier, "key to the lost paradise"?

The visitor passes the narthex, goes through the "processional area" and past the baptistery, positioned up front as in Le Corbusier's work, and spirals round clockwise into the vaulted nave,[34] turning right to face the altar (Fig. 7.13). The elegant curved wooden pews gather and unify the rather sprawling spaces around them. The mirrored floor evokes the watery quality of the slate floor at La Tourette. There are many parallels between Le Corbusier's altars at Ronchamp and Saint Ignatius. Above the altar, and slightly to the right, a square panel protrudes into the nave, as at the Jubilee Church (Fig. 7.14). Although in a completely different building, it feels like the geometric echo of the dark void of the organ loft at La Tourette. Coloured light leaks into the church through its glazed sides. The crucifix on the left is in relative darkness, here sidelit in yellow. To the right of the altar is a blue glass niche recollecting Mary at Ronchamp (as well as Oubrerie's watery niche at Saint Pierre). It occupies the same side of the church as the baptismal font, the reflective pool, the chapel of reconciliation and indeed the "bride's room". This is the tallest, brightest side (the glass is clear), again as at Ronchamp. Is it possible, given Holl's interest in Teilhard, that this side of the chapel reflects this enlightened Jesuit's belief in the importance of woman in giving access to the divine, or does Saint Ignatius reuse the themes of Ronchamp minus its more political agenda? It is very hard to tell.

Liminal Liturgy: the Church of Santa Maria, Porto, by Alvaro Siza, 1996

Alvaro Siza, when commissioned to work on the Cistercian monastery of La Thoronet in 2006, acknowledged the influence of Le Corbusier on an unquantifiable level, not at the level of "direct transposition",[35] recognising publicly the importance of his work – particularly La Tourette,[36] his legacy and its role as an "irreplaceable object of learning", and supported the candidature of Le Corbusier's work for Unesco's world heritage programme.[37] Our focus here is on Siza's treatment of the Liturgy which, like Holl, builds on that of Ronchamp, but brings in elements of the natural environment usually reserved for Le Corbusier's domestic work.

Siza's church of Santa Maria in Marco de Canaveses near Porto, Portugal (1990-1996) is now part of a parochial complex with auditorium, catechism classrooms and presbytery (built years later, finished in 2006). The church sits, resolutely white, on the little hill Siza describes, in Corbusian fashion, as an "acropolis"[38] overlooking a nondescript area of town, surrounded by beautiful rolling hills and mountains (Fig. 7.15). The parish sanctuary is reached by two different paths on either side of the church. As the commissioning priest, since turned philosopher, Nuno Higino wrote: "The access to the Santa Maria church requires diverse paths. It requires the cross and the crossing, it requires movements, detours and diagonal lines, restraint, it requires conditioning and calculation. It requires a critical effort."[39] In this way it echoes the complex routes of La Tourette.

Siza worked closely with local theologians to try to respond to the liturgical needs of the church with Vatican II. At the same time he drew inspiration from the regional church-building traditions of northern Portugal.[40] Despite this he spoke of experiencing "more freedom than usual" in this commission.[41] It is this close attention to the Liturgy

7.13 – Chapel of Saint Ignatius, interior

7.14 – Chapel of Saint Ignatius, elevation and plan

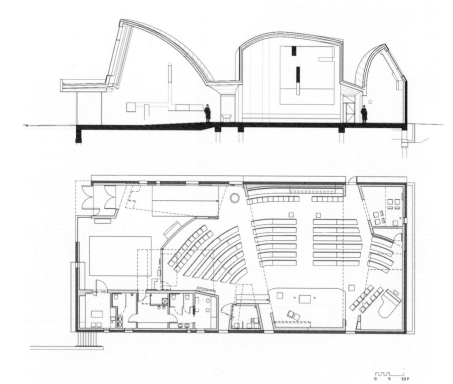

7.15 – Church of Santa Maria, exterior showing church in 'Acropolis' position

7.16 – Church of
Santa Maria,
exterior showing
entrance facade

7.17 – Church of
Santa Maria, interior
of main sanctuary

7.18 – Church
of Santa Maria,
detail of cross

and his emphasis on "fraternal relationship" developed through engagement with the local community that his work most closely echoes that of Le Corbusier and is most interesting to those who want more than aesthetics from their architecture.[42]

The exterior of Santa Maria is deceptively simple-looking: a parallelepiped with its front punched out (two tower-like protrusions on either side of the main doors, one enclosing the bell tower, the other the baptistery whose font is also a subtly burbling fountain). The back of this space, which is adorned with a Matisse-like silhouette drawing of a baptism on one of its tile-lined walls, is punched inwards echoing that of the apses of churches past. The vast ten metre high ceremonial door in the main facade is used only for special occasions. To the right are a modest set of glass doors for everyday use (Fig. 7.16). The thirty-meter-long nave, made to seat four hundred people on simple wooden chairs, extends to the choir space (Fig. 7.17). On the right wall, when facing the choir, a low horizontal band of windows the length of the nave opens out onto the landscape beyond. The wall opposite rises up in a convex curve, interrupted by three grand clerestory windows which let in diffuse light from the unevenly thick walls, reminiscent of Ronchamp's south wall, though the overall shape and the horizontal band of windows bring to mind La Tourette. Two openings behind the altar in the choir space let in light from a periscope source above and behind which also lights the mortuary chapel behind and below it. In front of the openings, the white marble altar seems to dissolve into light itself when seen from afar.

Like Le Corbusier, Siza spoke of the importance of liturgical furnishing and the difficulties he experienced in designing the altar:[43]

> Around the altar, the ambo, the tabernacle, the seats and the cross have been slowly defined, and have contributed in turn to the configuration of the space, being organized according to the established movements of the mass. In this way the church has acquired its shape as a negative sculpture, and tensions and connections of continuity have been defined between the various parts.[44]

This idea of "negative sculpture" draws attention to space in a manner similar to Le Corbusier. Space here takes on the character of plastic form encouraging meditation on the duality of matter and spirit.

Siza was interested in Le Corbusier's treatment of the crosses for Ronchamp and La Tourette.[45] For Santa Maria Siza would finally make a Franciscan T cross, with a very Corbusian insertion of a cross within the cross at its apex (Fig. 7.18). It is set to the left of the altar in relative darkness, the right side of the altar expanding out to views of nature. The left half of Siza's choir is "brought down" to human scale by the curved wall that is cut off just above the height of the back-lit openings behind the altar. This also allows for the introduction of a discrete entrance onto the sacristy behind, on the north side of the church, just as at Ronchamp, where it is the raised, curved music stall that creates this same effect. The other most important element is light, which Siza saw as key in defining the atmosphere of the church.[46] He insisted that light was central to the liturgical function of spatial relationships and liturgical function of the church.[47] As at Ronchamp there are no electrical wall or ceiling-mounted lights.[48] Here the white stucco of the walls, the off-white tiles that wrap around the lower part of three of its four walls and line the baptistery, as well as the blond wood on the floors and of the chairs, all contribute to its ethereal quality.

While the overall set-up of the church is, according to Siza, fairly conservative (especially with its traditional elongated nave), his attention to reform shaped the church in all its details. Two are of special interest here. The horizontal ribbon window (a classic Le Corbusier detail with origins in the Villa Savoye) creates the connection with the outside world. At the far end of this window, in the space on the wall demarcating the transition between the nave and the choir, is the statue of the Virgin Mary, the only effigy in the church. She occupies the zone between congregation and clergy, secular and spiritual. Being next to the window she watches over the outside world. As at Ronchamp she is the mediator.

The Framing of Nature: the Meditation Space for Unesco, Paris, by Tadao Ando, 1995

When Tadao Ando was not yet fifty years old he received and completed three commissions for Christian churches, all located in Japan. The Chapel on Mount Rokko, Kobe, the Church on the Water in Hokkaido, and the Church of Light in Ibaraki, Osaka, were conceived and built over a four-year period of time (1985–1989).[49] They are here discussed as a unit.[50] Each embodies an example of Ando proposing cosmic order through architecture, much in the way Le Corbusier's churches attempted to do through the use of strong, simple – and coded – geometry for the spaces; careful manipulation of rising and descending flooring (slopes and steps abound); varying wall heights and the highly contrived architectural promenade culminating in the church sanctuary. Ando's churches, like Le Corbusier's, have a very strong engagement with their environment and the cosmic dimensions of geometry.[51] In the words of Ando: "Nature, organic and constantly changing, must be captured by geometric forms that give it a spiritual dimension."[52] The framing of nature, such a characteristic of Le Corbusier's work, is taken to extremes by Ando. Here through variously manipulated openings (including those of ventilation), the visitor is encouraged to focus on the natural world: a "wall" of green grass; a "floor" of water (Fig. 7.19); a "cross" of light (Fig. 7.20), all representative of the cosmos:

> I believe that a sacred space must be related in some way to nature. Of course this has nothing to do with Japanese animism or pantheism. I also believe that my idea of nature is different from that of nature-as-is. For me, the nature that a sacred space must relate to is a man-made nature, or rather an architecturalized nature. I believe that when greenery, water, light or wind is abstracted from nature-as-is according to man's will, it approaches the sacred.[53]

7.19 – Church on the Water, Tadao Ando, view of water 'floor'

7.20 – Church of the Light, Tadao Ando, view of cross of light

Nature gains stature being framed by man, a quintessentially Corbusian concept. In this discussion we have frequently alluded to Le Corbusier's penchant for using the word "human" to describe architecture at its geometrical best. Ando takes this cue stating, "I hope that, lacking in distractions, space might succeed in optimising people's humanity." Further, "The presence of nature – water, wind, light, open sky – is what humanises spaces."[54]

In a conversation with Ando, William Curtis (himself steeped in Le Corbusier's architecture) proposed that what linked his work to that of architects such as Le Corbusier was a shared concern for the "psychological character of space". "A year ago in London I heard you give a lecture in which you explained how central Le Corbusier's Ronchamp had been in your early development and how it continues to haunt you because it is a vessel filled with filtered light, a resonant object in the landscape, a sculptural work creating an 'ineffable space'."[55] While Ando ducked from a direct response to this observation, his long-term interest in Le Corbusier is one of the founding myths of this self-taught architect's practice. The first architecture books he bought were the multiple volumes of Le Corbusier's *Œuvres complètes* specifically designed as an alternative to architecture school for autodidacts such as Ando[56] who spent the better part of his "formative years" in the 1960s travelling the globe, much like his spiritual master, looking and drawing (Cistercian monasteries such as Le Thoronet also figure prominently in his biography). Indeed one of his foremost motivations for going to France in 1965 was to meet Le Corbusier who, to his dismay, had recently died.

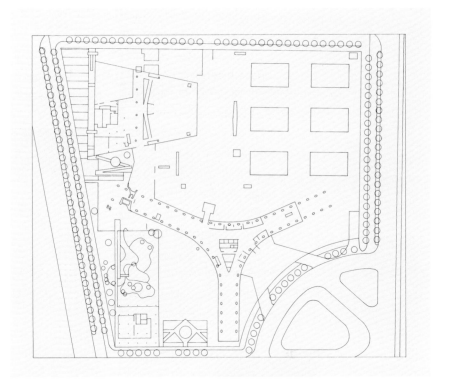

Echoing Le Corbusier's own famous line, "some things are spiritual and others are not, whether or not they are religious," [57] Curtis continued: "It seems you think of architecture as having a spiritual mission, and some of your buildings encourage one to reflect upon the place of the secular and the sacred in today's societies and today's architecture." [58] This comment sets the scene for a discussion of Ando's non-denominational Meditation Space, designed and built for the Unesco Headquarters in Paris (1994-1995) which echoes the three church projects from the 1980s. In a way it summarises them, incorporating green nature, water, light and air as wind, deftly bound together on an improbable patch of crowded land. Le Corbusier intended his churches to appeal to people of all religions. Ando's work, combining aspects of Shinto, Buddhism and Christianity shares this quality of synchretism – geometry being an important element in the mix.

Ando's Meditation Space was built for the Unesco headquarters in Paris on the occasion of its fiftieth anniversary. It is tucked in behind Isamu Noguchi's Zen garden and Pier Luigi Nervi's auditorium (Fig. 7.22), both built in 1958. The promenade to the Meditation Space begins by first traversing the garden, punctuated by a wall on which hangs "The Angel of Nagasaki", a stone-carved statue from a church in the atomic bomb decimated city. In the words of Ando: "This wall clearly cuts off and sanctifies the domain of the prayer space. A ramp leads to the prayer space. The site is narrow, but feels deep because you have to go one way and another." [59] The ramp actually cuts right through this area, which is a simple concrete cylinder six metres high and in diameter (Fig. 7.21). The only natural light sources are a ring circling the outer edge of the ceiling and the two entry openings (Fig. 7.23). Its only inhabitants are two simple chairs (used in all Ando's churches). This is an experience to be shared.

7.23 – Meditation Space for Unesco, ceiling from interior

A pond surrounds the Meditation Space and flows beneath the ramp; it is lined with stones exposed to the atomic bomb, brought in from Hiroshima, designed as a cleansing feature to "appease the souls of the dead."[60] These elements prepare the visitor for a moment of meditation within the circular space. Noguchi's greenery, the water of the pond, and the penetrating light, combined with the wind that sweeps through it at will, all contribute to the other-worldly, filtering character of the space. Focus comes back to the body and the senses. It is a version of Ando's Christian churches in Japan in condensed form.

Cosmic Light and Time: the Private Chapel at Valleaceron, Spain, by Estudio Sancho-Madridejos (S-M.A.O.), 2001

The chapel at Valleaceron (conceived in 2000, built in 2001) designed by the Madrid-based Estudio Sancho-Madridejos (Sol Madridejos and Juan Carlos Sancho Osinaga) is part of a residential complex in southern Spain. It forms a beacon, sitting high over the rest of the property, overlooking a vast and arid landscape (Fig. 7.24). It is less about the promenade than Ando's work but seems to share his Corbusian preoccupation with space and nature.

The route to the chapel is up a hill. The scrubby surface of the landscape, almost Biblical in character, contrasts violently with the crystal form of the chapel itself. Approached from below, the building has no preface. The visitor is compelled to circle the multi-faceted, but somehow four-facaded, building before entry and a further circuit, this time interior, taking in the angles and folds of this extraordinary space – a constricted, simple promenade, but one that changes again and again depending on the the time of day, weather and season (Fig. 7.25).

The small one-volume structure is made of reinforced concrete and glass, but the architects claim that the two materials used were in fact concrete and light; a shift of vocabulary that suggests immediately the play of matter and spirit, the intermediary here being geometry (Fig. 7.26). The chapel is completely unoccupied, with no tell-tale details giving any sense of its scale. The architects were particularly interested in Le Corbusier's use of the promenade, "the object and the space characteristics, the way of using the light to concepts related with phenomenology and perception."[61] The concrete is striated in panels, presumably traces of its construction, but the finish does not evoke the rough *béton brut* of the Unité, more the fine angles of the Carpenter Centre.

A single metal Greek cross hangs on the back wall, off-centre to the right, near the chapel's only right-angled corner, picking out the joints in the concrete behind it (Fig. 7.27).[62] The Greek cross is less hierarchical and directional than the traditional crucifix, suggesting the importance of space in all dimensions. To the left of the cross is a tiny square opening in the wall, again on a line with the panels of construction. This gives a sense of depth to the wall, evoking the voids characterised by "ineffable space".

7.24 – Private chapel
at Valleaceron, exterior
of chapel from 'front'

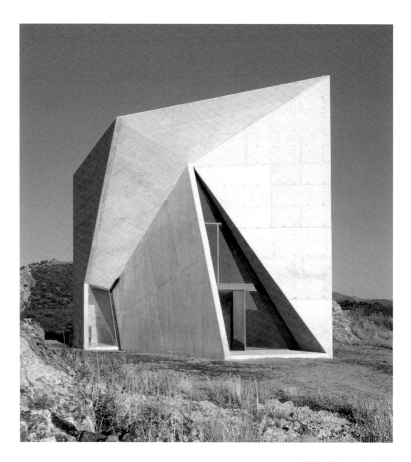

7.26 – Private chapel at
Valleaceron, elevations

7.25 – Private chapel
at Valleaceron, con-
trasting exterior view

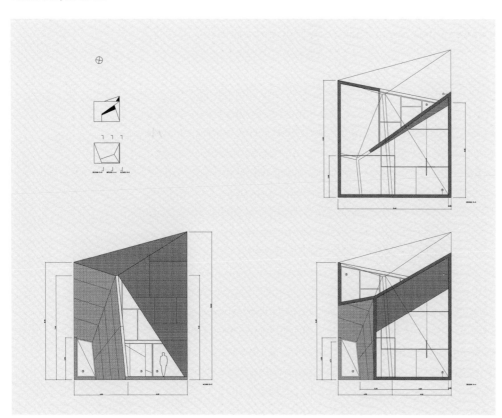

7.27 – Private chapel at
Valleaceron, interior
featuring Greek cross

7.28 – Private chapel at Valleaceron,
interior view

The small size of the opening is again confusing for our sense of scale. The cross and the opening are in conversation, washed over and constantly revised by the changing light that comes in from the exterior. As at Ronchamp there is no artificial lighting. According to the architects the interior-exterior relationship of form and light gives the chapel its meaning (Fig. 7.28). The sacred space becomes a sundial, a measuring instrument, a cosmic clock – a markedly Corbusian concern and, we argue, the Spanish chapel's *raison d'être*.

Jerzy Soltan wrote disdainfully of working in offices "after Corbu time" when "any void, any hole, began to be glorified as INEFFABLE SPACE"[63] with no real understanding of its meaning. There is a danger, when playing spatial games, of falling into this trap, something that S-M.A.O. are clever to avoid. Their engagement with the possibilities of cutting edge technology and theory helps with any sense of datedness that Corbusian spatial games might begin to attract. However theirs, like Le Corbusier's, is the kind of "simplicity" that does not come cheap.

Community and Context: the Chapel of Reconciliation, Berlin, by Rudolf Reitermann and Peter Sassenroth, 2000

Adam Sharr describes Berlin architects Rudolf Reitermann and Peter Sassenroth's 2000 Chapel of Reconciliation as the most "critically acute" of the Berlin projects that "deal conspicuously with the past."[64] Like many of the memorials in Berlin it plays on the issues of presence and absence (Fig. 7.29).

> This tactic exploits present fabric to reveal metaphorically what was once in existence, and exploits the idea of past fabric to imbue with significance that which now stands in its place. It involves a phenomenological appeal to material substance: to the tangible quiddity of something which is physically there and manifestly un-negotiable; and to the evocation of something or someone no longer present.[65]

There are thought provoking parallels here between this and the twin concepts of immanence and transcendence which, of course, involve the additional element of faith.

Le Corbusier's work was not an explicit influence on the design of the chapel. When asked about this Sassenroth observed that their work could perhaps be connected to that of Le Corbusier through their mutual pre-occupation with the early Christian church.[66] Le Corbusier, Reitermann and Sassenroth draw on a shared area of concern which we read as a preoccupation with light, austerity, materiality, movement and still earlier forms of religion. Early sketches reveal the chapel as double-layered ovaloids distinctly womblike in quality, its curves – as at Ronchamp – penetrated by a series of orthogonal events framed within the wall (Fig. 7.30).

7.29 – Chapel of
Reconciliation

7.30 – Chapel of Rec-
onciliation, plan

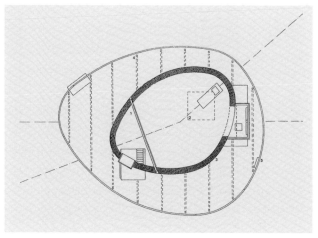

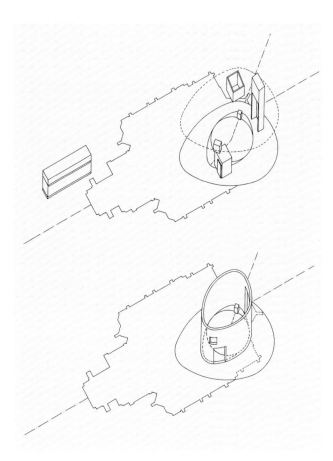

7.31 – Chapel of Reconciliation, plan showing placements of the old and new church

7.32 – Chapel of Reconciliation, altar space before the installation of seats

7.33 – Chapel of Reconciliation, within the screen wall

Although Ronchamp is on a hill in the middle of the countryside and the Chapel of Reconciliation is on a city site razed into flatness by events – the "Death Zone" between the layers of the Berlin wall (demolished in 1989) – both share a deeply charged relationship with their terrain. Similar in scale both are rebuilt out of the remains of an old church destroyed in war. Both are a symbol of peace. Ronchamp seems so solid, so defensive in its form – a quality taken to extremes at Sainte Bernadette. The Chapel of Reconciliation is the opposite, a form seemingly solid, but diaphanous and light at night time.

The land belonging to the former Chapel of Reconciliation was given back to the parish in 1995. It had little money – the number of parishioners having decreased dramatically in the intervening years[67] – so a pared down solution was needed. Reitermann and Sassenroth originally proposed to use glass and concrete for the site, but the parishioners did not want materials that reminded them of the hated Wall. It was decided instead to build the chapel out of the crushed aggregate of the old church, clay and timber. It is perhaps an irony, given his early emphasis on the redemptive power of whiteness that, for Le Corbusier, life within rough earth, as in the pisé housing for La Sainte Baume, would be a cleansing and ascetic experience. Similar ideas, possibly archetypal, underpin the use of clay in Berlin. Ronchamp was, of course, reconstructed out of the rubble of the old church used as infill within its concrete frame hidden behind a layer of Gunnite. In Berlin shards of old material protrude from the tactile surface of the rammed earth wall – its layers echoing the strata of time.

The Chapel of Reconciliation was conceived of as a "healing border", a visible threshold into sacred space.[68] Like Le Corbusier's architecture it is clearly conceived of as a journey. At Ronchamp you enter the chapel through the extraordinary depth of its walls, in the Chapel of Reconciliation you proceed subversively through its layers (Fig. 7.20). Sharr writes of "a lack of comfortable familiarity and the once-charged void between the walls. Its outward orientation resists an easy introversion, configuring instead 360-degree contact with the surrounding landscape."[69] Further, "this space does not reject the architectural conventions of the side aisle so much as rework them, making something familiar and at once also curiously unfamiliar."[70]

The Chapel of Reconciliation is positioned slightly off centre over the old foundations in order to make the difference between old and new discernible[71] (Fig. 7.31). There is a similar spatial twist at Ronchamp – two axes, one focusing on the altar and one on the east door. As Sharr observes:

> Care is taken to ensure that these axes have an equivalent presence in the building: the dominance of the axis implied by the niche is subverted by the laying-out of chairs parallel to the altar cube, by the placement of the square roof light and by the line of the organ loft which is expressed as a mezzanine at the rear of the chapel.[72]

The motivations may be different but they result in a similar feel. Something more profound is at work than a reshuffling of the different elements.

In keeping with the early Christian origins of the project Reitermann and Sassenroth, like Le Corbusier, were reluctant to include seating in their chapel (Fig. 7.32). Indeed there were no "proper" seats in the chapel for a few months after its opening. In the words of Sassenroth:

> We only had folded cardboard-boxes out of brown recycling paper to sit on. These stools without any backrest did fit perfectly, we thought – not only aesthetically but also because of their provisional character. They were very light – very easy to move around – easy to move away in one corner – to stack in order to make the room free again from any seating.
> They showed by its low-cost-character that there was no fixed concept for assembly – but a deliberate flexible one that includes forms of assembly with no seating. Different constellations of seating were also asked by the parish. And the chapel is indeed used like that. The seating constellation is in constant change (from quite formal, circular assembly forms to very reduced forms of seating to actually no seating – sometimes a few times within days).
> We liked those cardboard boxes! – They even looked great ...[73]

The architects suggested some "very basic" chairs but they were too expensive for the parish committee and did not suit the needs of the many old people in the congregation – arm rests, back and so on. Sassenroth wanted something "more 'beautiful', more precious (I mean not necessarily expensive), maybe just well crafted. Maybe that would be more appropriate because it is not at all a profane space / place – it is a sacred place in the end." After much discussion the parish bought cheaper ones, "very ordinary, also stackable, normal chairs". These Sassenroth describes as "profane" adding significantly: "And that might be an all-right-solution, actually." His dilemma is exactly that experienced by Le Corbusier, and indeed by many architects, at that moment when it is important and indeed necessary to let go, achieving what seems to us integral to a real state of simplicity and truth – humility. Which are the most simple and true seats – the cheap practical, readily available chairs or the more expensive, well crafted, rarified alternatives? Which are the most worthy of God?

It is perhaps ironic that our last example, Reitermann and Sassenroth's Chapel of Reconciliation, that ostensibly owes least to Le Corbusier, somehow manages to capture the spirit of his architecture more than any of the others. It is a beacon, of the earth and deeply engaged with its site, politics and community. Whilst engaging with the ordinary it is more than this. Structured around a route, it uses clever shifts of geometry to suggest alternate ways of seeing and indeed being. It plays with oppositions of solid and void, light and dark, rough and smooth matter and spirit with delicacy. It is organic without being too literal. There is a narrative of detail that subtly influences those within, the tiny fragments of the previous church set within its earthen walls, a reminder of human scale, fallibility and, ultimately, the importance of *savoir habiter*.

Summary

Wolfgang Jean Stock writes that "at the close of the twentieth century, the overall image of the Catholic Church and of its architectural representation in church buildings is above all vague and confused."[74] This, we argue, is because the Catholic Church is not a monolithic entity. The churches in this chapter represent a small section of Christian communities and a small, high architecture, spectrum of opinion on the best way to express our relationship with God through building.

With the rise and fall of Post-Modernism and the increased academicism of architectural commentary, the last few decades have brought about a significant decrease in interest in the social aspects of architecture. In most of these examples there is minimal engagement with the more politically challenging aspects of Le Corbusier's church architecture. In certain cases these aspects do surface, with some prodding, such as: communal play before God (and so questions of communal harmony); the sensory and initiatory promenade (experience bringing knowledge); Mary's place in the liturgical configuration (and by extension woman's place in society); syncreticsm and the links between world religions (a strong feature in Ando); memory both ancestral and recent (articulated history always informs the present's social-political climate); and cosmic harmony (which in Corbusian thinking has direct and major impact on daily life and so society as a whole). Most of the architects described in this chapter have perhaps been more concerned with issues of route, light and form than in the issues of social cohesion. Holl and Meier, in particular, are known for their engagement with phenomenology which, emphasising individual experience, has a tendency to neglect the social. Perhaps there are "political" issues at stake that we have been unable to unearth here, like the relationship with the client body and the socio-economic impact of these churches within their particular sites. Alas such narratives are rarely foregrounded in commentaries by the architects themselves or within an architectural press more concerned with impressive images than buildings in use. Then again it could be because the political dimension of Le Corbusier's work is frail and neglected.

Conclusion

The study of Le Corbusier's church architecture reveals a series of core social issues at the heart of modernism – politics lived out through attitudes to the salvation economy and embedded in an architecture of emancipation. Christianity is, after all, often portrayed as the ultimate counter-culture, particularly nowadays when market forces seem to have become our dominant value system and a rejection of materialism goes firmly against the grain. The term "freedom", when used in the dogma of the anarchists of the Spanish Civil War, means freedom to act unhindered by systems of hierarchy. "Freedom" when used by Couturier is freedom to achieve salvation within the context of modernism (it is often assumed erroneously that modernism and secularisation are much the same thing). "Freedom" for Le Corbusier would be within the liberating constraints of the Radiant City plan, a very different freedom to that of the Spanish anarchists, but still deeply marginal to mainstream politics. The individual is free to play out his or her life at a small scale within the overall order of this vision, presented as an immutable higher order, its benefits modelled by the intelligentsia, adopted through choice not coercion, leading ultimately to a state of Super Unification with nature such as that described by Teilhard de Chardin. Whether now, in the face of the Climate Change Emergency, we have any other choice is another matter.

Although Le Corbusier embraced the *L'Art sacré* belief in "simplicity, poverty and truth" even the, in reality, quite small chapel at Ronchamp was considered a stumbling block for those trying to promote all that was not monumental and it was seen as sparking a trend that was considered harmful to the cause of modesty.[1] "The watch-word 'poverty' in art and architecture, the intense plea that the spiritual richness of modern art with the poverty of its means and the firmness of the moral condemnation of ecclesiastic luxury were not without conveying an obvious political and social dimension,"[2] writes Gérard Monnier. Le Corbusier generally embraced reform. When he did not, rather than blaming ignorance or indifference on the architect's part, one must conclude he had other agendas at stake. We argue that his churches were about the promulgation of women's role in religion, central to the Radiant City plan as well as what we might nowadays call sustainability. This is however a message that has not filtered through the orthodox modernist narratives of the architectural hegemony which has had a long term vested interest in consumption.

In the last section of this book we set out to illustrate the way in which Le Corbusier's churches have influenced other more recent church architecture. We used the experience of route, the *promenade architecturale* as a means to unpack the journey. An analysis of the 'spatial dramaturgy'[3] of these churches reveals some fundamental differences between Le Corbusier's and those of his followers, most notably in terms of political meaning.

Whether Le Corbusier's was a truly democratic vision is never made clear. It is almost impossible to classify his work in the usual political terms. "I am an architect; no one is going to make a politician out of me."[4] The charitable amongst us would see Le Corbusier's rejection of politics as a disgust with party politics in favour of the moneyless world represented by the Radiant City. Others might see it as a cold blooded effort not to alienate clients. One might think that the fact that he was brazenly apolitical would increase his chances of securing work, but it actually appears to have had the opposite effect in post World War II France. Le Corbusier was not above using the dark arts of persuasion, rhetoric, advertising, and targeted marketing to convert people to his cause – indeed the sensory assault of his church architecture seems to have been designed to do precisely that. A telling editorial in *L'Art sacré*, "From Pagan temple to Christian Church", notes the way in which artists at that time purposefully maintained "confusions under the approving eye of the clergy and faithful whose judgement in this area is sometimes uncertain."[5]

Le Corbusier lost no opportunity to proselytise his religion of *savoir habiter*, a form of wisdom, indeed *gnosis,* that built upon the ideas of classical philosophy, notably the Orphic theories of Pythagoras and Plato. It involved life led in a balanced, harmonious and cyclical manner, in tune with the passing of the days and the seasons including close appreciation of the important and pleasurable things in life, "sun, space, greenery", water, sitting by the fire, food in amicable company, dancing, jokes, music and love – brought into relief through temperance, not surfeit and through the choreography of good architecture. In many ways Le Corbusier's architecture anticipated our twenty-first century preoccupation with 'mindfulness', slowness and minimal living. Taken further it involved an appreciation of ineffable space, the underlying meaning of mathematical harmony and its connection to the divine spark of energy latent within us all.[6]

His own harshest critic, Le Corbusier was quick to dissolve into agonies of disillusion, cynicism and doubt, particularly in later life, causing him to portray himself as Don Quixote tilting at the windmill of his own ideals (Fig. 8.1). As Le Corbusier himself observed in a discussion of the flaws in the concrete of the Unité in Marseilles, to err is to be human.

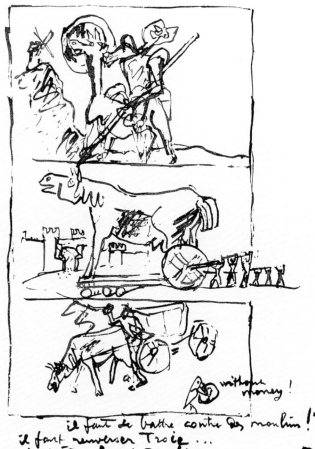

il faut de battre contre des moulins !
il faut renverser Troie ...
il faut être cheval de fiacre
tous les jours !
6 octobre 53   Bon Courage ! votre L-C

without money !

8.1 – Le Corbusier,
Don Quichotte, 1964

8.2 – Detail of
Le Corbusier's grave

8.3 – Le Corbusier's
grave, Roquebrune

In this book we have tried to understand Le Corbusier in his own terms, the terms of
the society in which he lived, as Pierre Bourdieu writes, "to make up for the absence
of the (true) understanding immediately available to an indigenous contemporary, one
must perform the task of *reconstructing* the code found invested there."[7] This is by no
means a straightforward matter. The ambiguity of his work leaves Le Corbusier open
to multiple, often conflicting, interpretations that can be drawn upon as necessary
by the "professional interpreters" in accordance with their particular situated needs,
as has been seen in the last chapter.[8] By making his work deliberately multivalent
Le Corbusier has extended its shelf life immeasurably, meaning that his work continues
to exercise its influence, even today, particularly in the realm of religious architecture.

Le Corbusier was preoccupied by his legacy, the focus of his "last" paper *Mise au
Point,* "Nothing is Transmissible but thought", written shortly before his death in
July 1965. He spent much time pondering over the design for the grave that he was
to share with his wife Yvonne. It is perched high above the sea in the cemetery in
Roquebrune, an eloquent full stop to all his achievements (Fig. 8.3). The square
concrete slab, carefully proportioned to the Modulor, has an underlying geometric
structure of two halves. The one on the left is the site of a small orthogonal box
– not a cube, but more like a lectern – fronted by one of his enamels subdivided

horizontally. The top half of the enamel plaque framing Le Corbusier's name is yellow, the colour of sun and spirit. It meets and reflects Yvonne's blue watery half below in a zone of red, the colour of fusion.

Next to the box on the right half of the slab, is a cylindrical pot – together the two creating a marriage of contrasting lines straight and curved. A pebbled planter extends along the back of the slab and then round, past the cylinder, to form a strip in front, its mottled surface contrasting handsomely with the smooth surface of the concrete. The cylinder is thus allied to the earth, to plants and to nature, feminine according to Le Corbusier's world view.

Objects arranged in Le Corbusier's "technique of grouping" normally come in a trinity – the tomb is no exception. Quietly tucked in between the two sculptural forms is a tiny bronze byzantine crucifix (Fig. 8.2). This crucifix is not adorned with Christ as is normal. It instead contains a representation of Mary – like the one from Santa Maria Antigua that found her way into *Le poème de l'angle droit*. She is large, without halo, benignly overshadowing the small torso of a man on her right with whom she shares a gaze. She is allied through her position and orientation with the masculine orthogonal box on the left – he with the feminine cylindrical planter on the right. There is here a flipping back and forth of meaning in terms of gender and hierarchy. Le Corbusier's name may be at the top of the tomb, Yvonne's beneath, but the Mary figure is much bigger than Jesus and they are clearly linked. Here at Roquebrune this tiny "unity" celebrates the importance of woman in the life of man. To the left of the orthogonal box is a playful gesture the imprint of a cockle shell – symbol of the Magdalene and of nature – now worn through erosion to a simple pit. Is it coincidence that the cockle also appears on the east door at Ronchamp, so evocative of the stone that sealed Christ's tomb? Whilst to a non-believer Corbusier's identification with Jesus might smack of grandiosity, Christians have a strong personal sense of affinity with Christ.

We have, in fact, seen all the elements of this tiny unity, which could be read as an open-air chapel in miniature, at Ronchamp with Notre Dame's outdoor choir: the altar (lectern), the rounded and elevated choir stall protruding from the south wall (planter), the cross and Mary presiding above it all from her niche. Standing before the grave, one looks out over *la mer* (the sea), *la mère* (the mother), just as at Ronchamp one looks out over the billowing green horizon, a sea of hills. Thoughts return to the windows of the chapel where indeed the *mer* is explicitly convoked. In the west wall tucked in the lower tier, one finds a vertical window, divided like the enamel of the grave's lectern. It reads in partial pictogram in much the same way as the lectern: in the upper section a dark bird soars (this time on a blue background), the Corbu. The sun cuts across the middle in a blaze of fusion red. On the lower half, on a green slab of glass, is written *la mer*. The window, the closest one to the interior choir, is another version of the painted enamel on the grave.

Yvonne, who died in October 1957, two years after Ronchamp was finished and while La Tourette was in the pipeline, is one key to understanding Le Corbusier's intentions. His mother, Marie Charlotte Amélie Jeanneret-Perret, is the other. Venerated by Le Corbusier to an almost obsessive degree, she died in 1960 at the age of 101, just as he was working on the Firminy commissions. The drawing that he made of her in September 1951, the letter he wrote to her two days after the Ronchamp inauguration, June 27, 1955 and a wealth of other material indicate the importance of her role, both in his life and in the chapel. She is pictured as a sphinx, placed between moon and sun, face raised to take in the sky (Fig. 4.17). Eardley has suggested that Saint Pierre Firminy's silhouette has similarities to the Easter Island sculptures, poised for communication with the cosmos. We would suggest this face-facade could also be that of the architect's mother, raised to take in the cosmos beyond the community of Firminy-Vert. She was after all his guide, his confidant, his rock and the standard against which he measured everything. He told her in the letter that Ronchamp was the most revolutionary architecture to be made in some time in terms of Catholicism, rite and ritual. Despite her great age (96) at this time, and her life-long Protestantism he urged her to visit Ronchamp, instructing her to enter through the small door, to go behind the main altar and over by the stairs next to the sacristy. Precisely what she would see there was left as a surprise, but was clearly conceived to give her pleasure. In this area inaccessible to the common visitor, "hidden" and virtually unphotographable, she would have found a wall of royal purple[9] punched with multiple windows in praise of "Marie", his own mother and mother of God, the ideal and the real here overlaid.

Le Corbusier believed that women had most to gain from his vision of the harmonious future and played a central role in making it happen, but they were being held back by religion. Woman was key to religion and religion was key to woman's advancement as it still is today in many parts of the world. This, we argue, is the main lesson to be learnt from Le Corbusier's churches, one that seems unlikely to be heard for some time.

NOTES

INTRODUCTION

1 Michel Ragon, *Histoire mondiale de l'architecture et de l'urbanisme modernes, tome 2: pratiques et méthodes 1911-1985* (Paris: Casterman, 1986), p. 297.

2 Just as Le Corbusier liked to return to the roots of religion to discover its pure form, we turn here to the etymology of the word. According to Cicero "religion" connects to *religare*, to "go through again, read again", "to bind fast" while creating a "bond between humans and gods". Twelfth-century interpretations link it to a "state of life bound by monastic vows". Significantly it is not linked to "a particular system of faith" until 1300. Religion is used here in its early sense – a merging of these themes. www.etymonline.com. Accessed November 3, 2011.

3 Nikolaus Pevsner, *Pioneers of Modern Design* (Harmondsworth: Pelican, 1975), p. 217. First published under the title *Pioneers of the Modern Movement* in 1936.

4 Nikolaus Pevsner, *An Outline of European Architecture* (Harmondsworth: Pelican, 1981), p. 414. First published in 1943.

5 André Wogenscky, *Les Mains de Le Corbusier* (Paris: Éditions de Grenelle, 1987), p. 41.

6 Le Corbusier, *Modulor* (London: Faber, 1954), p. 224. Originally published as *Le Modulor* (Paris: Éditions de l'Architecture d'Aujourd'hui, 1950), p. 112.

7 Le Corbusier, *Journey to the East* (Cambridge: MIT, 1987), p. 176.

8 Le Corbusier, *New World of Space* (New York: Reynal and Hitchcock), 1948, p. 16.

9 Richard A. Moore, "Alchemical and Mythical themes in the Poem of the Right angle 1947-65", *Oppositions* 19/20 (winter/spring 1980), pp. 110–139.

10 Peter Carl, "Le Corbusier's Penthouse in Paris: 24 Rue Nungesser et Coli", *Daidalos*, 28 (June 15, 1988), pp. 65–75. Peter Carl, "Architecture and time: a prolegomena", *AA Files*, 22 (autumn 1991), pp. 49–64. Peter Carl, "Ornament and time: a prolegomena", *AA Files*, 23 (summer 1992), pp. 49–64.

11 Jaime Coll, "Le Corbusier. Taureaux: An Analysis of the Thinking Process in the last Series of Le Corbusier's Plastic Work", *Art History*, 18, 4 (December 1995), pp. 537–568.

12 Danièle Pauly, *Le Corbusier: Drawing as Process* (New Haven: Yale University Press, 2018). Originally published as *Le Corbusier et le dessin, "Ce labeur secret"* (Lyon: Fage éditions, Paris: Fondation Le Corbusier, 2015).

13 Luisa Martina Colli, "Le Corbusier e il colore; I Claviers Salubra," *Storia dell'arte*, 43 (1981), pp. 271–291.

14 Nadir Lahiji, "The Gift of the Open Hand: Le Corbusier's Reading Georges Bataille's La Part Maudite", *Journal of Architectural Education*, 50, 1 (1996), pp. 50–67.

15 Henry Plummer, *Cosmos of Light, The Sacred Architecture of Le Corbusier* (Bloomington and Indianapolis: Indiana University Press, 2013, p. xi).

16 Ibid., p. 14

17 See for example Ross Anderson and Maximillian Sternberg, *Modern Architecture and the Sacred: Religious Legacies and Spiritual Renewal* (London: Bloomsbury, 2020).

18 Martin Purdy's essay "Le Corbusier and the Theological Program". In Russell Walden (ed.), *The Open Hand, Essays on Le Corbusier* (Cambridge: MIT Press, 1986), pp. 286–321.

19 Catherine de Lorenzo, "Creativity Against Fundamentalism: The Struggles of a Little Church in Sydney", Modern Catholic Space, Jesuit Centre, London, December 9, 2011.

20 Marc Chauveau and Anselm Kiefer, *Anselm Kiefer à la Tourette* (La Garenne-Colombes: Couleurs contemporaines and Bernard Chauveau Édition, 2019).

21 See for example the recent publishing project *Cher Corbu* undertaken by the editor close La Tourette for which twelve architects were invited to write "letters" to Le Corbusier. Almost all (8 of 12) cite at least one of his sacred commissions in these short, dense missels. See *Cher Corbu... Douze architects écrivent à Le Corbusier / Dear Corbu... Twelve Architects Write to Le Corbusier* (Suresnes: Couleurs contemporaines and Bernard Chauveau Édition, 2014).

22 Guiliano and Glauco Gresleri (eds.), *Le Corbusier: il programma liturgico* (Bologna: Editrice Compositori, 2001).

23 Albert Christ-Janer and Mary Mix Foley, *Modern Church Architecture* (New York: McGraw Hill, 1962), p. 102.

24 Ibid.

25 Karla Britton, *Constructing the Ineffable: Contemporary Sacred Architecture* (New Haven: Yale University Press, 2011)

26 Jean Capellades, *Guide des églises nouvelles en France* (Paris: Éditions du Cerf, 1969).

27 Georges Mercier, *L'architecture religieuse contemporaine en France* (Tours: Mame, 1968).

28 Suzanne Robin, *Églises modernes, évolution des edifices religieux en France depuis 1955* (Paris: Hermann, 1980).

29 Wolfgang Jean, Stock, *European Church Architecture 1950–2000* (Munich: Prestel, 2002), p. 7.

30 Ibid., p. 11.

31 Phyllis Richardson, *New Sacred Architecture* (London: Laurence King Publishing, 2004). Edwin Heathcote and Laura Moffat, *New Church Architecture* (London: Wiley-Academy, 2004).

32 Richard Kieckhefer, *Theology in Stone: Church Architecture from Byzantium to Berkeley* (Oxford: Oxford University Press, 2004).

33 In this we take our cue from MarkTorgerson, *The Architecture of Immanence: Architecture for Worship and Ministry Today* (Grand Rapids: Michigan: William B. Eerdmans, 2007).

34 Pierre Bourdieu, *The Rules of Art*, trans. Susan Emanuel (Cambridge: Polity, 2005), p. 128.

35 Peter, Hammond (ed.), *Towards a Church Architecture* (Architectural Press: London, 1962), p. 15.

36 Jerzy, Soltan, "Working with Le Corbusier" in H. Allen Brooks (ed.), *The Le Corbusier Archive, Volumes XVII*, (New York: Garland, 1983), p. iii.

37 Cristina Garduno Freeman, *Participatory Culture and Social Value of an Architectural Icon* (London: Routledge 2017).

38 In Le Corbuiser's inauguration speech of the chapel at Ronchamp on 25 June 1955, addressing the archbishop of Besançon. See Jean Petit (ed.), *Textes et Dessins pour Ronchamp, Le Corbusier* (Geneva: Coopi, Ronchamp: Association Œuvre Notre-Dame-du-Haut, 1995). Originally published in Geneva: Jean Petit, 1965, not paginated. We have translated the word "loyal" as "loyal" and not "honest" as formerly published; this subtle shift has its importance.

CHAPTER 1

1 For an in-depth discussion of these issues see Eamon Duffy's *Saints and Sinners, a History of the Popes* (New Haven and London: Yale University Press, 2006), specifically the chapters on the nineteenth and twentieth-century popes. Originally published in 1997.

2 Available from http://www.papalencyclicals.net/Pius09/p9syll.htm (accessed November 30, 2011). The *Syllabus* was attached to the encyclical *Quanta Cura* (Encyclical, December 8, 1864).

3 Eamon Duffy names theologian Father Alfred Loisy and his sensational, condemned *The Gospel and the Church* as one such modernist. Duffy, *Saints and Sinners*, p. 326. An encyclical is an open letter from the pope to bishops, and sometimes a wider audience, on major issues of concern.

4 Ibid., pp. 326–327.

5 The *motu proprio* (a document written and signed by the pope) *Sacrorum antistitum* was a requirement of priests until 1967, ibid., pp. 328–329.

6 Ibid., p. 329, p. 334.

7 Ordered by Pope Pius X, coordinated by Cardinal Pietro Gasparri, completed under and promulgated by Benedict XV, effective in 1918.

8 An updated *Code of Canon Law* was promulgated by Pope John Paul II on January 25, 1983. It now contains 1752 canons. Available from http://www.vatican.va/archive/ENG1104/__P1.HTM (accessed November 30, 2011).

9 Eamon Duffy, *Saints and Sinners*, p. 341.

10 Ibid., p. 311.

11 Despite being involved in the left wing Regional Syndicalist movement prior to World War II Le Corbusier actively courted the Fascist Vichy Regime in an effort to secure building contracts as well as the title "architect", as did Auguste Perret. Perret was to redeem himself through association with the Resistance while Le Corbusier's name remains tainted by his actions during this period.

12 Eamon Duffy, *Saints and Sinners*, p. 352.

13 Alain Rey (ed.), *Dictionnaire historique de la langue française* (Paris: Robert, 1995) p. 1258.

14 Eamon Duffy, *Saints and Sinners*, p. 296.

15 Blaise Wilfert, "Les Chantiers du Cardinal, une œuvre attendue", in Simon Texier (ed.), *Églises parisiennes du XXe siècle, architecture et décor* (Paris: Action artistique de la Ville de Paris, 1996), p. 27.

16 Jean-Pie Lapierre and Philippe Levillain, "Laïcisation, union sacrée et apaisement (1895-1926)", in Jacques Le Goff and René Rémond (eds.), *Histoire de la France religieuse*, volume 4 (Paris: Seuil, 1992), p. 52.

17 Ibid., p. 65.

18 Robert Pincus Witten, *Occult Symbolism in France: Joséphin Péladan and the Salons de la Rose-Croix* (New York: Garland, 1976), p. 55.

19 Jean-Pie Lapierre and Philippe Levillain, "Laïcisation, union sacrée et apaisement (1895-1926)", in Le Goff and Rémond (eds.), *Histoire de la France religieuse*, volume 4, p. 100.

20 Also his *Essais de philsophie religieuse*, 1901, and *Le Réalisme chrétien et l'idéalisme grec*, 1902, were condemned in 1907. Ibid., p. 107.

21 Ibid., p. 74.

22 See Freddy Raphaël, "Les juifs de France, de l'Affaire Dreyfus au bicentenaire de la Révolution, la synthèse 'franco-judaïque' et sa fragilité", in Le Goff and Rémond (eds.), *Histoire de la France religieuse*, volume 4, pp. 260-266.

23 Étienne Fouilloux, "'Fille aînée de l'Église' ou 'pays de mission'? (1926-1958)", in Le Goff and Rémond (eds.), *Histoire de la France religieuse*, volume 4, p. 131.

24 Jean-Pie Lapierre and Philippe Levillain, "Laïcisation, union sacrée et apaisement (1895-1926)", in Le Goff and Rémond (eds.), *Histoire de la France religieuse*, volume 4, p. 125.

25 Étienne Fouilloux, "'Fille aînée de l'Église' ou 'pays de mission'? (1926-1958)", in Le Goff and Rémond (eds.), *Histoire de la France religieuse*, volume 4, p. 136.

26 Eamon Duffy, *Saints and Sinners*, p. 352.

27 Étienne Fouilloux, "'Fille aînée de l'Église' ou 'pays de mission'? (1926-1958)", pp. 242, 246-248.

28 History and heritage were privileged over invention: the National Historical Monuments Council was founded, Eugène Viollet-le-Duc undertook major restoration campaigns. See the section "Le Patrimoine" in Pierre Nora (ed.), *Les lieux de mémoire, II. La Nation*, volume 2 (Paris: Éditions Gallimard, 1986), pp. 405-650.

29   For a concise overview of international early twentieth-century church architecture see for example Edwin Heathcote, "The 20th-Century Church, The Enigma of Sacred Objectivity", in Edwin Heathcote and Laura Moffatt (eds.), *Contemporary Church Architecture* (Chichester: Wiley-Academy, 2007), pp. 8–71.

30   A handful of pictures of Böhm's and Bartning's churches featured in the issue of *L'Architecture d'Aujourd'hui* dedicated to religious architecture in 1934. *L'Architecture d'Aujourd'hui, "Architecture religieuse"*, July 1934; pp. 38, 39, 45, 53. Bartning's work also featured in *L'Architecture d'Aujourd'hui, "Architecture religieuse"*, July 1938, p. 46. Le Corbusier had thus at least surely seen some pictures of this work.

31   In France, the church that came closest aesthetically to Böhm's and Bartning's work was Sainte-Jeanne d'Arc by the architect Jacques Droz, built in Nice from 1926–33. It featured in *L'Architecture d'Aujourd'hui, "Architecture religieuse"*, July 1934; pp. 34, 38, 40, 96.

32   Peter Collins, *Concrete, The Vision of a New Architecture* (New York: Horizon Press, 1959) p. 202. 2nd edition 2004.

33   The first reinforced concrete church built in France was St Jean de Montmartre, 1894–1904. It is covered in brick.

34   Simon Texier, "Les matériaux ou les parures du béton", in Texier (ed.), *Églises parisiennes du XXe siècle, architecture et décor*, pp. 81–82.

35   For this issue concerning the Raincy church, see for example, ibid., pp. 74–75.

36   Agnès Delannoy, "Le prieuré de Maurice Denis à Saint-Germain-en-Laye, ou le travail avec l'existant", in J., Abram, J.-L., Cohen, G., Lambert (eds.), *Encyclopédie Perret*, (Paris: Monum, Éditions du Patrimoine, Institut français d'architecture, Le Moniteur, 2002), pp. 152–153.

37   Joseph Abram, "Une vie", in ibid., p. 17.

38   Guy Lambert, "Brevets", in ibid., p. 64.

39   For example, the churches of Saint-Anthony by Karl Moser, 1927, considered one of the most important modern churches, and All Saints by Hermann Baur, 1950, both in Basel. See Frédéric Debuyst, *Le renouveau de l'Art sacré de 1920 à 1962* (Paris: Nouvelles Éditions Mame, 1991),

p. 23, and Edwin Heathcote, "The 20th-Century Church, The Enigma of Sacred Objectivity", in Heathcote and Moffat (eds.), *Contemporary Church Architecture*, p. 40. For other examples see Texier "Les matériaux ou les parures du béton", in Texier (ed.), *Églises parisiennes du XXe siècle, architecture et décor*, pp. 83–85.

40   See Bruno Reichlin, "Le vocabulaire du béton armé, Tectonique: quel langage architectural pour le mono-lithisme?", in Abram et al. (eds.), *Encyclopédie Perret*, p. 112.

41   Blaise Wilfert, "Les Chantiers du Cardinal, une œuvre attendue", in Texier (ed.), *Églises parisiennes du XXe siècle, architecture et décor*, p. 26.

42   Ibid., p. 30.

43   Frank Debié and Pierre Vérot, *Urbanisme et art sacré, une aventure du XXe siècle* (Paris: Criterion, 1991), p. 49.

44   Emmanuel Bréon, "L'art sacré s'expose 1925-1931-1937", *L'Art sacré au XXe siècle en France* (Thonon-les-Bains: Éditions de l'Albaron, Société Présence du Livre; Boulogne-Billancourt: Musée Municipale de Boulogne-Billancourt, Centre Culturel de Boulogne-Billancourt, 1993), p. 87.

45   Blaise Wilfert, "Les Chantiers du Cardinal, une œuvre attendue", in Texier (ed.), *Églises parisiennes du XXe siècle, architecture et décor*, p. 27.

46   Étienne Fouilloux, "'Fille aînée de l'Église' ou 'pays de mission'? (1926–58)", pp. 155–159.

47   The notion of a de-christianised France must be nuanced. See ibid., p. 197.

48   Ibid., p. 155.

49   Blaise Wilfert, "Les Chantiers du Cardinal, une œuvre attendue", in Texier (ed.), *Églises parisiennes du XXe siècle, architecture et décor*, p. 39.

50   Simon Texier, "Les architectes, entre audace et compromis", in Texier (ed.), *Églises parisiennes du XXe siècle, architecture et décor*, p. 59 and ibid., "Les matériaux ou les parures du béton", p. 105.

51   Frédéric Debuyst, *Le renouveau de l'Art sacré de 1920 à 1962*, p. 11.

52   The scheme was first built temporarily in 1931 by the *Chantiers* for the important *Exposition Coloniale* as the chapel representing the *Mission catholique*.

53   Frédéric Debuyst, *Le renouveau de l'Art sacré de 1920 à 1962*, p. 58.

54   Quoted by Marcel Billot in "Le père Couturier et l'art sacré", in *Paris-Paris 1937-1957* (Paris: Centre Georges Pompidou, 1981) p. 300.

55   Simon Texier, "Les architectes, entre audace et compromis", in Texier (ed.), *Églises parisiennes du XXe siècle, architecture et décor*, p. 59.

56   Letter from Le Corbusier to Madame de Salle, June 5, 1929. In Mathilde Dion and Gilles Ragot, *Le Corbusier en France, projets et réalisations* (Paris: Le Moniteur, 1997), pp. 142–143. The authors caution us to consider that Le Corbusier may have simply been too busy to accept the commission.

57   For the history of this competition and the ensuing scandal see Simon Texier, "Les matériaux ou les parures du béton", in Texier (ed.), *Églises parisiennes du XXe siècle, architecture et décor*, pp. 90–96.

58   Eamon Duffy, *Saints and Sinners*, pp. 322–323.

59   Frédéric Debuyst, *Le renouveau de l'Art sacré de 1920 à 1962*, p. 29.

60   According to Romano Guardini (discusssed later in this chapter), quoted by Debuyst, *Le renouveau de l'Art sacré de 1920 à 1962*, p. 24. See also Edwin Heathcote, "The 20th-Century Church, The Enigma of Sacred Objectivity", in Edwin Heathcote and Laura Moffatt (eds.), *Contemporary Church Architecture*, p. 39. A picture of Schwarz' church in Aachen featured in *L'Architecture d'Aujourd'hui, "Architecture religieuse"*, July 1934, p. 71.

61   *The Church Incarnate, the Sacred in Christian Architecture*, translated by Cynthia Harris (Chicago: Henry Regnery Company, 1958). Originally published as *Vom Bau der Kirche* (Heidelberg: Verlag Lambert, 1938).

62   Debuyst, *Le renouveau de l'Art sacré de 1920 à 1962*, pp. 32–33.

63   These are printed in full in Peter Hammond (ed.), *Towards a Church Architecture* (Architectural Press: London, 1962), pp. 248–254.

64   Edwin Heathcote, "The 20th-Century Church, The Enigma of Sacred Objectivity", in Heathcote and Moffatt (eds.), *Contemporary Church Architecture*, p. 45.

65   *L'Art sacré*, n. 7–8, March-April 1954, pp. 28–31.

66   See *L'Art sacré "Allemagne 1950"* (3-4 November-Decem-

ber 1950), and also especially the issues "À la recherche d'un plan" (5–6 January–February 1957), "Détruisez le Temple… Le problème des églises provisoires" (9–10 May–June 1958), "Nos amis d'Allemagne" (3–4 November–December 1959), "La Bible et l'ambon" (5–6 January–February 1960). The dates of these issues correspond to Le Corbusier's period of church building.

67   Thanks to Rosemary Crumlin for pointing this out.

68   "Constitution on the Sacred Liturgy (Sacrosanctum Concilium)", in *The Documents of Vatican II*, Walter M. Abbott, S.J., (ed.), (London: Geoffrey Chapman, 1966), pp. 137–178.

69   Frédéric Debuyst, *L'Art chrétien contemporain de 1962 à nos jours* (Paris: Éditions Mame, 1988), p. 35.

70   "To Artists", in "Closing Messages of the Council", in Walter M. Abbott (ed.), *The Documents of Vatican II*, p. 732.

71   See "Sacred Art and Sacred Furnishings", the final chapter of "Constitution on the Sacred Liturgy (Sacrosanctum Concilium)", in Walter M. Abbott (ed.), *The Documents of Vatican II*, pp. 174–177.

72   Cited by Françoise Caussé in *La revue "L'Art sacré", le débat en France sur l'art et la religion (1945–1954)*, (Paris: Les Éditions du Cerf, 2010) p. 587.

73   This was the title of the internal report of the French episcopate: *Faut-il encore construire des églises?*, 1971. See Blaise Wilfert, "Les Chantiers du Cardinal, une œuvre attendue", in Simon Texier (ed.), *Églises parisiennes du XXe siècle, architecture et décor*, p. 42, footnote 24.

74   The name of which means Hebrew for "prophet".

75   Frédéric Debuyst, *Le renouveau de l'Art sacré de 1920 à 1962*, p. 20.

76   *On Priestly Formation* in Walter M. Abbott (ed.), *The Documents of Vatican II*, pp. 437–457.

77   Ibid., p. 452, footnote 52.

78   Le Corbusier owned Paul Choisnard, *Saint Thomas d'Aquin et l'influence des astres* (Alcan, 1926).

79   For example, *Nouvelles théories sur l'art moderne, sur l'art sacré, 1914–1921* (Paris: L. Rouart et J. Watelin, Éditeurs, 1922), *Histoire d'art religieux* (Paris: Flammarion, 1939).

80   Rosicrucianism's roots go back to late-medieval Germany and quickly spread internationally. It is a philo-

sophical secret society with Christian branches of esoteric knowledge. It saw a revival in the nineteenth and twentieth centuries. Many artists were involved; Rouault and Desvallières, Maurice Denis' partner, all had connections with the Rosicrucian movement. David Hopkins, *Marcel Duchamp and Max Ernst: the Bride Shared* (Oxford: Oxford University Press, 1997), p. 194. Maurice Denis was dismissive of mystical Rosicrucianism. Ibid., p. 78.

81   The windows were first temporarily installed, then hand painted by Denis and Couturier, then replaced with the permanent windows done after Denis' designs, executed by the masterglass woman, Marguerite Huré. See Marcel Billot, "Le père Couturier et l'art sacré", in *Paris-Paris 1937–1957*, p. 296. There is still much to be done to document the scope of Couturier's artistic production.

82   See Geneviève et Henri Taillefert, "Les Sociétés d'Artistes et la fondation de l'Art catholique", in *L'Art sacré au XXe siècle en France*, pp.15–25.

83   Frédéric Debuyst, *Le renouveau de l'Art sacré de 1920 à 1962*, p. 21.

84   See Marcel Billot "Le père Couturier et l'art sacré", in *Paris-Paris 1937–1957*, p.293, and in Huysmans' *Les Foules de Lourdes* (Paris: Plon, 1906). It is the devil himself who proclaims he will get his revenge on the Virgin by making sacred art as ugly as possible. Lapierre and Levillain, "Laïcisation, union sacrée et apaisement (1895-1926)", in Le Goff et Rémond (eds.), *Histoire de la France religieuse*, volume 4, p. 114.

85   Marcel Billot "Le père Couturier et l'art sacré", in *Paris-Paris 1937–1957*, p. 297.

86   The journal was founded in 1935 by Joseph Pichard, who remained editor when the Dominicans were named directors, see Françoise Caussé, *La revue "L'Art sacré", le débat en France sur l'art et la religion (1945-1954)*, p. 51.

87   Marie-Alain Couturier, "Religious Art and the Modern Artist", *Magazine of Art*, November 1951 reprinted in Albert Christ-Janer and Mary Mix Foley, *Modern Church Architecture* (New York: McGraw Hill, 1962), p. 83.

88   No issues were produced between 1939 and 1945. Régamey mostly did the issues from 1945 to 1948, then both until Couturier's death in 1954, after which Fathers

Augustin-Marie Cocagnac and Marie-Robert Capellades directed the journal until it stopped in 1969. The last issue (*L'Art sacré*, 2, 1969) was tellingly themed "Architecture spontanée", see Françoise Caussé, *La revue "L'Art sacré", le débat en France sur l'art et la religion (1945–1954)*, especially the chapter "Deux dominicains", pp. 223–288.

89 He even published a defence of abstract art as having spiritual values in *Art et Catholicisme*, 1945, see Marcel Billot, "Le père Couturier et l'art sacré", in *Paris-Paris 1937–1957*, p. 302.

90 Marie-Alain Couturier, *Se garder libre, journal (1947–1954)*, (Paris: Éditions du Cerf, 1962).

91 Antoine Lion, "Postlude", in Antoine Lion (ed.) *Marie-Alain Couturier, un combat pour l'art sacré* (Nice: Serres Editeur, 2005), p. 199.

92 Marie-Alain Couturier, "L'Appel aux maîtres de l'art moderne", in *Paris-Paris 1937–1957*, p. 305.

93 Ibid.

94 Anne de Margerie (ed.), *Vallauris, La Guerre et la Paix, Picasso* (Paris: Réunion des Musées Nationaux, 1998).

95 Paul Scortesco, *Saint Picasso, peignez pour nous, ou les deux conformismes* (Paris, Nouvelles Éditions Latines, 1953).

96 As Henri Matisse famously stated "Do I believe in God? Yes, when I am working" in his artist's book, *Jazz* (Paris: Tériade, 1947), p. 102. 250 copies printed, facsimile published by George Braziller, Inc., 1983.

97 Marie-Alain Couturier, "L'Appel aux maîtres de l'art moderne", in *Paris-Paris 1937–1957*, p. 304.

98 Pierre Bourdieu, *Distinction: A Social Critique of the Judgement of Taste* (Cambridge: Harvard University Press, 1984). Originally published 1979. See also Frank Burch Brown, *Good Taste, Bad Taste, and Christian Taste, Aesthetics in Religious Life* (Oxford: Oxford University Press, 2000).

99 Marcel Billot "Le père Couturier et l'art sacré", in *Paris-Paris 1937–1957*, p. 303. Billot cites Couturier in an unnamed article from *Le Figaro*, dated October 24, 1951.

100 *Life*, June 19, 1950, volume 28, n. 25, pp. 72–76.

101 Lipchitz inscribed on the back of his sculpture, "Jacob Lipchitz, Jew, faithful to the religion of his ancestors, has made this Virgin to foster understanding between men on earth that the life of the Spirit may prevail." Chagall wrote on his, "In the name of Peace and tolerance among all men." (Chagall received numerous church commissions until the end of his long career.)

102 Thanks to Charles Pickstone for pointing this out. See his essay "Germaine Richier: Secular Theologian of Sacred Space", *Theology*, January 2007 volume 110, 853, pp. 31-39.

103 In the early-deceased brother's (age 36) obituary by Father Augustin-Marie Cocagnac that featured in *L'Art sacré* (3–4 November-December 1956) he wrote "He meditated on Le Corbusier. I can still see him in his room, brandishing a book by the architect, saying to me: the chapel came out of here.", p. 29. Rayssiguier also designed and built the very Corbusian hermitage forest chapel Saint-Rouin-en-Argonne (1954-1961). *L'Art sacré* (3-4, November-December 1961) was dedicated to the chapel.

104 See Marie-Alain Couturier, Henri Matisse, L.-B. Rayssiguier, *The Vence Chapel, the Archive of a Creation*, Marcel Billot (ed.) (Milan: Skira, Houston: Menil Foundation, 1999), translated by Michael Taylor. Originally published as *La chapelle de Vence, Journal d'une création* (Paris: Éditions du Cerf, Geneva: Skira, Houston: Menil Foundation, Inc., 1993) and Soeur Jacques-Marie, *Henri Matisse, la chapelle de Vence* (Nice: Grégoire Gardette Éditions, 1992, 2003). English edition 2001.

105 Ibid., *La chapelle de Vence*, p. 93.

106 Antoine Lion, "Postlude", in Antoine Lion (ed.), *Marie-Alain Couturier, un combat pour l'art sacré*, p. 198.

107 Marie-Alain Couturier, untitled article, *L'Art sacré*, "Vence" (11–12, July-August 1951). Couturier attributes to an old lady passing by, "it's much better that the Holy Virgin doesn't have a face, that way each person can see it as they want." p. 19.

One could also imagine that the androgynous St Dominic figure has an alternative identity, a Dominican sister, perhaps even Sister Jacques-Marie. After all, she had served for Matisse as a model many times before. In any case, it is easy to imagine that the worshipping sisters, facing the picture during offices seated in their stalls, could relate to the image as their own.

108 We are grateful to Charles Pickstone for this observation which brings to mind the connection that Le Corbusier, and others, would make between the crucifix and the tree to be discussed in chapter 4.

109 See Sarah Wilson "La Bataille des 'humbles'? Communistes et catholiques autour de l'art sacré", in Barthélémy Jobert (ed.), *Histoires d'art, Mélanges en l'honneur de Bruno Foucart* (Paris: Norma Éditions, 2008), pp. 448–466.

110 For example, Pope Pius XI's inaugural address for the Vatican's Pinacoteca museum on October 27, 1932, and in the aforementioned 1947 *Mediator Dei*.

111 The article subsequently circulated widely in several languages. It targeted Assy's *Crucifix* directly as "an indecent pastiche", an insult to God, and a scandal.

112 Issued on June 30, 1952, written by Giuseppe Cardinal Pizzardo (1877–1970) and Alfredo Ottaviani (1890–1979).

113 *L'Art sacré*, "Bilan d'une querelle" (9–10, May–June 1952). Tract of Angers reprinted, p. 4.

114 Pie-Raymond Régamey, *Art sacré au XXe siècle ?* (Paris: Éditions du Cerf, 1952).

CHAPTER 2

1 According to André Wogenscky, his long-term assistant, he was agnostic, "he did not know if God existed". Translated from André Wogenscky, *Les Mains de Le Corbusier* (Paris: Éditions de Grenelle, n.d.), p. 18.

2 Le Corbusier, *When the Cathedrals were White: a journey to the country of the timid people* (New York: Reynal and Hitchcock, 1947), p. xvii. Originally published as *Quand les cathédrales étaient blanches* (Paris: Plon, 1937).

3 Edward A. Sovik, "Review of The Radiant City", *Liturgical Arts*, p. 120.

4 Le Corbusier, *My Work* (London: Architectural Press, 1960), p. 9.

5 H. Allen Brooks, *Le Corbusier's Formative Years* (London: University of Chicago Press, 1997), p. 20. Letter Le Corbusier to his mother, 10.11.1931, in J. Jenger, *Le Corbusier, Choix de Lettres* (Basel: Birkhäuser, 2002), p. 215.

6 Jan Birksted has amply illustrated the prevalence of Masonic activity in Jeanneret's La Chaux-de-Fonds milieu although there is no evidence that Le Corbusier ever became a Freemason. Jan Birksted, *Le Corbusier and the Occult* (Cambridge MA: MIT, 2009).

7 For a discussion of Le Corbusier's library see Paul Turner, *The Education of an Architect* (New York: Garland, 1977).

8 Robert Pincus Witten records that in 1883 there was a burgeoning interest in the occult in Paris that focussed on a bookshop, the *Librairie de l'Art Indépendant* which published books on alchemy and Kabbalism and attracted a number of writers and poets including Huysmans and Schuré. Robert Pincus Witten, *Occult Symbolism in France: Joséphin Péladan and the Salons de la Rose-Croix* (New York: Garland, 1976), p. 55.

9 Extract from Édouard Schuré *Les Grands Initiés* (Paris: Perrin, 1908) quoted in Mogens Krustrup, 'Ineffable Space, B Arkitekturtidsskrift, 50 (1993)', p. 65.

10 Letter January 31, 1908. In the archives at La Chaux-de-Fonds (CdF LCms 34, transcription supplied by Françoise Frey) quoted in Tim Benton, "The Sacred and the Search for Truths", in Tim Benton (ed.) *Le Corbusier Architect of the Century* (London: Arts Council, 1987), p. 239.

11 Graham Livesey, 'The Van de Leeuw House: Theosophical Connections with Early Modern Architecture', *Architronic*, 8, 1, 1. corbu2.caed.kent.edu/architronic/v8n1/v8n1o2.pdf

12 Jean Jenger, *Le Corbusier, Architect of a New Age* (London: Thames and Hudson, 1996), p. 41. Amongst Le Corbusier's collection of books is Guillaume Apollinaire, *Alcools. Poèmes 1898–1913* (Paris: NRF, 1947) in Fondation Le Corbusier (hereafter referred to as FLC).

13 Le Corbusier, *New World of Space*, (New York: Reynal and Hitchcock, 1948), p. 11.

14 Ibid., p. 36.

15 Julia Fagan-King, "United on the Threshold of the Twentieth-Century Mystical Ideal", *Art History*, 11, 1 (1988), p. 94.

16 Virginia Spate, "Orphism", in Nikos Stangos (ed.), *Concepts of Modern Art* (London: Thames and Hudson, 1997), p. 194.

17 For a detailed discussion of all these influences on Le Corbusier's thinking see Flora Samuel, *Orphism in the Work of Le Corbusier with Particular Reference to his Scheme for La Sainte Baume*, unpublished PhD thesis, Cardiff University, 2000.

18 William Keith Chambers Guthrie, *Orpheus and Greek Religion* (London: Methuen, 1935), p. 39.

19 Ibid., p. 41.

20 Ibid., p. 114.

21 Ibid., p. 41.

22 Ibid., p. 18.

23 Ibid., p. 41.

24 Ibid., p. 39.

25 Ibid., p. 31.

26 Ibid., p. 29.

27 Ibid., p. 9.

28 Ibid., p. 220.

29 Ibid., p. 217.

30 Le Corbusier also referred to the discussion of Pythagoras at the Milan Triennale of 1951 dedicated to "de divina Proportione". Le Corbusier, *Modulor 2* (London: Faber, 1955), p. 145. Originally published as Le Corbusier, *Le Modulor II* (Paris: Éditions de l'Architecture d'Aujourd'hui, 1955), p. 146. See also Le Corbusier, *Modulor 2*, p. 193.

31 Ibid.

32 Ibid., p. 142.

33 Le Corbusier, *The Decorative Art of Today* (London: The Architectural Press, 1987), p. 167. Originally published as Le Corbusier, *L'Art décoratif d'Aujourd'hui* (Paris: Éditions Crès, 1925).

34 Arthur Rüegg (ed.), *Polychromie Architecturale: Le Corbusier's Colour Keyboards from 1931 to 1959* (Basel: Birkhäuser, 1997), p. 101.

35 Le Corbusier, *The Decorative Art of Today*, p. 169.

36 Elie Faure, *Equivalences* (Paris: Robert Marin, 1951). Elie Faure, *Histoire de l'art. L'esprit des formes* (Paris: Germain Crès, 1927) with a dedication from the author to Jeanneret. Elie Faure, *Histoire de l'art, vols. I, II, III, IV* (Paris: Germain Crès, 1924) all in FLC. Le Corbusier read *Equivalences* in March 1951. Le Corbusier, *Sketchbooks Volume 2* (London: Thames and Hudson, 1981), sketch 372.

37 Plato, *Symposium*, in Scott Buchanan (ed.), *The Portable Plato* (Harmondsworth: Penguin, 1997), p. 144.

38 Ibid., p. 147.

39 C.G. Jung, "The Structure and Dynamics of the Self", *Collected Works 9, Part II* (London: Routledge, Kegan and Paul, 1951), p. 355.

40 Julia Fagan-King, "United on the Threshold", p. 90.

41 Moshe Idel, *Kabbalah, New Perspectives* (Yale: Yale University Press, 1988), p. 251.

42 Harry Sperling and Maurice Simon, trans., *The Zohar* (London: Soncino Press, 1933), p. 91.

43 *Encyclopaedia Britannica* (Cambridge: Cambridge University Press, 1911), p. 620.

44 Le Corbusier, *Sketchbooks Volume 3, 1954–1957* (Cambridge MA: MIT, 1982), sketch 1011.

45 Le Corbusier, *Journey to the East* (Cambridge: MIT, 1987), p. 62. Le Corbusier, *Le Voyage d'Orient* (Paris: Parenthèses, 1987), p. 55. Originally published in 1966.

46 Le Corbusier, *Le poème de l'angle droit* (Paris: Éditions Connivance, 1989), section A3 Milieu.

47 Le Corbusier, *Precisions* (Cambridge MA: MIT, 1991), p. 77. Originally published as *Précisions sur un état présent de l'architecture et de l'urbanisme* (Paris: Crès, 1930).

48 Le Corbusier, *Sketchbooks Vol. 3*, sketches 645–646.

49 Louis Réau, *Iconographie de l'art Chrétien Volume 1* (Paris: Presses Universitaires de France, 1955), p. 68.

50 Émile Mâle, *The Gothic Image* (London: Fontana, 1961), p. 11. Originally published as *L'Art Religieux du XIII Siècle en France* (Paris: Librairie Armand Colin, 1925), p. 11. I am grateful to Judi Loach for drawing my attention to this passage of Mâle's writing.

51 Ghyka wrote "In Pythagorean Number-Mystic, seven was the Virgin-Number". Matila Ghyka, *The Geometry of Art and Life* (New York: Dover, 1977), p. 21. Originally published in 1946.

52 Réau, *Iconographie de l'art Chrétien Volume 1*, p. 68.

53 Le Corbusier, *Le poème de l'angle droit*, section B4 Esprit.

54 Réau, *Iconographie de l'art Clrétieu Volume 1*, p. 68.

55 From introduction to American edition of Le Corbusier, *When the Cathedrals were White, A Journey to the country of the Timid People* (New York: Reynal and Hitchcock, 1947) p. xvii.

56 Le Corbusier, *Le poème de l'angle droit* , section A1 Milieu.

57 Giovanni Pico della Mirandola, *On the Dignity of Man* (Indianapolis: Hackett, 1998), p. 15.

58 Le Corbusier, *Le poème de l'angle droit* , section A1 Milieu.

59 Mogens Krustrup, *Porte Email* (Copenhagen: Arkitektens Forlag, 1991), p. 128.

60 Réau, *Iconographie de l'art Chrétien Volume 1*, p. 121.

61 Plato, *The Republic V*, in Buchanan (ed.), *The Portable Plato*, p. 507.

62 Giovanni Pico della Mirandola, *On the Dignity of Man*, p. 16.

63 In an entry dated December 15, 1955, he wrote 'Retour à Paris reprendre un dessins grand format Chandigarh le bestiaire anthropocentrique de ces dernières années.' Le Corbusier, *Sketchbooks Volume 3*, sketch 426. Paul Claudel was also interested in the Bestiaries. Paul Claudel, "Quelques Planches du Bestiaire Spirituel", *Œuvre complète vol. 5* (Paris: Gallimard, 1953), pp. 249–280.

64 Émile Mâle, *The Gothic Image* (London: Fontana, 1961), pp. 33–34. Originally published as *L'Art Religieux du XIII en France* (Paris: Librairie Armand Colin, 1925). pp. 33–34.

65 Emile Mâle, *Religious Art in France: the Twelfth Century* (Princeton: Bollingen, 1978), p. 333.

66 Ibid., p. 336.

67 Guillaume Apollinaire, *Le Bestiaire ou Cortège d'Orphée* in Michel Décaudin (ed.), *Œuvres complètes de Guillaume Apollinaire* (Paris: André Balland et Jacques Lecat, 1966), pp. 40–41.

68 Henry Provensal, *L'Art de Demain* (Paris: Perrin, 1904), p. 70 in FLC.

69 Le Corbusier, *Sketchbooks Vol. 3*, sketch 257.

70 These words are from a poem by Stéphane Mallarmé. Erica Billeter, *Le Corbusier Secret* (Lausanne: Musée Cantonal des Beaux Arts, 1987), plates 121–132.

71 Le Corbusier, *Poésie sur Alger* (Paris: Éditions Connivances, 1989).

72 Le Corbusier's siren has the head of a horned animal, not that of a bird. It is possible that she was associated with a unicorn.

73 Femme cornée avec des ailes. Erica Billeter, *Le Corbusier Secret* (Lausanne: Musée Cantonal des Beaux Arts, 1987), plate 132.

74 Le Corbusier, *Sketchbooks Vol. 4, 1957-1964* (Cambridge, MA: MIT, 1982), sketch 41.

75 Jaime Coll., "Structure and Play in Le Corbusier's Art Works", *AA Files* 31 (1996), p. 10.

76 C.G Jung, "The Lapis-Christ Parallel", in *Psychology and Alchemy* (London: Routledge, Kegan and Paul, 1993), pp. 345-342.

77 One of the housing schemes for La Sainte Baume was to take the form of a *vesica piscis*.

78 Le Corbusier, *The Radiant City* (London: Faber, 1964), p. 185. Originally published as Le Corbusier, *La Ville Radieuse* (Paris: Éditions de l'Architecture d'Aujourd'hui, 1935), p. 185.

79 Flora Samuel, "Le Corbusier, Teilhard de Chardin and the Planetisation of Mankind", *Journal of Architecture*, 4, 1999, pp. 149–165.

80 Flora Samuel, "Le Corbusier, Teilhard de Chardin and *La Planétisation humaine*: spiritual ideas at the heart of modernism", *French Cultural Studies*, 11,2, 2000, p. 192.

81 Pierre Teilhard de Chardin, *On Love* (London: Collins, 1972), p. 14.

82 H. de Lubac, *L'Éternel Féminin: étude sur un texte du Père Teilhard de Chardin* (Paris: Aubier, 1968), p. 24. Written from the gendered point of view of man, what it means if you are a woman is a moot point.

83 Pierre Teilhard de Chardin, *L'Énergie humaine* (Paris: Seuil, 1962), p. 146.

84 Mary McLeod, *Urbanism and Utopia: Le Corbusier from Regional Syndicalism to Vichy*, DPhil thesis, Princeton University (1985), p. iv.

85 Jeremy Jennings, *Syndicalism in France: A Study of Ideas* (London: Macmillan 1990), p. 203.

86 McLeod, *Urbanism and Utopia*, p. 131.

87 Le Corbusier, *The Radiant City*, p. 177.

88 Ibid.

89 Le Corbusier, *Modulor 2* (London: Faber, 1955), p. 26. Originally published as *Le Modulor II* (Paris: Éditions de l'Architecture d'Aujourd'hui, 1955).

90 "Cultiver le corps et l'esprit mettre dans des conditions favorables positive ou négative". Le Corbusier, *Sketchbooks Volume 2* (London: Thames and Hudson, 1981) sketch 503.

91 Daphne Becket-Chary, *Le Corbusier's Poem of the Right Angle*, Unpublished MPhil Thesis, Cambridge (1990).

92 Le Corbusier, *When the Cathedrals were White*, p. 154.

93 Le Corbusier, *Modulor* (London: Faber, 1954), p. 224.

94 Le Corbusier, *Le Modulor*, p. 113.

95 Le Corbusier, *The Radiant City*, p. 78.

96 Ibid. We have changed the published word "inexpressible" to "ineffable" for the sake of consistency. Both are translations of "indicible".

97 Le Corbusier, *Modulor*, p. 220.

98 Le Corbusier, *Precisions*, (Cambridge: MIT, 1991), p. 29.

99 Pico noted that "Orpheus covered the mysteries of his doctrines with the wrappings of fables, and disguises them with a poetic garment, so that whoever reads his hymns may believe that there is nothing underneath but tales and the purest nonsense". Pico della Mirandola, *On the Dignity of Man*, p. 33.

100 Le Corbusier, *Precisions*, p. 29. Abortion was made illegal in France in 1942. "Therapeutic" abortion was made legal in France in 1955. It was therefore a hot political topic.

101 See Antoine Mesclon, *Le Féminisme et l'homme* (Paris: A, Mesclon, 1931) in Fondation Le Corbusier. Also Flora Samuel, *Le Corbusier Architect and Feminist* (London: Academy, 2004), p. 42.

102 Louis Réau, *Iconographie de l'art Chrétien Volume 2*, p. 59.

103 Le Corbusier, *Journey to the East*, p. 162.

104 Le Corbusier, *Sketchbooks, Vol. 3*, sketch 549.

105 Translated from André Gide, *Thesée* (Paris: Gallimard, 1946), p. 62 in Fondation Le Corbusier.

106 "En une heure = 60 minutes, Paris Genève. J'ai eu le Temps de lire Thésée (Gide) Arianne et Dédale: + Marg., et avoir changé d'atmosphère. Etre// jeune, à nouveau!!" Le Corbusier, *Sketchbooks Vol. 4*, sketch 62.

CHAPTER 3

1 Le Corbusier, *Œuvre complète vol. 5* (Zurich: Les Éditions d'Architecture, 1995), p. 24.

2 A.-M. Cocagnac, "Ronchamp", *L'Art sacré*, 1–2, September-October 1955.

3 P. Devoucoux du Buysson, *Le Guide du Pèlerin à la grotte de sainte Marie Madeleine* (La Sainte-Baume: la Fraternité Marie-Madeleine, 1998), p. 20.

4 Trouin gave his date of birth in a letter to Le Corbusier. Letter Trouin to Le Corbusier, January 24, 1959, FLC 13 01 163.

5 Letter Henriette Trouin to Flora Samuel, November 22, 1999.

6 Le Corbusier, *Œuvre complète vol. 5*, p. 24.

7 Ibid.

8 Françoise Caussé, *La Revue "L'Art Sacré", le débat en France sur l'art et la religion (1945–1954)*, (Paris: Cerf, 2010), p. 289.

9 Letter Henriette Trouin to Flora Samuel, May 3, 2000.

10 Letter Le Corbusier to Trouin, July 13, 1963, FLC 13 01 206.

11 Caussé, *La Revue "L'Art Sacré"*, p. 292.

12 M.-A. Couturier, *Dieu et art dans la vie* (Paris: Cerf, 1965), p. 291. The editor of this book added a note making it clear that the underground church referred to was La Sainte Baume.

13 Ibid., p. 29. Couturier was to refer to the scheme even earlier in a note in his journal dated October 24, 1940. Ibid., p. 246.

14 He was a diplomat in the Far East from 1895-1909 before returning to be consul in a variety of countries nearer to home. *Robert Dictionaire Universel des Noms Propres* (Paris: Robert, 1974).

15 Paul Claudel, *L'Annonce faite à Marie* (Paris: Nouvelle Revue Français, 1912). Le Corbusier's own edition is not annotated. See "L-C relire 'la Ville' Claudel." Le Corbusier, *Sketchbooks Volume 3, 1954–1957* (Cambridge, MA: MIT, 1982), sketch 333. Originally published in 1893, in it Claudel used the city as metaphor for the inner world within a person. Paul Claudel, *La Ville* (Paris: Mercure de France, 1967). Le Corbusier also owned Paul Claudel, *Connaissance de l'est* (Paris: Mercure, 1907) in FLC.

16 P.R. Régamey, "Paul Claudel et l'art chrétien", in *La Pensée religieuse de Claudel* (Paris: Desclée de Brouwer, 1969), p. 151. Cited in Claude Bergeron, "La Basilique souterraine de la Sainte-Baume", *Revue de l'Art* 118 (1997), p. 29.

17 Letter Claudel to Couturier January 28, 1937, Bibliothèque du Saulchoir, Paris, C- 5D 9.

18 Paul Claudel, "Project d'une église souteraine à Chicago", *Positions et propositions vol. 2* (Paris: Gallimard, 1934), pp. 229-242. See also H.F., "Le Plateau Provençal de La Sainte-Baume: abritera-t-il un jour une église rupestre?", *Le Monde* (July 5, 1948), p. 3.

19 Curiously, Couturier records these events in the entry dated October 24, 1946 by which time Trouin and Le Corbusier were fully involved. Couturier, *Dieu et art dans la vie*, p. 246.

20 Ibid.

21 Antonin Raymond, *Antonin Raymond, an Autobiography* (Rutland Vermont: Charles E. Tuttle Co., 1973), p. 183.

22 Ibid., p. 184.

23 Translated from Paul Claudel, "Projet d'une église souteraine à Chicago", *Positions et propositions vol. 2* (Paris: Gallimard, 1934), p. 234.

24 He wrote an article in a 1946 edition of *L'Art sacré* dedicated to the subject.

25 Claudel, "Projet d'une église souteraine à Chicago", p. 241.

26 Raymond, *An Autobiography*, p. 184.

27 At the culmination of the initiation into the mysteries of Eleusis, a cult linked to that of Orpheus, the initiate was given a grain of seed.

28 Translated from Claude Bergeron, "La Basilique souterraine de la Sainte-Baume", p. 33.

29 Le Corbusier, *Modulor* (London: Faber, 1954), p. 222. Originally published as *Le Modulor* (Paris: Éditions de l'Architecture d'Aujourd hui, 1950), p. 222.

30 Claudel visited the grotto at La Sainte Baume on two occasions, once in 1925 and once in 1936 and had found the experience extremely moving. P. Claudel, *Contacts et circonstances* (Paris: Gallimard, 1940), p. 185.

31 Letter Henriette Trouin to Flora Samuel, October 6, 1999.

32 Trouin, "Presentation de La Sainte-Baume", January 27, 1962, FLC 13 01 193.

33 P. Devoucoux du Buysson, *Le Guide du Pèlerin à la grotte de sainte Marie Madeleine* (La Sainte-Baume: la Fraternité Marie-Madeleine, 1998), p. 32.

34 See annotations to Coincy Saint Palais, *Esclarmonde de Foix: Princesse Cathare* (Toulouse: Privat, 1956), p. 27 in FLC.

35 Frédéric Mistral, *Mirèio* (Avignon: Roumanille, 1859). See Sully-André Peyre, *Essai sur Frédéric Mistral* (Paris: Pierre Seghers, 1959), p. 24.

36 J.-C. Vigato, "Le Choix du Sud", in G., Viatte (ed.), *Le Corbusier et la Mediterranee* (Marseilles: L'université de Provence, 1991), p. 218.

37 *Marseille Magazine*, no 5, April 1957, FLC P5 02 120.

38 Le Corbusier, *Œuvre complète vol. 5*, p. 24.

39 Ibid., pp. 26-7.

40 Luke, 7: 37.

41 Luke, 7: 36-9.

42 Letter Trouin to the Princesse de C.[sic], June 1945, FLC 13 01 279.

43 Victor Saxer, *Le Culte de Marie Madeleine en Occident des orgines à la fin du moyen âge* (Paris: Auserre, 1959), p. 234.

44 Haskins, *Mary Magdalene*, (London: Harper Collins, 1993), p. 122. See also Louis Réau, *Iconographie de l'Art Chrétien Volume 3.2*, pp. 854-5.

45 33 is significant for being the age at which Jesus was crucified.

46 Emile Mâle, *Religious Art in France: the Twelfth Century* (Princeton: Bollingen, 1978), pp. 216-7.

47 Trouin wrote that the Compagnons du Tour de France, of which Moles was leader, were thinking about building an "unité Corbu". He also mentioned that Le Corbusier knew Moles. Letter Trouin to Le Corbusier, February 8, 1955, FLC 13 01 301.

48 On the frontispiece of this book are printed the words "Exemplaire imprimé pour: Monsieur Charles Le Corbusier". Perret contributed to the introduction. Antoine Moles, *Histoire des charpentiers* (Paris: Librairie Gründ, 1949) in FLC. Moles, who lived in Marseilles, tried to interest Le Corbusier in working on a scheme with him. Letter André Wogenscky to Antoine Moles, January 3, 1950, FLC G3 159.

49 Moles, *Histoire des Charpentiers*, p. 114. See also p. 119. Frédéric Mistral, *Calendal* (Avignon: Roumanille, 1867).

50 Moles, *Histoire des Charpentiers*, p. 114. For Moles it was significant that Jesus was the son of a carpenter and that he chose simple workers for his Apostles. Ibid., p. 21.

51 Jean Gimpel, *Les Bâtisseurs de Cathédrales* (Paris: Éditions Seuil, 1959) in FLC. These words are underlined in notes on p. 181. Interestingly Gimpel notes that there were female masons and that "the thirteenth century woman had more rights than women in France today", p. 78.

52 Le Corbusier, *Œuvre complète vol. 5*, p. 27.

53 Saintes-Maries-de-la-Mer a town on the Provençal coast is named after the Marys, indicating that the idea of Marys in plural is a familiar one in that part of France.

54 John, 19: 25.

55 Mark, 15: 40.

56 Trouin, "Rapport du Secrétaire Général (Edouard Trouin) sur nos projets en cours: Les Fastes Européens de La Sainte-Baume et le 'Museon Madalanen [sic].'" FLC 13 01 380, February 8, 1955.

57 Jacobus de Voragine, *The Golden Legend*, vol. 1 translated by William Granger Ryan (Princeton: Princeton University Press, 1993), p. 380.

58 Voragine, *The Golden Legend*, vol. 1, p. 375.

59 Letter Le Corbusier to Trouin, March 9, 1957, FLC13 01 123. Le Corbusier suggested the use of 'la lumière noire' in his theatre, an idea that delighted Trouin.

60 Edouard Trouin, "Appel au Monde en faveur du Plan d'Aups". n.d., FLC 13 01 348.

61 Ibid., FLC 13 01 355.

62 Letter Trouin to Picasso, FLC P5 02 37, February 23, 1956.

63 Ernest Renan, *La Vie de Jesus* (Paris: Calmann-Levy, 1906), p. 128 in FLC.

64 Ibid., p. 176 in FLC.

65 Le Corbusier's own copy published in Paris in 1906 (originally published 1863), is signed Ch.E. Jeanneret in ink. On the frontispiece Le Corbusier wrote the page numbers of several passages that were of particular interest to him.

66 Coincy Saint Palais, *Esclarmonde de Foix: Princesse Cathare*, p. 41 in FLC.

67 Saint-Palais, *Esclarmonde de Foix: Princesse Cathare*, p. 121 in FLC. According to the Albigensian Cathars Mary Magdalene was Christ's concubine. See Haskins, *Mary Magdalen*, p. 135.

68 Unnamed document within the file FLC P5 02 08, May 22, 1948.

69 Unnamed document within notes by Trouin, May 22, 1948, FLC P5 02 08.

70 Louis Réau, *Iconographie de l'art Chrétien Volume 1*, p. 59.

71 Edouard Trouin, "Appel au Monde en faveur du Plan d'Aups", n.d., FLC 13 01 365.

72 It may be significant that Henri Provensal identified two main types of religious monuments in India, those that were subterranean and "monuments monoliths creusés dans le roc" (subterranean monoliths dug/drilled/cut (you choose) in the rock". Henry Provensal, *L'Art de demain* (Paris: Perrin, 1904), p. 202 in FLC.

73 Le Corbusier, *The Modulor* (London: Faber, 1951), p. 18. Originally published as Le Corbusier, *Le Modulor* (Paris: Éditions de l'Architecture d'Aujourd'hui, 1950), p. 18.

74 Trouin, "Table provisoire" for book entitled *La Sainte-Baume et Marie Madeleine*," n.d., FLC 13 01 399.

75 St Teresa of Jesus, *The Way of Perfection* (London: Thomas Baker, 1911).

76 St Teresa of Jesus, *The Interior Castle* (London: Thomas Baker, 1912), originally written in 1577.

77 Catherine Swietlicki, *Spanish Christian Cabala* (Columbia: University of Missouri Press, 1986), pp. 9 and 43.

78 Edouard Trouin, "La Cité de Contemplation", undated pamphlet found interleaved within Edouard Trouin [Louis Montalte pseud.], *La Basilique Universelle de la Paix et du Pardon* (Levallois Perret: Imprimerie Schneider, Fres et Mory, 1948), FLC 13 01 401.

79 Ibid.

80 Trouin, "Plan d'Aups ou Plan-Plan d'Aups," n.d., FLC 13 01 368. See also Caussé, p. 289.

81 "Déclaration d'amour à La Sainte-Baume." Trouin, "Table provisoire" for book entitled *La Sainte-Baume et Marie Madeleine*, n.d., FLC 13 01 396.

82 Letter Trouin to Le Corbusier, December 18, 1957, FLC 13 01 141.

83 Le Corbusier, *Œuvre complète vol. 5*, p. 29.

84 Trouin [Montalte pseud.], *La Basilique Universelle de la Paix et du Pardon*, FLC 13 01 403.

85 There are similarly a number of allusions to the number seven in the architecture of Ronchamp. Seven beams in the roof, seven steps to the outdoor pulpit and seven levels in the pyramid to the north east of the chapel.

86 Émile Mâle, *L'Art religieux du XIII Siècle en France*, p. 11.

87 Ibid.

88 Trouin [Montalte pseud.], *La Basilique Universelle de la Paix et du Pardon*, FLC 13 01 403.

89 Letter Trouin to Le Corbusier, January 10, 1947, FLC 13 01 4.

90 Ibid.

91 Letter Trouin to Le Corbusier, February 8, 1955, FLC 13 01 301.

92 Trouin [Montalte pseud.], *La Basilique Universelle de la Paix et du Pardon*, FLC 13 01 403.

93 Ibid.

94 Réau noted that this became a very popular theme within Christian art and literature, especially in the work of Matthias Grünewald. Réau, *Iconographie de l'art Chrétien Volume 2*, p. 87.

95 Trouin [Montalte pseud.], *La Basilique Universelle de la Paix et du Pardon*, FLC 13 01 403.

96 Ibid.

97 Réau, *Iconographie de l'art Chrétien Volume 1*, pp. 67-68.

98 Trouin [Montalte pseud.], *La Basilique Universelle de la Paix et du Pardon*, FLC 13 01 403.

99 Trouin, "Table provisoire" for book entitled *La Sainte-Baume et Marie Madeleine*, FLC 13 01 396.

100 Réau, *Iconographie de l'art Chrétien Volume 1*, p. 268.

101 Charles Lalo, "L'esthétique sans amour", in two consecutive editions of *Esprit Nouveau*, No. 5 and 6, (New York: Da Capo Press, 1969), pages not numbered.

102 Sheila Hassell Hughes, "A Woman's Soul is her Castle: Place and Space in St Teresa's Interior Castle", *Literature and Theology* 11, 4 (1997), p. 378.

103 Trouin, "Table provisoire" for book entitled *La Sainte-Baume et Marie Madeleine*, FLC 13 01 399.

104 For a more detailed discussion of St Teresa's role in the scheme see Flora Samuel, "The Philosophical City of Rabelais and St Teresa; Le Corbusier and Edouard Trouin's scheme for St Baume", *Literature and Theology* 13, 2 (1999), pp. 111-126.

105 St Teresa of Jesus, *The Way of Perfection*.

106 Trouin, "La Cité de Contemplation", undated pamphlet found interleaved within Trouin [Montalte pseud.], *La Basilique Universelle de la Paix et du Pardon*, FLC 13 01 403.

107 Letter Le Corbusier to Trouin, dated September 14, 1953, FLC 13 01 77.

108 Le Corbusier, *Œuvre complète vol. 5*, p. 31.

109 Le Corbusier, *Œuvre complète vol. 5*, p. 25.

110 Mircea Eliade, *Images and Symbols* (London: Harville Press, 1961), p. 53.

111 Ibid., p. 53.

112 Jaime Coll, "Le Corbusier's Taureaux; An Analysis of the Thinking Process", *Art History*, 18, (December 4, 1995), p. 548.

113 Moles, *Histoire des charpentiers*, p. 73, in FLC.

114 Le Corbusier, *Sketchbooks vol. 2*, sketch 799.

115 See also Letter Trouin to Le Corbusier, June 7, 1955, FLC P5 02 18.

116 Trouin [Montalte pseud.], *La Basilique Universelle de la Paix et du Pardon*, FLC 13 01 403.

117 Le Corbusier, *Œuvre complète vol. 5*, p. 25.

118 Letter Le Corbusier to J. Arthuys, July 6, 1948, FLC 13 01 27.

119 Ibid., p. 25.

120 Le Corbusier, *Œuvre complète vol. 5*, p. 27.

121 Caussé, *La revue "L'Art Sacré"*, p. 296, p. 302.

122 Ibid., p. 297.

123 Ibid., p. 296

124 Ibid., p. 298.

125 Ibid., p. 295.

126 Ibid., p. 304.

127 Ibid., p. 307.

128 Translated from André Billy, "La Sainte-Baume contre Lourdes!", *Figaro*, December 9, 1948, front page.

129 Ibid.

130 Translated from a letter by M.-A. Couturier in *Le Figaro*, February 12, 1949 quoted in Paul Claudel, *Journal, vol. II 1933–1955*, (Paris: Gallimard, 1969), pp. 672-3. His editors added the information that the article was called "La Basilique du Pardon et de la Paix" and was actually dated February 7, 1949.

131 Caussé, *La Revue L'Art sacré*, pp. 309-310.

132 Translated from a letter by M.-A. Couturier in *Le Figaro*, February 12, 1949 quoted in Claudel, *Journal, vol. II*, pp. 672-73.

133 Caussé, *La Revue "L'Art sacré"*, p. 308.

134 Le Corbusier, *Œuvre complète vol. 5*, p. 30.

135 Letter Le Corbusier to Trouin, October 8, 1951, FLC 13 01 68.

136 Mallarmé, the French writer of the Symbolist period.

137 In other words "baroque". *The Oxford English Dictionary* definition of gongorism is "An affected type of diction and style introduced into Spanish literature by the poet Don Luis de Gongora y Argote (1561–1627), akin to euphemism in England."

138 Trouin to Picasso regarding the memorial to Couturier, February 23, 1956, FLC P5 2 37.

139 Letter Le Corbusier to Trouin, March 25, 1956, FLC 13 01 108.

140 Letter Le Corbusier to Trouin, March 19, 1956, FLC 13 01 41. For Trouin's response see Letter Trouin to Le Corbusier, March 18, 1956, FLC P5 02 39.

141 Caussé, *La Revue "L'Art sacré"*, p. 194.

142 "Rapport présenté par M. Edouard Trouin", March 12, 1949, FLC 13 01 378.

143 It became part of the legislation of the French planning system that when a building was listed all the land within a 500 metre radius of the building would be safeguarded too. See Judi Loach, "Le Corbusier at Firminy-Vert", in Benton (ed.), *Le Corbusier, Architect of the Century* (London: Arts Council, 1987), p. 342.

144 "Pour la réalisation du CHEMIN DU PARDON et de LA PAIX." "Rapport Trouin", April 11, 1949, FLC 13 01 02.

145 Ibid.

146 Le Corbusier, *Œuvre complète vol. 5*, p. 31.

147 "Pour la réalisation du CHEMIN DU PARDON et de LA PAIX." "Rapport Trouin", April 11, 1949, FLC 13 01 02.

148 Le Corbusier. *Precisions*, p. 142.

149 Le Corbusier, *Le Poème de l'angle droit*, section A4, "Milieu".

150 Réau, *Iconographie de l'art Chrétien Volume 1*, p. 98.

151 Réau, *Iconographie de l'art Chrétien Volume 2*, p. 58.

152 "Deuxième Rapport Trouin", April 5, 1949, FLC 13 01 379.

CHAPTER 4

1 Le Corbusier, *The Chapel at Ronchamp* (London: Architectural Press, 1957), p. 6.

2 Daniele Pauly, *Ronchamp lecture d'une architecture* (Paris: Éditions Ophrys, 1980). Daniele Pauly, "The Chapel at Ronchamp", *AD Profile 60*, 55, 7/8 (1985), pp. 30–37. Pauly, *Le Corbusier: La chapelle de Ronchamp, The chapel at Ronchamp* (Basel, Boston, Berlin: Birkhäuser, 1997).

3 For a history of the committee and their work, see Annick Flicoteaux, "La commision d'art sacré de Besançon, 1945–1955", in *Bulletin du centre de recherche d'art comtois*, n. 12, 1998–1999 (Besançon: Université de Franche-Comté, 2000) pp. 41–52 and Françoise Caussé, *La revue "L'Art sacré", le débat en France sur l'art et la religion (1945–1954)*, (Paris: Les Éditions du Cerf, Paris, 2010) pp. 338–411.

4 André Wogenscky, *Les mains de Le Corbusier* (Paris: Édition de Grenelle), p. 18.

5 Ibid., p. 18.

6 Le Corbusier, *The Chapel at Ronchamp*, p. 52.

7 Caussé, *La revue "L'Art sacré"*, p. 406.

8 Valerio Casali, "Marie-Alain Couturier et Le Corbusier", *Marie-Alain Couturier, un combat pour l'art sacré* (Nice: Serre éditeur, 2005), p. 93.

9 The same day the plans for the important church at Audincourt were approved, also in the diocese, architect Novarina – like the Assy church – with art by Léger and Bazaine. Couturier was present at this meeting in Besançon. Caussé, *La revue "L'Art sacré"*, p. 399.

10 "Le Corbusier Ronchamp" p. 29–31, on p. 31, in *L'Art sacré*, "Espagne", 11–12, July–August 1953.

11 Letter Le Corbusier to M. Delgado Chalbaud July 26, 1951, FLC 8 52 32.

12 Letter Le Corbusier to Couturier, FLC E1 17, Paris, May 11, 1953.

13 Le Corbusier, *Texts et Dessins pour Ronchamp*, ed. Jean Petit (Geneva: Coopi: Ronchamp: Association Œuvre Notre-Dame du Haut, 1995). Originally published in 1965, not paginated. See also Alfred Manessier, "témoignage", in *Un artisan de l'art sacré: Le chanoine Lucien Ledeur de Besançon*, (Dijon: 1977), pp.5–6, reprinted in Annick Flicoteaux, "Le Chanoine Lucien Ledeur et la Commission d'art sacré du diocese de Besançon de 1945-1955, thesis, Institut Catholique de Paris, 1998, Annexe 1.

14 Jean-François Mathey in an interview with Inge Linder-Gaillard, January 14, 2012.

15 Jean Gimpel, *The Cathedral Builders* (Evergreen: London, 1961).

16 Christian Luxeuil in an interview with Inge Linder-Gaillard, January 14, 2012.

17 James Stirling, "Ronchamp: Le Corbusier's Chapel and the Crisis of Rationalism", *Architectural Review*, March 1956, pp. 155–161.

18 Le Corbusier, *Precisions*, (Cambridge MA: MIT, 1991), pp. 128–133.

19 Ibid., p. 160.

20 Flora Samuel, *Le Corbusier and the Architectural Promenade* (Basel: Birkhäuser, 2010).

21 See Le Corbusier *Poésie sur Algier* (Paris: Éditions Connivances, 1989). Originally published in 1950, p. 8.

22 Genesis, 28:11–19.

23 Le Corbusier and Pierre Jeanneret, *Œuvre complète, vol. 1, 1910–1929* (Zurich: Girsberger, 1943), p. 136. Originally published in 1937. There are various edited versions of this film but the 1971 Chaplin edited version does not contain an image of the Jacob's Ladder. There is however an extraordinary dream sequence in which Chaplin's alter ego the tramp dreams of his slum home translated to heaven, bedecked in flowers in which all the people that he knows have sprouted wings, including the dog. The dialectical nature of these two worlds is then broken down.

24 J. Peter, *The Oral History of Modern Architecture* (New York: Harry N. Abrams, 1994), p. 146.

25 Mogens Krustrup, *Porte Email* (Copenhagen: Arkitektens Forlag, 1991). More recently Jan Birksted has argued that the 'FF' symbols on the door have their origins in Le Corbusier's involvement in Masonry. Jan Kenneth Birksted, "Beyond the clichés of the hand-books: Le Corbusier's architectural promenade", *The Journal of Architecture*, 11, 1 (2006), pp. 55–132.

26 Email Louis Mauvais to Inge Linder-Gaillard, December 7, 2011.

27 Le Corbusier and Pierre Jeanneret, *Œuvre complète, volume 3, 1934-38* (Zurich: Les Éditions d'Architecture, 1995), p. 157. Originally published in 1938.

28 See Jaime Alberto Sarmento, *La Capilla de Ronchamp de Le Corbusier*, Unpublished Thesis, Universitat Politecnica de Catalunya, 1997, p. 146 for an extensive discussion of anthropomorphism.

29 Albert Christ-Janer and Mary Mix Foley, *Modern Church Architecture* (London: McGraw Hill, 1962), p. 110.

30 Le Corbusier, *Towards an Architecture* (London: Architectural Press, 1982), p. 183. Originally published as *Vers une Architecture* (Paris: Crès, 1923).

31 Letter Le Corbusier to his mother, June 27, 1955, Jean Jenger (ed.), *Le Corbusier Choix de lettres* (Basel: Birkhäuser, 2002), p. 388.

32 Robin Evans, *The Projective Cast* (Cambridge, MA: MIT, 1995), p. 284.

33 Mogens Krustrup, "Les Illustrations de Le Corbusier pour l'Illiade", in Germain Viatte (ed.), *Le Corbusier et la Mediterranée* (Marseilles: L'Université de Provence, 1991), p. 107.

34 Le Corbusier, *Towards an Architecture*, p. 126.

35 Jean Petit, *Ronchamp: Corbusier* (Fidia Edizioni d'Arte a Lugano, 1997), not paginated.

36 Le Corbusier, *Le poème de l'angle droit* (Paris: Éditions Connivance, 1989). Originally published in 1955, Section A5, Milieu, p. 45.

37 Email from Louis Mauvais, priest incumbent, to Inge Linder-Gaillard, December 7, 2011.

38 Robert Maguire and Keith Murray, *Modern Churches of the World* (London: Studio Vista, 1965), p. 48. Stirling, "Ronchamp: *Architectural Review*, March 1956, pp. 155–161.

39 Le Corbusier, *Texts et Dessins pour Ronchamp*, not paginated.

40 Ibid., footnote 18.

41 Le Corbusier, *Talks with Students* (New York, Princeton: 2003), p. 46.

42 See Samuel, *Le Corbusier and the Architectural Promenade* (2010).

43 Flora Samuel, *Le Corbusier in Detail* (London: Architectural Press, 2007).

44 Email from Louis Mauvais, priest incumbent, to Inge Linder-Gaillard December 7, 2011.

45 Le Corbusier, *Sketchbooks, vol. 3, 1954–1957* (Cambridge, MA: MIT, 1982), sketch 551.

46 Ibid., sketch 551.

47 Le Corbusier, *Œuvre complète, vol. 6, 1952–1957* (Zurich: Les Éditions d'Architecture, 1995). Originally published in 1957, p. 18.

48 Le Corbusier, *The Chapel at Ronchamp*, pp. 131–133.

49 Richard Keickhefer, "Christocentric and Theocentric Church Design", December 9, 2011, Modern Catholic Space Conference, London.

50 There was a special edition of *L'Architecture d'Aujourd'hui* devoted to "Architecture religieuse", dated July 6, 1934, containing several examples of churches by Dominikus Böhm. There is a further special edition on the subject in July 1938. From 1950 Régamey, Couturier and Claudius-Petit were on its Patronage committee. *L'Architecture d'Aujourd'hui*, 31, September 1950.

51 "Allemagne 1950", *L'Art sacré*, 3–4, November–December 1950.

52 Keickhefer, "Christocentric and Theocentric Church Design".

53 Wolfgang Jean Stock, *European Church Architecture 1950–2000* (Munich: Prestel, 2002), p. 59.

54 A.-M. Cocagnac, "Ronchamp", *L'Art sacré*, 1–2, September–October 1955.

55 Le Corbusier, *Œuvre Complète, vol. 6*, p. 21.

56 Le Corbusier, *Towards an Architecture*, p. 177.

57 See for example Flora Samuel, *Le Corbusier: Architect and Feminist* (London: Architectural Press, 2004), pp. 145–147.

58 Thomas Schumacher, "Deep Space Shallow Space". *Architectural Review*, vol. CLXXXI, No 1079, 1987, pp. 37–43.

59 See Mark Torgerson, *The Architecture of Immanence: Architecture for Worship and Ministry Today* (Grand Rapids: Michigan: William B. Eerdmans, 2007), pp. 3–5 for a discussion of immanence.

60 Le Corbusier, *New World of Space*, p. 20.

61 Le Corbusier, *Modulor 2*, p. 71.

62 Le Corbusier, *The Chapel at Ronchamp*, p. 47.

63 Le Corbusier letter to Pierre Betz, October 10, 1955, FLC B2. 19.405. Quoted in Roberto Gargiani and Anna Rosellini, *Le Corbusier Béton Brut and Ineffable Space, 1940–1965* (EPFL: Lausanne, 2011), p. 146.

64 Gil Perry, *Women Artists and the Parisian Avant Garde* (Manchester: Manchester University Press, 1995), p. 142.

65 For ample illustration of Le Corbusier's interest in feminism see Samuel, *Le Corbusier: Architect and Feminist* (2004).

66 Eamon Duffy, *Saints and Sinners, a History of the Popes* (New Haven and London: Yale University Press, 2006), p. 291.

67 Ibid., p. 292.

68 Marina Warner, *Alone of All her Sex* (London: Vintage, 2000), p. 338.

69 Duffy, *Saints and Sinners*, p. 300.

70 Ibid.

71 Marina Warner, *Alone of All her Sex* (London, 1976), p. 334.

72 "The Role of the Blessed Virgin Mary, Mother of God, in the Mystery of Christ and the Church", *On the Church*, in Walter M. Abbott (ed.), *The Documents of Vatican II*, pp. 85–96.

73 Encyclical *Christi Matri*, September 15, 1966. Available from http://www.vatican.va/holy_father/paul_vi/encyclicals/documents/hf_p-vi_enc_15091966_christi-matri_en.html (accessed November 30, 2011).

74 *On the Church*, in Walter M. Abbott (ed.), *The Documents of Vatican II*, p. 19.

75 M le Chanoine Belot Curé de Ronchamp, *Notre Dame du Haut à Ronchamp: Manuel du Pèlerin* (n.d.–1930?), p. 12.

76 Ibid., p. 30.

77 Ibid., p. 22.

78 Ibid., p. 27.

79 Caussé, *La revue "L'Art sacré"*, p. 399.

80 Le Corbusier, *Sketchbooks Volume 3*, sketch 150.

81 Mogens Krustrup, *Porte Email*, p. 143.

82 Le Corbusier, *Œuvre complète vol.10*, p. 21.

83 Charles Jencks, *Le Corbusier and the Tragic View of Architecture* (London: Allen Lane, 1973).

84 Le Corbusier, *The Radiant City* (London: Faber, 1967), p. 152. Originally published as Le Corbusier, *La Ville Radieuse* (Paris: Éditions de l'Architecture d'Aujourd'hui, 1935).

85 Marjorie M. Malvern, *Venus in Sackcloth: The Magdalen's Origins and Metamorphoses* (Carbondale, Il.: Southern Illinois University Press, 1975), p. 39.

86 Le Corbusier, *Œuvre Complete vol. 5*, p. 24.

87 Le Corbusier, *The Chapel at Ronchamp*, p. 46.

88 Geoffrey Ashe, *The Virgin* (London: Routledge, Kegan and Paul, 1976), p. 213.

89 Joseph Campbell, *The Mythic Image* (Princeton: Princeton University Press, 1974), p. 254.

90 Ibid., p. 91. See C.G. Jung, *Psychology and Alchemy* (London: Routledge, 1993), p. 78 (first published in Zurich in 1944) for a discussion of the symbolism of the rose.

91 H. Allen Brooks (ed.), *Le Corbusier Ronchamp, Maison Jaoul, and other Projects 1951–52* (New York: Garland, 1983), p. 260.

92 Le Corbusier, *Œuvre complète vol. 5*, p. 72.

93 Lucien Hervé, *Le Corbusier, The Artist/Writer* (Neuchatel: Éditions du Grifon, 1970), p. 35.

94 Ibid., p. 28.

95 Le Corbusier, *Le poème de l'angle droit* (1989), p. 89.

96 Jean Labasant, "Le Corbusier's Notre Dame du Haut at Ronchamp", *Architectural Record* 118/4 (1955), p. 170.

97 Le Corbusier quotes in Heidi Weber (ed.), *Le Corbusier the Artist* (Zurich: Éditions Heidi Weber, 1988), pages not numbered.

98 Christopher Pearson, "Integrations of Art and Architecture in the work of Le Corbusier. Theory and Practice from Ornamentalism to the 'Synthesis of the Major Arts'". PhD Thesis, Stanford University (1995), p. 140.

99 André Gide., *Thésée* (Paris: Gallimard, 1946), p. 62. Le Corbusier, *Sketchbooks Volume 4*, sketch 62.

100 Jaime Coll, "Structure and Play in Le Corbusier's Art Works", *AA Files* 31 (1996), pp. 3–15.

101 Julia Kristeva, "Stabat Mater", in Susan Robin Sulieman (ed.), *The Female Body* (Cambridge MA: Harvard University, 1986), p. 108.

102 Le Corbusier, *Œuvre complète vol. 6* (Zurich: Éditions d'Architecture, 1976), p. 20.

103 Warner, *Alone of All her Sex*, p. 37.

104 Ibid.

105 Le Corbusier, *Sketchbooks Volume 3*, sketches 85–88. For an expansion of this discussion see Flora Samuel, "Le Corbusier, Rabelais and the Oracle of the Holy Bottle", *Word and Image*, 16 (2000), pp. 1–13.

106 Le Corbusier, *Sketchbooks vol. 3*, p. 10.

107 Ibid., p. 91.

108 Interview with Jean-François Mathey by Inge Linder-Gaillard, January 14, 2012, Ronchamp. In other words it was not cheap. In 1970 a large middle class house in the area could be bought for 1,000,000 old francs.

109 For a highly detailed account of the construction process see Gargiani and Rosellini, *Le Corbusier Béton Brut and Ineffable Space*, pp. 126–145.

110 Wolfgang Jean Stock, *European Church Architecture 1950–2000* (Munich: Prestel, 2002), p. 11.

111 M.-A. Couturier, "Magnificence de la Pauvreté", *L'Art sacré*, 1950, p. 8. Quoted in Philippe Potié, *The Monastery of Sainte Marie de La Tourette* (Basel: Birkhäuser, 2001), p. 62.

112 Richard Keickhefer, *Theology in Stone* (Oxford: OUP, 2004), p. 252.

113 Nikolaus Pevsner, *An Outline of European Architecture*, seventh edition in new format (London Penguin: 1964), p. 429.

114 The principles are reprinted in Peter Hammond (ed.), *Towards a Church Architecture* (Architectural Press: London, 1962), p. 249.

115 Quoted in Richard Keickhefer, *Theology in Stone*, p. 252.

116 Peter Hammond (ed.), *Towards a Church Architecture*, p.161.

117 Robert Maguire and Keith Murray, *Modern Churches of the World* (London: Studio Vista, 1965), p. 103.

118 His pre-war publication *Des Canons, des munitions ? Merci, des logis s.v.p.* (Boulogne-sur-Seine: Éditions de l'Architecture d'Aujourd'hui, Collection de l'équipement de la civilisation machiniste, 1938) set the stage for this.

119 Ernest Renan, *Vie de Jesus* (Paris: Calmann-Levy, 1906), p. 124 in FLC.

120 Le Corbusier, *The Final Testament of Père Corbu: a Translation and Interpretation of Mise au Point by Ivan Zaknic* (New Haven: Yale University Press, 1997), p. 120. Originally published as *Mise au point* (Paris: Éditions Forces-Vives), 1966.

121 Mary McLeod, "Charlotte Perriand, Her First Decade as a Designer", *AA Files*, 15, 1987, p. 8.

122 Stirling, "Ronchamp: Le Corbusier's Chapel and the Crisis of Rationalism", p. 158.

123 M.-A. Couturier, "Pour les Yeux", *L'Art sacré*, 5–6, January–February 1950, p. 4.

124 He is of course open to the charge of being paternalistic. Le Corbusier admired the 'primitive' people for their innate connection to nature and he admired intellectuals for advancing the cause of knowledge. His aim was instilling a sense of understanding of the principles of *savoir habiter* amongst the confused middle ground – his main target being women as they had most to gain from his emancipatory agenda.

125 Le Corbusier, *The Chapel at Ronchamp*, p. 25.

126 Le Corbusier, *Œuvre complète vol. 5*, p. 52.

127 Ibid., p. 27.

128 M.-A. Couturier, "Pour les Yeux", *L'Art sacré*, 5–6, January–February 1950, pp. 3–5.

129 André Vigneau, "La Lumière et la Liturgie", *L'Art sacré*, September–October 1957, p. 18.

139 Le Corbusier, *Œuvre complète vol. 5*, p. 52.

131 Letter Le Corbusier to his mother, June 27, 1955, Jean Jenger (ed.), *Le Corbusier Choix de lettres* (Basel: Birkhäuser, 2002), p. 388.

132 Cocagnac, "Ronchamp", *L'Art sacré*, 1–2, September–October 1955.

133 Le Corbusier, *Sketchbooks Volume 3*, sketch 722.

CHAPTER 5

1 Father Belaud was to visit Le Corbusier's atelier in April 1954 voicing his concern about the ways in which the plans lapsed from tradition.

He objected to the cloister being used as a means of communicating from one place to another when traditionally it was used for contemplation. Philippe Potié, *Le Corbusier: The Monastery of Sainte Marie de La Tourette* (Basel: Birkhäuser, 2001), p. 70.

2   Le Corbusier, *Œuvre complète vol. 7, 1957–1965* (Zurich: Les Éditions d'Architecture, 1995), p. 32. Originally published in 1965.

3   Potié, *Le Corbusier: The Monastery of Sainte Marie de La Tourette*, p. 52.

4   Jean-Marie Gueullette, "Le Corbusier and the Dominicans", *La Tourette, le cinquantenaire, 1959–2009* (Paris: Éditions Bernard Chauveau, 2009), p. 54.

5   Jerzy Soltan, "Working with Le Corbusier", in H. Allen Brooks (ed.), *The Le Corbusier Archive, vol. XVII* (New York: Garland, 1983).

6   See for example Le Corbusier's correspondence with the young monk Claude Ducret, son of his associate Paul Ducret. Le Corbusier, *The Final Testament of Père Corbu: A Translation of Mise au Point* by Ivan Zacnic (New Haven: Yale, 1997), p. 65.

7   Letter Le Corbusier to Sigismond Marcel, January 28, 1925, Fondation Le Corbusier, Dossier La Roche, doc. 131. Quoted and translated by Tim Benton, "The Sacred and the Search for Myths", in Tim Benton (ed.), *Le Corbusier Architect of the Century* (London: Arts Council, 1987), p. 243.

8   Le Corbusier, *Journey to the East* (Cambridge MA: MIT, 1987), p. 206.

9   Drawing May 7, 1954, FLC 1234.

10   Gueullette, "Le Corbusier and the Dominicans", p. 54.

11   Flora Samuel, *Le Corbusier Architect and Feminist* (London: Academy, 2004), p. 52.

12   Phyllis Zagano, *The Dominican Tradition* (Collegeville: Liturgical Press, 2006), p. xviii.

13   There are strong parallels here with the ideas of C.G. Jung. For a discussion of the relationship between Le Corbusier and Jung see Flora Samuel, "Animus, anima and the architecture of Le Corbusier", *Harvest Journal for Jungian Studies*, 48, 2, 2002, pp. 42–60.

14   Iannis Xenakis, "The Monastery of La Tourette", in H. Allen Brooks (ed.), *The Le Corbusier Archive, Volume XXVIII*

(New York: Garland, 1983), p. xiii.

15   Le Corbusier, *Modulor* (London: Faber, 1954), p. 224. Originally published as *Le Modulor* (Paris: Éditions de l'Architecture d'Aujourd hui, 1950).

16   Colin Rowe, *The Mathematics of the Ideal Villa and Other Essays* (Cambridge, MA: MIT, 1976), p. 189. For a discussion of Rowe's critical approach see Anthony Vidler, "Up Against the Wall: Colin Rowe at La Tourette", *Log*, Winter/Spring 2012, 24, pp. 7–18.

17   Quoted in Potié, *Le Corbusier: The Monastery of Sainte Marie de La Tourette*, p. 7.

18   Valerio Casali, "Marie-Alain Couturier et Le Corbusier", *Marie-Alain Couturier, un combat pour l'art sacré*, Antoine Lion (ed.), (Nice: Serre éditeur, 2005), p. 97.

19   Ibid. Casali notes that Hervé had encouraged Le Corbusier to visit the monastery as well, in view to contributing to the book. Lucien Hervé, *La plus grande aventure du monde, l'architecture mystique de Cîteaux*, Arthaud, 1956. Published as *The Architecture of Truth* (London: Phaidon, 2001), p. 7.

20   Ibid.

21   Ibid., pp. 128–130.

22   Casali, "Marie-Alain Couturier et Le Corbusier", p. 101.

23   Ibid., letter Couturier to Le Corbusier, July 28, 1953.

24   Gueullette, "Le Corbusier and the Dominicans", p. 50.

25   Robert Maguire and Keith Murray, *Modern Churches of the World* (London: Studio Vista, 1965), p. 60.

26   Marie-Alain Couturier, "Le Corbusier", *L'Art sacré*, n. 7-8, March–April 1954, pp. 9–10.

27   Le Corbusier, untitled text in section "L'adieu de ses amis, les artistes", *L'Art sacré*, n. 7-8, March–April 1954, p. 6.

28   Casali, "Marie-Alain Couturier et Le Corbusier", p. 105.

29   For a detailed account of the design process see Potié, *Le Corbusier: The Monastery of Sainte Marie de La Tourette*, pp. 63.

30   Iannis Xenakis, "The Monastery of La Tourette", p. x.

31   Quoted in Philippe Potié, *Le Corbusier: The Monastery of Sainte Marie de La Tourette*, p. 64.

32   See the chapter "Réalisation" in Sergio Ferrao, Chérif Kebbal, Philippe Potié and Cyrille Simonnet, *Le Corbusier, Le Couvent de la Tourette* (Marseilles: Éditions Parenthèses, 1987), pp. 43–62.

33   Iannis Xenakis, "The Monastery of La Tourette", p. x., gives a slightly contradictory account.

34   Philippe Potié, *Le Corbusier: The Monastery of Sainte Marie de La Tourette*, p. 80.

35   Ibid., p. 114.

36   See FLC 1075 in H. Allen Brooks, *The Le Corbusier Archive, Volume XXVIII*, p. 8 for the details of the cell.

37   Sekler notes a "return to the very fundamentals of pier-and-lintel architecture" that characterises the boat club at Chandigarh. Eduard F. Sekler and William Curtis, *Le Corbusier at Work: The Genesis of the Carpenter Centre for the Visual Arts* (Cambridge MA: MIT, 1978), p. 253.

38   Conversation Robert Rebutato with Flora Samuel, Paris, December 9, 2006.

39   Ferrao et al., *Le Corbusier, Le Couvent de la Tourette*, p. 63, footnote 2.

40   Le Corbusier, *Precisions* (Cambridge MA: MIT, 1991), p. 91. Originally published as Le Corbusier, *Précisions sur un état présent de l'architecture et de l'urbanisme* (Paris: Éditions Crès, 1930).

41   Marie-Alain Couturier, *Se garder libre, Journal (1947–1954)* (Paris: Cerf, 1962), pp. 44–45.

42   Giuliano Grisleri, *Le Corbusier, il viaggio in Toscana, 1907*, exhibition catalogue, Florence, Palazzo Pitti: Cataloghi Marsilio (Venice, 1987), p. 17. See also Couturier, *Se garder libre*, pp. 49–50.

43   Notes made in the summer of 1955. Le Corbusier, *Sketchbooks vol. 3 1954–1957* (Cambridge, MA: MIT, 1982), sketch 520.

44   Le Corbusier, *The Final Testament of Père Corbu: A Translation of Mise au Point* by Ivan Zacnic (New Haven: Yale, 1997), p. 91. Originally published as *Mise au Point* (Paris: Éditions Forces-Vives, 1966).

45   A.-M.Cocagnac, "Ronchamp", *L'Art sacré*, 1–2, September–October 1955.

46   Casali, "Marie-Alain Couturier et Le Corbusier", p. 96.

47   Le Corbusier, *L'Homme et l'architecture*, 12–13 (1947), p. 5.

48   Le Corbusier, *The Modulor* (London: Faber and Faber), p. 140.

49   Ibid.

50   For a discussion of the spiritual concerns between the Unité see Flora Samuel, "Le Corbusier, Teilhard de Chardin and the Planetisation of Mankind", *Journal of Architecture*, 4 (1999) pp. 149–16.

51   Jean Petit, *Un Couvent de Le Corbusier* (Paris, Les Éditions de Minuit, 1961), p. 28.

52   This is endorsed by Roberto Gargiani and Anna Rosellini, *Le Corbusier Béton Brut and Ineffable Space, 1940–1965* (Lausanne: EPFL, 2011), p. 502 who describe it as an "ideogram" and note that Iannis Xenakis described the form as a "Neuma", in other words a musical notation of Gregorian chant, Iannjs Xenakis, *Musique de l'architecture* (Marseilles: Parenthèses, 2006), p. 91, caption.

53   Le Corbusier, *Œuvre complète vol. 7, 1957–1965* (Zurich: Les Éditions d'Architecture 1955). Originally published in 1965, p. 37.

54   Le Corbusier interviewed by the Dominican monks in October 1960; published in "Le Couvent Sainte-Marie de La Tourette construit par Le Corbusier", *L'Art sacré*, 7-8, March/April 1960 quoted in Philippe Potié, *Le Corbusier: The Monastery of Sainte Marie de La Tourette*, p. 66.

55   See sketches of the acoustic conch, FLC 1312, FLC 1280, FLC 1237. There is an article on church acoustic "abats son", *L'Art sacré*, 3–4, November-December, 1950, pp. 31–32.

56   Potié, *Le Corbusier: The Monastery of Sainte Marie de La Tourette*, p. 56.

57   Ferrao et al., *Le Corbusier, Le Couvent de la Tourette*, p. 21.

58   Rowe, "La Tourette", p. 186.

59   Wolfgang Jean Stock, *European Church Architecture 1950–2000* (Munich: Prestel, 2002), p. 65.

60   Le Corbusier, *Œuvre complète vol. 5* (Zurich: Les Éditions d'Architecture, 1995), pp. 189–224.

61   Rowe, "La Tourette", p. 188.

62   Various different floor numbering systems are in use. We are using the version from the *Œuvre complète*.

63   Flora Samuel, *Le Corbusier in Detail* (London: Wiley, 2007), p. 150.

64   Nicholas Fox Weber, *Le Corbusier: A Life* (New York: Knopf, 2008), p. 729.

65   Father Vincent de Couesnongle, "Remarques, Noël 1955", FLC K3.15.5, quoted in Roberto Gargiani and Anna Rosellini, *Le Corbusier Béton Brut and Ineffable Space, 1940–1965* (Lausanne: EPFL, 2011), p. 500.

66   Réjean Legault, "The Semantics of Exposed Concrete", in Jean-Louis Cohen and G. Martin Moeller (eds.), *Liquid Stone: New Architecture in Concrete* (Basel: Birkhäuser, 2006), pp. 46–56.

67   Le Corbusier, *Œuvre complète vol 5*, p. 191.

68   Le Corbusier, *Œuvre complète vol. 6, 1952–1957* (Zurich: Les Éditions d'Architecture, 1985), p. 42. Originally published in 1957.

69   There is a sub-route to the lower level of the church at this point which is suppressed by various architectonic means meaning that the reader barely notices it.

70   For a detailed discussion of this see Roberto Gargiani and Anna Rosellini, *Le Corbusier Béton Brut and Ineffable Space*, pp. 503–509.

71   This separation is no longer imposed. Brother Marc Chauveau, interview with Inge Linder-Gaillard, January 9, 2012.

72   Iannis Xenakis, "The Monastery of La Tourette", p. xiii.

73   Potié, *Le Corbusier: The Monastery of Sainte Marie de La Tourette*, p. 70.

74   Letter from father Couesnongle to Le Corbusier. December 25, 1959: "Rapport sur l'ameublement de l'église de La Tourette". Cited in Luis Burriel Bielza, "Altar y la puerta en la iglesia parroquial de Saint- Pierre de Firminy Vert", le corbuiserinpar.wordpress.com, p. 5.

75   Le Corbusier interviewed by the Dominican monks in October 1960; published in "Le Couvent Sainte-Marie de La Tourette construit par Le Corbusier", *L'Art sacré*, 7-8, March-April 1960, quoted in Potié, *Le Corbusier: The Monastery of Sainte Marie de La Tourette*, p. 120.

76   The term *opus optimum* is used in Le Corbusier, *Œuvre complète vol. 7*, p. 51.

77   Letter Trouin to Le Corbusier, January 29, 1958, FLC 13 01 143.

78   Le Corbusier flatly rejected the contractor's suggestion to cover the walls

of the church to reduce the reverberation time. Philippe Potié, *Le Corbusier: The Monastery of Sainte Marie de La Tourette*, p. 74.

79 Ferrao et al. *Le Corbusier Le Couvent de la Tourettte*, p. 31.

80 Iannis Xenakis, "The Monastery of La Tourette", p. xiii.

81 Letter Trouin to Le Corbusier, December 27, 1960, FLC 13 01 189.

82 The current state of the underground level of the sacristy, where one altar exists, shows evidence of the intention of additional ones being added, which never happened. The plans in Le Corbusier, *Œuvre complète vol. 6*, p. 46 also testify to this.

83 Robert Maguire and Keith Murray, *Modern Churches of the World*, p. 52.

84 Patrick Hodgkinson, "St Peter's Seminary, Cardross", *Mac Journal One*, 1994, p. 42.

85 Ibid., p. 43.

86 Hodgkinson, "St Peter's Seminary, Cardross", p. 42.

87 www.curia.op.org/en/ accessed June 17, 2009.

88 Le Corbusier, "Unités d'habitation de grandeur conforme", April 1957, FLC A3-1. Cited in Potié, *Le Corbusier: The Monastery of Sainte Marie de La Tourette*, p. 116.

89 Rowe, *'La Tourette'*, p. 194.

90 Guieuillette, "Le Corbusier and the Dominicans", p. 54.

91 André Malraux, "Funérailles de Le Corbusier", *Malraux, Oraisons funebres* (Paris: Gallimard, 1971), pp. 103–114.

92 Ibid.

93 Le Corbusier, *Œuvre complète vol 7*, p. 53.

94 Note from Le Corbusier to Andre Wogenscky, March 21, 1956. Quoted in Potié, *Le Corbusier: The Monastery of Sainte Marie de La Tourette*, p. 76.

CHAPTER 6

1 Le Corbusier, *Œuvre complète vol. 7, 1957–1965* (Zurich: Les Éditions d'Architecture, 1995). Originally published in 1965, p. 137.

2 A.-M. Cocagnac, untitled article in *L'Art sacré*, "Un projet d'église paroissiale de Le Corbusier", 3–4, November-December 1964, p. 3.

3 Le Corbusier, *The Final Testament of Père Corbu: A Translation of Mise au Point* by Ivan Zacnic

(New Haven: Yale, 1997), p. 91. Originally published as *Mise au Point* (Paris: Éditions Forces-Vives, 1966).

4 Originally three *unités d'habitation* were commissioned and also a swimming pool, which was finally designed and built by another of Le Corbusier's architects, André Wogensky, from 1969 to 1971 in proximity to the stadium and, now, the church.

5 The Association was founded in 1968 by Eugène Claudius-Petit and was then led by his son Dominique.

6 "Description de l'église paroissiale St Pierre de Firminy-Vert", typed document, February 10, 1964, FLC N1.2 (90).

7 *Le Corbusier in Detail* (London: Academy, 2007), p. 82.

8 The two roof skylights do not feature in the drawings or plans of December 1963 and are not mentioned in the final written descriptions of February 1964. They reappear however in the final model of 1964 and are essential to Le Corbusier's project, thus included here. One can speculate they briefly disappeared in an effort to demonstrate the architect's willingness to eliminate costly "details".

9 "Projet pour la construction de l'église St. Pierre de Firminy à Firminy-Vert", typed document, February 15, 1964, FLC N1.2 (100-104).

10 This statistic was provided by the Parish Association to Le Corbusier in early 1961. See "FY Vert – Paroisse St Pierre – Eglise et Centre paroissial", FLC U1.19 (9) and footnote 26.

11 Claudius-Petit solicited Le Corbusier for the church on January 31, 1960.

12 See Eugène Claudius-Petit, "Firminy-Vert", in Le Corbusier's *Œuvre complète vol. 8, Les dernières œuvres* (Zurich: Les Éditions d'Architecture, 1970), p. 10. This scene is described as taking place on June 19, 1960.

13 As cited in *Firminy, Le Patrimoine Le Corbusier*, Service Architecturel et Culturel de la Ville de Firminy, 1995, p. 32.

14 Le Corbusier rejected a commission offered by Louis Secretan, a pastor at La Chaux-de-Fonds, on the basis of the site. Martin Purdy, "Le Corbusier and the Theological Programme", in Russell Walden (ed.), *The Open Hand: Essays on Le Corbusier* (Cambridge MA: MIT, 1977), p. 291.

15 In Eugène Claudius-Petit, "Note sur l'implantation de St Pierre de Firminy-Vert", May 3, 1966, pp. 1–2, typescript, as cited by Anthony Eardley, "Grandeur is the Intention", in Ann Bremner (ed.), *Architecture Interruptus* (Columbus: Wexner Center for the Arts, The Ohio State University, 2007), p. 71, n. 11. Originally published in Kenneth Frampton and Silvia Kolbowski (ed.) *Le Corbusier's Firminy Church* (New York: Rizzoli, 1981).

16 In 1946, as the Minister of Reconstruction and Urbanism, Raoul Dautry had sent Claudius-Petit and Le Corbusier off together to the United States to study the workings of the Tennessee Valley Authority.

17 Letter Le Corbusier to Claudius-Petit, October 23, 1962, FLC N1.2 (129).

18 We thank Father Jean-Louis Reymondier and Jean-Michel Larois for this information provided in an interview conducted with Inge Linder-Gaillard on October 17, 2011 on the Parish Association and the diocese's involvement in the commission.

19 There is very little written on Father Tardy. Many thanks again to Father Jean-Louis Reymondier, who knew Father Tardy as a young person growing up in Firminy and from his involvement in the evolution of the church in Firminy since. Ibid.

20 Letter Jean-François Baud to Le Corbusier, March 29, 1963, FLC N1.2 (135).

21 See Olivier Chatelan, "Les catholiques et l'urbanisation française", *Vingtième Siècle. Revue d'histoire*, 2011/3 no. 111, p. 151.

22 Eardley, "Grandeur is the Intention", p. 61.

23 Citation by Claudius-Petit in "Firminy-Vert", in *Œuvre complète vol. 8*, p. 11.

24 Olivier Chatelan, "Les catholiques et l'urbanisation française", *Vingtième Siècle. Revue d'histoire*, 2011/3 no. 111, p. 155.

25 The Parish Association made a first, one page list in June 1960, FLC U1.19 (1), dated by Le Corbusier June 19, 1960; this was elaborated on several months later into a three page document with some changes, dated January 8, 1961, received by Le Corbusier on 11 February 1961, FLC U1.19 (9-11). This description refers to the 1961 document.

26 Ibid.

27 Ibid.

28 Le Corbusier, "Rome byzantine", *L'Art sacré*, "Rome", 9–10, May-June 1962, pp. 5–6.

29 Luis Burriel Bielza, "El Altar y la Puerta" en la iglesia parroquial de Saint-Pierre de Firminy Vert, le corbusierin-par.wordpress.com, p. 44.

30 Letter Le Corbusier to Claudius-Petit, June 22, 1961, FLC N1.2 (5).

31 "Un projet d'église paroissiale de Le Corbusier", *L'Art Sacré*, 3–4, November-December 1964.

32 Ibid., p. 6.

33 For an extensive discussion of this topos see Flora Samuel, *Le Corbusier in Detail* (London: Academy, 2007), pp. 199–206.

34 See a sketch by Le Corbusier of the Hagia Sofia dated 1936 that he provided to be featured in Keller Smith Jr. and Reyhan Tansal (eds.), *The Development by Le Corbusier of the Design for the Église de Firminy, a church in France*, Student Publications of the School of Design, North Carolina State University at Raleigh, Volume 14, number 2, 1964, not paginated.

35 See for example Jeffrey Kipnis' essay "A Time for Freedom", p. 15; José Oubrerie, "Architecture Before Geometry, or the Primacy of Imagination", p. 41, who states on the Chandigarh building that it "is a gigantic hyperboloid of revolution, piercing the square roof-platform of the Chandigarh building, as an expression of the primacy of the elected institution and also as a witness to Le Corbusier's fascination with the cooling towers and their power as skyline", and Eardley, p. 66, all in Brenner (ed.), *Architecture Interruptus*.

36 Eardley, "Grandeur is the Intention", p. 66.

37 According to a letter from Le Corbusier to Fernand Gardien dated June 26, 1961, FLC N1.2(6), he had just given the initial plans to the parish committee. Le Corbusier also sent the plans, dated June 10, 1961, to Claudius-Petit. Letter Le Corbusier to Claudius-Petit, July 6, 1961, FLC N1.2 (7).

38 This is best observed by going through the lengthy correspondence between all parties involved held at the FLC.

39 In *L'Église Saint-Pierre de Firminy-Vert, Ensemble, reprenons le chantier*, p. 10.

40 For a discussion of the spiral see Flora Samuel, *Le Corbusier and the Architectural Promenade* (Basel: Birkhäuser, 2010), pp. 56–57.

41 Jean Petit, *Le Corbusier lui-même* (Paris: Forces Vives, 1970), p. 184.

42 Le Corbusier, in "The development by Le Corbusier of the design for l'Église de Firminy, a church in France", pp. 14 and 39. Burriel Bielza, p. 8.

43 While Le Corbusier numbered the evolution of the project into four phases, Gilles Ragot convincingly presents six phases of project development, laid out in "'Cette église elle existe'. La construction de l'église Saint-Pierre de Firminy 1958–2006", in Xavier Guillot (ed.), *Firminy: Le Corbusier en heritage*, Publications de l'université Saint-Etienne, 2008, pp. 77–80.

44 For the written description see FLC N1.2 (90-98) dated February 10, 1964 and FLC N1.2 (100-104) dated February 15, 1964. For the drawings, sections (EG FIR 6104), elevations (EG FIR 6105), plans (EG FIR 6103) and model (wood, made by Claude Dirlik) dated December 23, 1963 see Frampton and Kolbowski (eds.), *Le Corbusier's Firminy Church*, pp. 80-83. Ragot points out that Le Corbusier had the plans dated December 12, 1962 published in *Œuvre complète vol. 7, 1957–65*, pp. 138–139 and did not publish in his lifetime the December 1963 plans, or the final changes proposed later in 1964–65 (though the famous drawing dated September 19, 1963 circulated widely). Ragot suggests Le Corbusier preferred the December 1962 plans, which may well have been, but for our purposes here the December 1963 plans and early 1964 description must be taken into account. Ragot, ibid., p. 79. It should be noted that the Dirlik model probably dates from later in 1964 (In *L'Art sacré* it is dated December 1964, p. 20).

45 Le Corbusier, *Œuvre complète vol. 7*, p. 137.

46 As pointed out by Gilles Ragot, citing Claudius-Petit's account of the clergy's request for the placement of the church in a document from his archives: "Note sur l'implantation de St-Pierre de Firminy-Vert", typed note, dated May 3, 1966, Eugène Claudius-Petit Archives, p. 1–2, in Gilles Ragot, "'Cette église elle existe'. La construction de l'église Saint-

Pierre de Firminy 1958–2006", in *Firminy: Le Corbusier en heritage*, p. 76.

47 Gilles Ragot, *Le Corbusier à Firminy-Vert, manifeste pour un urbanisme moderne* (Paris: Éditions du patrimoine, Centre des monuments nationaux, 2011), p. 318.

48 See Le Corbusier's sketches dated October 28, 1961 featured in Keller Smith Jr. and Reyhan Tansal (eds.), *The Development by Le Corbusier of the Design for the l'Eglise de Firminy, a church in France*, not paginated.

49 Eduard F. Sekler and William Curtis, *Le Corbusier at Work: The Genesis of the Carpenter Centre for the Visual Arts* (Cambridge MA: MIT, 1978), p. 18 and p. 182.

50 For a discussion of a similar space see Samuel, *Le Corbusier in Detail*, pp. 202–206.

51 The prominent lavabo at La Thoronet provides a case in point.

52 See Colin Rowe, *The Architecture of Good Intentions* (London: Academy Editions, 1994), p. 60 on the Villa Savoye as quoted by Flora Samuel in *Le Corbusier in Detail*, in the section on water, p. 185. She gives further examples in footnote 34 of this section.

53 See Samuel, *Le Corbusier in Detail*, p. 183; José Oubrerie reported to Samuel in an email letter, April 2006, that the Church rejected Le Corbusier's idea for the baptistery for total immersion. Apparently the gutter ring was created in Memory of Le Corbusier by Oubrerie but there are several versions of it on the design sketches made by Le Corbusier. Eardley, *Le Corbusier's Firminy Church*, p. 20.

54 As pointed out by Uwe Bernhardt in *Le Corbusier et le projet de la modernité, la rupture avec l'intériorité* (Paris: L'Harmattan, 2002), p. 44.

55 "Bâtir et aménager les églises. Le lieu de la célébration", *La Maison-Dieu* n. 63, 4th trimester 1960, Les Éditions du Cerf, p. 105 quoted in Burriel Bielza, "El Altar y la Puerta", p. 3.

56 Martin Purdy, "Le Corbusier's Theological Programme", in Walden (ed.), *The Open Hand*, p. 309.

57 Noted by Le Corbusier in his commentary on a sketch dated June 10, 1961, "outils de culte", as published in Smith and Tansal (eds.), *The Development by Le Corbusier of the Design for l'Église de Firminy*.

58 "Projet pour la construction de l'église St. Pierre de Firminy à Firminy-Vert", February 15, 1964, FLC N1.2 (100-104).

59 José Oubrerie based it on the Orion constellation.

60 Anthony Eardley, "Grandeur is the Intention", p. XX.

61 Featured in Frampton and Kolbowski (eds.), *Le Corbusier's Firminy Church*, p. 62.

62 Burriel Bielza, "El Altar y la Puerta", p. 50.

63 Ibid.

64 Burriel Bielza, "El Altar y la Puerta", p. 47.

65 Ibid., p. 7.

66 Ibid.

67 Todd Wilmert, "The 'Ancient fire, the hearth of tradition': creation and combustion in Le Corbusier's studio residences" *arq* (2006), 10, pp. 57–78.

68 See for example Letter Le Corbusier to Yvonne, October 24, 1928, in J. Jenger, *Le Corbusier Choix de Lettres* (Basel: Birkhäuser, 2002), p. 199. Also Flora Samuel, *Le Corbusier: Architect and Feminist* (London: Wiley, 2004), p. 14.

69 Document "Note sur une conversation entre Mazioux et Eugène Claudius-Petit", October 1, 1962, Archives of the Saint-Étienne Diocese.

70 See Eugène Claudius-Petit's text "Firminy-Vert", *Œuvre complète vol. 8, Le Corbusier les dernières œuvres/The Last Works* (Zurich, Éditions d'Architecture Artemis, 1970), pp. 10–11.

71 Anthony Eardley, "Grandeur is the Intention", pp. 61–72.

72 Even if in theory, the Parish Assocations were free to chose their own architects and establish their projects with them – the Office was meant to serve as a sort of consulting agency. See Chatelan, "Les catholiques et l'urbanisation française", *Vingtième Siècle. Revue d'histoire*, 2011/3 no. 111, p. 156.

73 We thank Jean-Louis Reymondier for information leading to this reading of the situation.

74 See the letter from Pelnard-Considère and Cie. to Le Corbusier warning this, January 17, 1963, FLC N1.2 (23).

75 Contract signed May 22, 1963, FLC N1.2, (138-139).

76 Letter Parish Association's new president, M. Portafaix, to Le Corbusier April 7, 1964, FLC N1.2 (51-52). It is speculated that Baud stepped down from his presidency in a refusal to renounce the project. J.L. Reymondier, interview October 17, 2011.

77 Letter Le Corbusier to Claudius-Petit, May 8, 1964, FLC N1.2 (53).

78 Letter Le Corbusier to Portafaix, asking him to reconsider, May 13, 1964, FLC N1.2 (54). Letter Tardy to Le Corbusier, with proposal for Tardy, Mazioux and Portafaix to go see him in Paris, June 2, 1964, FLC N1.2 (55). Letter Le Corbusier to Tardy, proposing July 8, 1964 as date for their visit, June 18, 1964, FLC N1.2 (58). Note Le Corbusier mentioning that meeting, but with Tardy and Portafaix, FLC U1.19 (102).

79 Issue assembled using the documents Le Corbusier had already prepared for the North Carolina book project earlier that year – a project he also probably accepted to drum up support. Smith and Tansal (eds.), *The Development by Le Corbusier of the Design for l'Eglise de Firminy.*

80 Letter Tardy to Le Corbusier, January 12, 1965, FLC U1 (19) 110.

81 Letter Le Corbusier to Tardy, January 28, 1965, FLC N1.2 (64-66).

82 Anthony Eardley, *Le Corbusier's Firminy Church*, p. 2.

83 Le Corbusier, interviewed in the journal *Le Progrès: le journal de Lyon*, October 20, 1960. Cited in Burriel Bielza, "El altar y la puerta".

84 Luke, 10: 38-42.

85 Ernest Renan, *La Vie de Jesus* (Paris: Calmann-Levy, 1906), p. 184, in FLC.

CHAPTER 7

1 Robert Maguire and Keith Murray, *Modern Churches of the World* (London: Studio Vista, 1965), p. 50.

2 Quoted from a talk arranged by the NCRG, in Hammond, Peter (ed.), *Towards a Church Architecture* (London: Architectural Press, 1962), p. 10.

3 Gilles Ragot, "'Cette église elle existe. La construction de l'église Saint-Pierre de Firminy 1958-2006", in *Firminy, Le Corbusier en héritage* (Publications de l'université de Saint-Étienne: Saint-Étienne, 2008), p. 75, footnote 2.

4 Charles Jencks, *Le Corbusier and the Continual Revolution in Architecture* (New York: The Monacelli Press, 2000), pp. 262–275.

5 Frédéric Migayrou, "Le monolithe fracturé", in Frédéric Migayrou (ed.), *Bloc: Le monolithe fracturé, édifices culturels, architecture de recherché*, (Orléans: Éditions HYX, 1996), small booklet version, p. 10.

6 The term "critical" is used here in the sense that the Frankfurt School employed the word, in their investigations of "critical theory", as developed by Max Horkheimer, Theodor W. Adorno, and others. See, for example, Rolf Wiggerhaus, *The Frankfurt School: Its History, Theories and Political Significance* (Cambridge, Massachusetts: MIT Press), 1995.

7 Claude Parent and Paul Virilio, "Sacred architecture, architecture of Transference", in Frédéric Migayrou (ed.) *Nevers, Architecture Principe, Claude Parent, Claude Virilio*, (Orléans: Éditions HYX, Frac Centre, 2010) p. 79. Originally published as "l'Architecture sacrée, architecture de transfert", in *L'Architecture d'Aujourd'hui*, 125, April–May, 1966, p. 26.

8 Monseigneur Vial and the Abbé Bourgoin were thanked openly for their support by the architects in their review. See "Nevers chantier" issue of *Architecture principe*, 4, May–June 1966.

9 See "Interview with Paul Virilio / Entretien avec Paul Virilio", in Frédéric Migayrou (ed.), *Nevers, Architecture Principe, Claude Parent, Claude Virilio*, (Orléans: Éditions HYX, Frac Centre, 2010), pp. 18–19.

10 See for example Steve Redhead (ed.), *The Paul Virilio Reader* (New York: Columbia University Press, 2004).

11 Paul Virilio, *Bunker Archaeology* (New York: Princeton University Press, 1994). Originally published as *Bunker Archéologie, étude sur l'espace militaire européen de la Seconde Guerre mondiale* (Paris: Centre Georges Pompidou, Centre de Creation Industrielle, 1975) and reprinted (Paris: Éditions du demi-cercle, 1994).

12 They called this phenomenon "the third urban order", the name of the second issue of their self-published review. "Le troisième ordre urbain", *Architecture principe*, March 2, 1966, p. 6.

13 See biographical information sheets for Grand Palais exhibition, *Claude Parent*, 1970, unpublished document kept at the Documentation of the Musée National d'Art Moderne.

14 Sainte Bernadette's liturgical furnishings were designed by sculptor Maurice Lipsi, member of *architecture principe*.

15 For a more detailed discussion of this comparison, see Inge Linder, "Pilgrimage to the Millennium, Sacred Art and Architecture in Late Twentieth-Century France", PhD Thesis, Courtauld Institute, University of London, 2000, pp. 104–107.

16 A differently shaped bunker-like presbytery was also designed for the plot but was not built for lack of funds – and also the priest reportedly wanted to remain living in an apartment in the neighbourhood amongst the people – in worker-priest fashion? So it was never built. Its absence created the open land in front of the church.

17 Paul Virilio, *Bunker Archéologie* (Paris: Éditions du demi-cercle, 1994), p. 29.

18 Ibid., p. 46.

19 Paul Virilio in unpublished speech delivered on occasion of thirtieth anniversary celebration of Sainte Bernadette du Banlay, December 8, 1996, Nevers. Nevers City Archives. Le Corbusier too experimented with the recoding of instruments of war. The light canons of La Tourette provide a case in point. For Le Corbusier the atom bomb, which features in the *Poème électronique*, seems to have represented both the strength and negative potential of radiance gone wrong.

20 Paul Virilio, *Bunker Archéologie*, p. 14.

21 Laurent Lemire, "L'église-manifeste de Claude Parent", *La Croix*, September 23, 1996.

22 André Bloc and Claude Parent. This citation is reprinted in Frédéric Migayrou (ed.), *Bloc: le monolithe fracturé, édifices culturels, architecture de recherches* (Orléans: Éditions HYX, 1996), full catalogue version, p. 63. It originally appeared in *L'Architecture d'Aujourd'hui*, 24, December 1959. André Bloc founded the magazine in 1930. Claude Parent became a member of the editorial board in the 1950s.

23 The "ouvrages et obstacles" of the Atlantic Wall, counted at over fifteen thousand in 1944 (including four

thousand major works, and over nine thousand artillery batteries), were built under the direction of the Todt Organisation, often using French workers against their will, as their STO (service du travail obligatoire). Paul Virilio, *Bunker Archéologie*, p. 62.

24 See Béatrice Simonot, "Claude Parent, present in posterity / Claude Parent, present dans la postérité", in Frédéric Migayrou (ed.), *Nevers, Architecture Principe, Claude Parent, Claude Virilio*, (Orléans: Éditions HYX, Frac Centre, 2010) pp. 162-171 for a discussion of contemporary secular architecture influenced by the church of Sainte Bernadette.

25 The church suffered significant criticism locally and nationally, even before it was finished. See Aurélien Vernant, "Sainte Bernadette, the hardship of a crossing / Sainte-Bernadette, l'épreuve de la traversée", in ibid., pp. 154-161 for a history of the church's reception.

26 See Richard Meier and Partners, LLP, press release October 26, 2003, available from www.richardmeier.com. The other architects were Tadao Ando, Günter Behnisch, Santiago Calatrava, Peter Eisenman and Frank Gehry.

27 Ibid.

28 Richard Meier, *Richard Meier, Architect, 1999-2003, vol. 4* (New York: Rizzoli, 2004), p. 354.

29 Richard Meier, "Jubilee Church", *Richard Meier* (Milan: Electra architecture, 2003), p. 370. Originally published in Italian in 2002.

30 Yoshio Futagawa, interview with Stephen Holl, "Studio", *GA Document Extra Stephen Holl* (Tokyo: A.D.A. Edita, 1996), p. 31.

31 Ibid., p. 33.

32 Pierre Teilhard de Chardin, quoted by Stephen Holl in *Urbanisms, Working with Doubt* (New York: Princeton Architectural Press, 2009), p. 93.

33 Ibid., p. 93.

34 Ibid.

35 Dominique Machabert, interview with Alvaro Siza, "Siza au Thoronet : 'Une architecture d'une admirable clarté'", *Siza au Thoronet, le parcours et l'œuvre* (Marseilles: Éditions Parenthèses, 2007), p. 28.

36 See Dominique Machabert, interview with Alvaro Siza, "Au couvent de La Tourette, où il fut question de l'église de Marco de Canaveses", in *Alvaro Siza, une question de mesure* (Paris: Le Moniteur, 2008), p. 176.

37 See Cité de l'architecture et du patrimoine, dossier, "Le Corbusier, World Heritage Architecture / Une œuvre pour le patrimoine mondiale, a day of meetings and debates, Monday 9 May 2011 / journée de rencontres et débats, lundi 9 mai 2011", p. 15.

38 Alvaro Siza, "The Church at Marco de Canaveses", in Kenneth Frampton (ed.), *Alvaro Siza, Complete Works* (London: Phaidon, 2000), p. 377. Originally published in Milan: Electa, 1999.

39 Nuno Higino, "L'église paroissiale de Marco de Canaveses, Portugal, 1990-1997, Les chemins du cérémonial", *Siza au Thoronet, le parcours et l'œuvre* (Marseilles: Éditions Parenthèses, 2007), p. 99. Higino left the priesthood in 2005 to write a doctoral thesis in philosophy on "Alvaro Siza's Creative Process Based on Deconstruction". According to Dominique Machabert, "Au couvent de La Tourette, où il fut question de l'église de Marco de Canaveses", in *Alvaro Siza, une question de mesure*, p. 179.

40 See Dominique Machabert, interview with Alvaro Siza, "Au couvent de La Tourette, où il fut question de l'église de Marco de Canaveses", in *Alvaro Siza, une question de mesure*, p. 179.

41 Ibid., p. 184.

42 Yoshio Futagawa, interview with Alvaro Siza, "Santa Maria Church of Marco de Canaveses", *GA Documents Extra* (Tokyo: A.D.A. Edita, 1998), p. 37.

43 Ibid.

44 Alvaro Siza, "The Church at Marco de Canaveses", *Alvaro Siza, Complete Works*, p. 377.

45 Alvaro Siza in interview with Yoshio Futagawa, "Santa Maria Church of Marco de Canaveses", p. 37.

46 Ibid.

47 Alvaro Siza, interview with Marianne Brausch, in *L'Architecture en question, 15 entretiens avec des architectes* (Le Moniteur: Paris, 1996), p. 228.

48 See Laura Moffat, "Church of Santa Maria", *Contemporary Church Architecture* (Chichester: Wiley-Academy, 2007), p. 164.

49 Planning stage for the Chapel on Mount Rokko, Kobe, began in 1985 and the chapel was built by early 1986. The planning stage for the Church on the Water in Hokkaido began just as construction for the Rokko Chapel was under way, and it was built in 1988-1989. Planning for the Church of Light in Ibaraki, Osaka, began just before construction of the Church on the Water, and it was completed before the Church on the Water, in early 1989.

50 Ten years after the Church of Light was built, Ando received the commission from the same community to build a Sunday School addition. This project is not included in our discussion here for question of space. It is a remarkably coherent addition to the earlier church project and deserves more attention than the mere mention it gets here.

51 See Philip Drew, *Church on the Water, Church of the Light, Tadao Ando* (London: Phaidon, 1996), pp. 10-11.

52 Yann Nussaume quotes Ando in "Le regard du milieu: nature, site, tradition", in Yann Nussaume (ed.), *Tadao Ando et la question du milieu* (Paris: Le Moniteur, 2000), p. 126. The citation is taken from "Comment by Tadao Ando", *TAS*, December 1985.

53 Tadao Ando, "From the Church on the Water to the Church of the Light", in *Tadao Ando, Complete Works* (Milan: Electa, 1995), p. 455. Originally published in Italian in 1994. The article originally appeared in *The Japan Architect*, 386, June 1989.

54 Tadao Ando in interview with Anatxu Zabalbeascoa, "Architecture and Spirit", *Architecture and Spirit/arquitectura y espiritu, Tadao Ando* (Barcelona: Editorial Gustavo Gili, 1998), pp. 57-58.

55 William Curtis, "A Conversation with Tadao Ando", *Tadao Ando 1983-2000* (Madrid: El Croquis editorial, 2000), p. 15.

56 Tadao Ando, "De la périphérie de l'architecture", in Yann Nussaume (ed.), *Tadao Ando et la question du milieu* (Paris: Le Moniteur, 2000), p. 240.

57 Le Corbusier in Jean Petit (ed.), *Le Corbusier lui-même* (Geneva: Editions Rousseau, 1970), p. 181.

58 William Curtis, "A Conversation with Tadao Ando", p. 16.

59 Yoshio Futagawa, interview with Tadao Ando, "Meditation Space, Unesco", *GA Documents Extra* (Tokyo: A.D.A. Edita, 1995) p. 148.

60 Ibid.

61 Email Juan Carlos Sancho Osinaga to Flora Samuel, October 17, 2011.

62 Laura Moffatt points this out in "Private Chapel", *Contemporary Church Architecture* (Chicester: Wiley-Academy, 2007). She wrote, "Other planes slip and slide into place around the one perpendicular corner in which the cross sits – a metaphor if ever there was for the ordering and calming presence of God." p. 114.

63 Jerzy Soltan, "Working with Le Corbusier", in Allen Brooks, H. (ed.), *The Le Corbusier Archive, Volume XVII* (New York: Garland, 1983), pp. ix-xxiv (p. xiv).

64 Adam Sharr, "The Sedimentation of Memory", *Journal of Architecture*, 15, 4, p. 499. We are grateful to Sharr for drawing our attention to this building.

65 Ibid., p. 503.

66 Email Peter Sassenroth to Flora Samuel, January 17, 2012.

67 Petra Bahr, *The Chapel of Reconciliation* (Berlin: Kunstverlag Josef Fink, 2008), p. 29.

68 Ibid., p. 30.

69 Adam Sharr, "The Sedimentation of Memory", p. 505.

70 Ibid., p. 508.

71 Petra Bahr, *The Chapel of Reconciliation*, p. 45.

72 Adam Sharr, "Sedimentation of Memory", p. 502.

73 Email Peter Sassenroth to Flora Samuel, May 6, 2012.

74 Wolfgang Jean Stock, *European Church Architecture 1950–2000* (Munich: Prestel, 2005), p. 19.

CONCLUSION

1 This is reported, for example, in Suzanne Robin's *Églises modernes, Évolution des édifices religieux en France depuis 1956*, (Paris: Hermann, 1980), p. 75.

2 Gérard Monnier, "Actualité de l'art sacré", *L'Art en Europe. Les années décisives. 1945-1953*, exhibition catalogue (Musée d'art moderne de Saint-Étienne, Skira: 1987), p. 52, cited by Françoise Caussé in *La Revue "L'Art Sacré", le Débat en France sur l'art et la religion (1945–1954)*, (Paris: Cerf, 2010), p. 456.

3 See Holger Kleine, *The Drama of Space* (Basel: Birkhäuser, 2017).

4 Le Corbusier, *The City of Tomorrow*, trans. Frederick Etchells (London, 1929), p. 298.

5 "Du temple Paien a l'église chrétienne", *L'Art sacré*, 9-10, May-June, 1958, p. 5.

6 For a very twenty-first-century take on this subject see Ingrid Fetell Lee, *Joyful: The Surprising Power of Ordinary Things to Create Extraordinary Happiness* (New York: Rider, 2018).

7 Pierre Bourdieu, *The Rules of Art*, trans. Susan Emanuel (Cambridge: Polity, 2005), p. 314.

8 Ibid.

9 Purple is the colour of royalty, in Catholic terms the colour of Lent, in alchemical terms the fusion of male and female, red and blue.

SELECTED BIBLIOGRAPHY

Abbott, W.M, S.J. (ed.), *The Documents of Vatican II* (London: Geoffrey Chapman, 1966).

Abram, J., Cohen, J.-L. and Lambert, G. (eds.), *Encyclopédie Perret* (Paris: Monum, Éditions du Patrimoine, Institut français d'architecture, Le Moniteur, 2002).

Ando, T., *Tadao Ando 1983-2000* (Madrid: El Croquis Editorial, 2000).

Ando, T., Rodriguez, M.J. and Zabalbeascoa, A., *Architecture and Spirit / arquitectura y espiritu, Tadao Ando* (Barcelona: Editorial Gustavo Gili, 1998).

Beaudouin, L. and Machabert, D., *Alvaro Siza, une question de mesure* (Paris: Le Moniteur, 2008).

Benton, T. (ed.), *Le Corbusier Architect of the Century* (London: Arts Council, 1987).

Billot, M., "Le père Couturier et l'art sacré", *Paris-Paris, 1937–1957* (Paris: Centre Pompidou, 1981) pp. 292–303.

Billot, M. (ed.), Couturier, M.-A., Matisse, H., Rayssiguier, L.B., *The Vence Chapel, the archive of a creation* (Milan: Skira, Houston: Menil Foundation, 1999), translated by Michael Taylor. Originally published as *La chapelle de Vence, Journal d'une création* (Paris: Cerf, Geneva: Skira, Houston: Menil Foundation, Inc., 1993).

Billy, A., "La Sainte-Baume contre Lourdes!", *Figaro*, December 9, 1948, front page.

Billy, A., "Sainte Baume", *Figaro*, December 16, 1948, p. 2.

Biot, F., Bourdeau, M., Duverger, A., Perrot, F., Tournié, L., *Le Corbusier et l'architecture sacrée, Sainte-Marie-de-la-Tourette-Éveux* (Lyon: La Manufacture, 1985).

Birksted, J., *Le Corbusier and the Occult* (Cambridge MA: MIT, 2009).

Blanchet, C. and Vérot, P., *Architecture et arts sacrés de 1945 à nos jours* (Paris: Archibooks + Satereau Éditeur, 2015).

Bony, J., *L'art sacré au XXe siècle en France* (Thonon-les-Bains: Éditions de l'Albaron, Société Présence du Livre; Boulogne-Billancourt: Musée Municipale de Boulogne-Billancourt, Centre Culturel de Boulogne-Billancourt 1993).

Brausch, M. and Emery, M. (eds.), *L'Architecture en question, 15 entretiens avec des architectes* (Paris: Le Moniteur, 1996).

Bremner, A. (ed.), *Architecture Interruptus* (Columbus, Ohio: Wexner Center for the Arts, The Ohio State University, 2007).

Breton, A., *Arcane 17* (Paris: Jean-Jacques Pauvert, 1971). Originally published in 1947.

Brooks, H.A., *Le Corbusier's Formative Years* (London: University of Chicago Press, 1997).

Brunet-Weinmann, M., *Le souffle et la flamme, Marie-Alain Couturier au Canada et ses lettres à Louise Gadbois* (Quebec City: Les éditions du Septentrion, 2016).

Buchanan, S. (ed.), *The Portable Plato* (Harmondsworth: Penguin, 1997).

Cali, F., *The Architecture of Truth: The Cistercian Abbey of le Thoronet in Provence* (London: Thames and Hudson, 1957). Originally published as *La plus grande aventure du monde, l'architecture mystique de Cîteaux* (Grenoble: Arthaud, 1956). Photographs by Lucien Hervé, preface by Le Corbusier, foreword by R.P. Régamey.

Capellades, J., *Guide des églises nouvelles en France* (Paris: Cerf, 1969).

Carl, P., "Le Corbusier's Penthouse in Paris: 24 Rue Nungesser et Coli", *Daidalos*, 28 (June 15, 1988), pp. 65–75.

Carl, P., "Architecture and time: a prolegomena", *AA Files*, 22 (autumn 1991), pp. 48–65.

Carl, P., "Ornament and time: a prolegomena", *AA Files*, 23 (summer 1992), pp. 49–64.

Caussé, F., *La Revue "L'Art sacré", le débat en France sur l'art et la religion (1945–1954)*, (Paris: Cerf, 2010).

Caussé, F. and Crippa, M.-A., *Le Corbusier: The Chapel of Notre-Dame du Haut at Ronchamp* (London: Royal Academy of Arts, 2015). Originally published as *Le Corbusier: Ronchamp, La cappella di Notre-Dame du Haut* (Milan: Editoriale Jaca Book SpA, 2014).

Chatelan, O., "Les catholiques et l'urbanisation française", *Vingtième Siècle. Revue d'histoire*, 2011/3, 111, pp. 147–158.

Chauveau, M. and Kiefer, A., *Anselm Kiefer à la Tourette* (La Garenne-Colombes: Couleurs contemporaines and Bernard Chauveau Édition, 2019).

Christ-Janer, A. and Mix Foley, M., *Modern Church Architecture* (London: McGraw Hill, 1962).

Cocagnac, A.-M., "Ronchamp", *L'Art sacré*, 1–2, 1955.

Cocagnac, A.-M., "Un projet d'église paroissiale de Le Corbusier", *L'Art sacré*, 3–4, 1964.

Coll, J., "Le Corbusier. Taureaux: An Analysis of the thinking process in the last series of Le Corbusier's Plastic work", *Art History*, 18, 4 (December 1995), pp. 537–568.

Coll, J., "Structure and Play in Le Corbusier's Art Works", *AA Files*, 31 (1996), pp. 4–14.

Colli, L.M., "Le Corbusier e il colore; I Claviers Salubra", *Storia dell'arte*, 43 (1981), pp. 271–291.

Collins, P., *Concrete, The Vision of a New Architecture* (New York: Horizon Press, 1959).

Couturier, M.-A., "Aux grands hommes, les grandes choses", *L'Art sacré "Le Prêtre et la création artistique"*, 9–10 (1950), pp. 3–7.

Couturier, M.-A., "Religious Art and the Modern Artist", *Magazine of Art*, November 1951.

Couturier, M.-A., "Le Corbusier, Ronchamp", *L'Art sacré "Espagne"*, 11–12 (1953) pp. 28–31.

Couturier, M.-A., "Le Corbusier", *L'Art sacré*, 7–8 (1954) pp. 9–11.

Couturier, M.-A., *Se garder libre, Journal (1947-1954)* (Paris: Cerf, 1962).

Couturier, M.-A., *Dieu et art dans la vie* (Paris: Cerf, 1965).

Couturier, M.-A., "L'appel aux maîtres de l'art moderne", *Paris-Paris, 1937–1957* (Paris: Centre Pompidou, 1981) pp. 304–307.

Couturier, M.-A., *Sacred Art* (Austin: University of Texas Press, Houston: Menil Foundation, 1989). Originally published as *Art sacré* (Paris: Herscher, Houston: Menil Foundation, 1983).

Culot, M., Peyceré, D. and Ragot, G. (eds.), *Les frères Perret, l'œuvre complète, les archives d'Auguste Perret (1874–1954) et Gustave Perret (1976–1952) architectes-entrepreneurs* (Paris: Institut français d'architecture, Norma, 2000).

Dal Co, F., *Tadao Ando, Complete Works* (London: Phaidon, 1995). Originally published as *Tadao Ando. Le opere, gli scritti, la critica* (Milan: Electa, 1994).

Debuyst, F., *L'Art chrétien contemporain de 1962 à nos jours* (Paris: Mame, 1988).

Debuyst, F., *Le renouveau de l'Art sacré de 1920 à 1962* (Paris: Mame, 1991).

de Smet, C. *Vers une architecture du livre. Le Corbusier: édition et mise en pages 1912–1965* (Baden: Lars Müller Publishers, 2007).

Devoucoux du Buysson, P., *Le guide du pèlerin à la grotte de sainte Marie Madeleine* (La Sainte Baume: La Fraternité Sainte Marie Madeleine, 1998).

Dion, M. and Ragot, P., *Le Corbusier en France, projets et réalisations* (Paris: Electa Moniteur, 1987).

Donada, J., Liaudet, D., Mathey, J.-M. and Parent, C., *Ronchamp, Le Corbusier/Photographies de Charles Bueb* (Orléans: Œuvre photographique Charles Bueb, 2018).

Drew, P., *Church on the Water, Church of the Light, Tadao Ando* (London: Phaidon, 1996).

Duffy, E., *Saints and Sinners, a History of the Popes* (New Haven and London: Yale University Press, 2006). Originally published in 1997.

Dupont, R., "Près de Marseille dans les forêts millénaires de la Sainte-Baume la 'cathédrale engloutie' surgira pour devenir la basilique de la Paix", *L'Aube* (June 2, 1948), front page.

Fagan-King, J., "United on the Threshold of the Twentieth Century Mystical Ideal", *Art History*, 11, 1 (March 1988), pp. 89–113.

Faure, É., *Fonction du Cinéma: de la cinéplastique à son destin social* (Paris: Éditions Gonthier, 1995), p. 12. Originally published in 1953.

Flicoteaux, A., "La commission d'art sacré de Besançon, 1945–1955", *Bulletin du centre de recherche d'art comtois, no. 12, 1998–1999* (Besançon: Université de Franche-Comté, 2000), pp. 41–52.

Frampton, K. (ed.), *Alvaro Siza, Complete Works* (London: Phaidon, 2000), p. 377. Originally published at Milan: Electa, 1999.

Frampton, K. and S. Kolbowki (eds.), *Le Corbusier's Firminy Church* (New York: Institute for Architecture and Urban Studies and Rizzoli, 1981).

Futagawa, Y. (ed.), *Tadao Ando, GA Documents Extra* (Tokyo: A.D.A. Edita, 1995).

Futagawa, Y. (ed.), *Stephen Holl, GA Document Extra* (Tokyo: A.D.A. Edita, 1996).

Futagawa, Y. (ed.), *Alvaro Siza, GA Documents Extra* (Tokyo: A.D.A. Edito, 1998).

Gargiani, R., *Auguste Perret, la théorie et l'œuvre* (Milan: Gallimard/Electa, 1993, 1994 for French edition), translated from Italian to French by Odile Ménégaux.

Ghyka, M., *Esthétique des proportions dans le nature et dans les arts* (Paris: Gallimard, 1927).

Ghyka, M., *Nombre d'or: rites et rhythmes Pythagoriciens dans le développement de la civilisation occidentale* (Paris: Gallimard, 1931).

Gimpel, J., *Les Bâtisseurs de Cathédrales* (Paris: Éditions Seuil, 1959), in FLC.

Gorringe, T. J., *A Theology of the Built Environment: Justice: Empowerment, Redemption* (Cambridge: Cambridge University Press, 2001).

Gresleri, G., "Prima da Ronchamp La Sainte Baume: Terra e cielo, ombra e luce", *Parametro*, 207, 1995, pp. 34–43.

Gresleri, G. and Gresleri, G. (eds.), *Le Corbusier il programma liturgico* (Bologna: Editrice Compositori, 2001).

Guardini, Romano, *The Spirit of the Liturgy* (Crossroads US, 1998). Originally published in 1918.

Gueullette, J.-M., "Le Corbusier and the Dominicans", *La Tourette, le cinquantenaire, 1959–2009, rencontre Le Corbusier-François Morellet: regards contemporains [de] Philippe Chancel, Stéphane Couturier, Pascal Hausberr* (La Garenne-Comombes: Couleurs contemporaines, Éditions Bernard Chauveau, 2009).

Guillot, X. (ed.), *Firminy: Le Corbusier en heritage* (Saint-Étienne: Publications de l'Université Saint-Étienne, 2008).

Guthrie, W.K.C., *Orpheus and Greek Religion* (London: Methuen, 1935).

Hammond, P., "A Liturgical Brief", *Architectural Review*, April 1958.

Hammond, P., *Towards a Church Architecture* (London, Architectural Press, 1962).

Haskins, S., *Mary Magdalene* (London: Harper Collins, 1993).

Heathcote, E., and Moffat, L., *Contemporary Church Architecture* (London: Wiley-Academy, 2007).

Heft, J., *A Catholic Modernity* (Oxford University Press, 1999).

H.F., "Le Plateau Provençal de La Sainte Baume: abritera-t-il un jour une église rupestre?", *Le Monde*, July 5, 1948, p. 3.

Holl, S., *Urbanisms, Working with Doubt* (New York: Princeton Architectural Press, 2009).

Jacques-Marie, Soeur, *Henri Matisse: The Vence Chapel* (Nice: Gardette, 2001) translated by B. Freed. Originally published as *Henri Matisse: La chapelle de Vence* (Nice: Gardette, 1992), new edition published in 2003.

James-Chakraborty, K., *German Architecture for a Mass Audience* (London: Routledge, 2000).

Jencks, C., *Le Corbusier and the Tragic View of Architecture* (London: Allen Lane, 1973).

Jencks, C., *Le Corbusier and the Continual Revolution in Architecture* (New York: The Montacelli Press, 2000).

Jenger, J., *Le Corbusier Choix de Lettres* (Basel: Birkhäuser, 2002).

Jung, C.G., *Alchemical Studies, Collected Works 13* (London: Routledge, Kegan and Paul, 1951).

Kieckhefer, R., *Theology in Stone* (Oxford University Press, 2004).

Kilde, J. H., *Sacred Power, Sacred Space* (Oxford University Press, 2008).

Kleine, H., *The Drama of Space* (Basel: Birkhäuser, 2017).

Krustrup., M., *l'Iliade Dessins* (Copenhagen: Borgen, 1986).

Krustrup, M., "Poème de l'Angle Droit", *Arkitekten*, 92 (1990), pp. 422-432.

Krustrup, M., *Porte Email* (Copenhagen: Arkitektens Forlag, 1991).

Lahiji, N., "The Gift of the Open Hand: Le Corbusier's Reading Georges Bataille's La Part Maudite", *Journal of Architectural Education*, 50, 1 (1996), pp. 50–67.

Le Corbusier, *Journey to the East* (Cambridge: MIT, 1987). Originally published as *Le Voyage d'Orient* (Paris: Parenthèses, 1887).

Le Corbusier, *Towards an Architecture* (London: Architectural Press, 1982). Originally published as *Vers une architecture* (Paris: Crès, 1923).

Le Corbusier, *The Decorative Art of Today* (London: The Architectural Press, 1987). Originally published as *L'Art décoratif d'aujourd'hui* (Paris: Crès, 1925).

Le Corbusier, *Urbanisme* (Paris: Éditions Arthaud), 1980. Originally published in 1925.

Le Corbusier, *Une Maison – un palais, À la recherche d'une unité architecturale* (Paris: Crès, 1928).

Le Corbusier, *Precisions on the Present State of Architecture and City Planning* (Cambridge, MA: MIT, 1991). Originally published as *Précisions sur un état présent de l'architecture et de l'urbanisme* (Paris: Crès, 1930).

Le Corbusier, "Perret par Le Corbusier", *L'Architecture d'Aujourd'hui*, 3,7 (1932), pp. 6–9.

Le Corbusier and Pierre Jeanneret, *Œuvre complète Volume 2, 1929–34* (Zurich: Les Éditions d'Architecture, 1995). Originally published in 1935.

Le Corbusier, *The Radiant City* (London, Faber, 1967). Originally published as *La Ville Radieuse* (Paris: Éditions de l'Architecture d'Aujourd'hui, 1935).

Le Corbusier and Pierre Jeanneret, *Œuvre complète Volume 1, 1910-1929* (Zurich: Girsberger, 1943). Originally published in 1937, new edition Zurich: Les Éditions de l'Architecture, 1995.

Le Corbusier, *When the Cathedrals were White: A Journey to the Country of the Timid People* (New York: Reynal and Hitchcock, 1947). Originally published as *Quand les cathédrales étaient blanches* (Paris: Plon, 1937).

Le Corbusier and Pierre Jeanneret, *Œuvre complète Volume 3, 1934-38* (Zurich: Les Éditions Girsberger, 1945). Originally published in 1938, new edition Zurich: Les Éditions de l'Architecture, 1995.

Le Corbusier, *Le Corbusier Talks with Students* (New York: Orion, 1961). Originally published as *Entretien avec les étudiants des écoles d'architecture* (Paris: Denoël 1943), new edition: New York: Princeton Architectural Press, 2003.

Le Corbusier, *Œuvre complète Volume 4, 1938-1946* (Zurich: Les Éditions d'Architecture, 1995). Originally published in 1946.

Le Corbusier, *The City of Tomorrow* (London: Architectural Press, 1946).

Le Corbusier, *A New World of Space* (New York: Reynal Hitchcock, 1948).

Le Corbusier, *Poésie sur Alger* (Paris: Éditions Connivances, 1989). Originally published in 1950.

Le Corbusier, *Modulor* (London: Faber, 1954). Originally published as *Le Modulor* (Paris: Éditions de l'Architecture d'Aujourd'hui, 1950).

Le Corbusier, *Œuvre complète Volume 5, 1946-1952* (Zurich: Les Éditions d'Architecture, 1973). Originally published in 1953.

Le Corbusier, *Le Poème de l'angle droit* (Paris: Éditions Connivance, 1989). Originally published in 1955.

Le Corbusier, *Modulor 2* (London: Faber, 1955). Originally published as *Le Modulor II* (Paris: Les Éditions de l'Architecture d'Aujourd'hui, 1955).

Le Corbusier, *Œuvre complète Volume 6, 1952–1957* (Zurich: Les Éditions d'Architecture, 1985). Originally published in 1957.

Le Corbusier, *The Chapel at Ronchamp* (London: Architectural Press, 1957).

Le Corbusier, *Le Poème Electronique* (Paris: Les Cahiers Forces Vives aux Éditions de Minuit, 1958).

Le Corbusier, *Œuvre complète Volume 7, 1957–1965* (Zurich: Les Éditions d'Architecture, 1995). Originally published in 1965.

Le Corbusier, *The Final Testament of Père Corbu: A Translation and Interpretation of Mise au Ppoint by Ivan Zaknic* (New Haven: Yale University Press, 1997). Originally published as *Mise au Point* (Paris: Éditions Forces-Vives, 1966).

Le Corbusier, *Sketchbooks Volume 1* (London: Thames and Hudson, 1981).

Le Corbusier, *Sketchbooks Volume 2* (London: Thames & Hudson, 1981).

Le Corbusier, *Sketchbooks Volume 3, 1954-1957* (Cambridge, MA: MIT, 1982).

Le Corbusier, *Sketchbooks Volume 4, 1957–1964* (Cambridge, MA: MIT, 1982).

Le Goff, J. and Rémond, R., (eds.), *Histoire de la France religieuse, Tome 4* (Paris: Seuil, 1992).

Linder, I., "Pilgrimage to the Millennium: Sacred Art and Architecture in Late Twentieth-Century France", unpublished PhD thesis, Courtauld Institute, University of London (2000).

Linder-Gaillard, I., "La chapelle de Ronchamp et son influence sur l'architecture ecclésiastique contemporaine", in Association Œuvre Notre-Dame-du-Haut (ed.), *Ronchamp, l'exigence d'une rencontre, Le Corbusier et la chapelle Notre-Dame-du Haut* (Lyon: Fage éditions, Ronchamp: Association Œuvre Notre-Dame-du-Haut, 2007), pp. 94–101.

Linder-Gaillard, I., "Modern Art and Catholicism", in Fastiggi, R.L. (ed.), *New Catholic Encyclopedia: Supplement 2011* (Detroit: Gale, 2011), 2 vols., pp. 557–565.

Lion, A. (ed.), *Marie-Alain Couturier (1897–1954) un combat pour l'art sacré, Actes du colloque de Nice, 3-5 décembre 2004* (Nice: Éditions Serre, 2005).

Loach, J., "Le Corbusier and the Creative use of Mathematics", *British Journal of the History of Science* 31 (1998), pp. 185–215.

Machabert, D. (ed.), *Siza au Thoronet, le parcours et l'œuvre* (Marseilles: Éditions Parenthèses, 2007).

Maguire, R. and Murray, K., *Modern Churches of the World* (London: Studio Vista, 1965).

Mâle, E., *The Gothic Image* (London: Fontana, 1961). Originally published as *L'Art Religieux du XIIIe siècle en France* (Paris: Armand Colin, 1910).

Mâle, E., *Religious Art in France: the Twelfth Century* (Princeton: Bollingen, 1973). Originally published as *L'Art religieux du XIIe siècle en France. Étude sur l'origine de l'iconographie du Moyen Age* (Paris: Armand Colin, 1922).

Margerie, A. de (ed.), *Vallauris, La Guerre et la Paix, Picasso* (Paris: Réunion des Musées Nationaux, 1998).

Maritain, J., *Art and Scholasticism* (New York: Sheed and Ward, 1930). Originally published as *Art et scholastique* (Paris: Art catholique, 1920).

Masheck, J., "Post Tenebras Lux, Speculations on Ronchamp", *Building-Art, Modern Achitecture Under Cultural Construction* (Cambridge: Cambridge University Press, 1993), pp. 110–121.

Matisse, H., *Chapelle du Rosaire des dominicaines de Vence par Henri Matisse* (Paris: Murlot Frères, 1951).

McLeod, M., *Urbanism and Utopia: Le Corbusier from Regional Syndicalism to Vichy*, 1985, DPhil Thesis, Princeton.

Meier, R., *Richard Meier* (Milan: Electra architecture, 2003). Originally published in Italian in 2002.

Meier, R., *Richard Meier, Architect, vol. 4 (1999–2003)*, (New York: Rizzoli, 2004).

Mercier, G., *L'architecture religieuse contemporaine en France* (Tours: Mame, 1968).

Migayrou, F. (ed.), *Bloc: Le monolithe fracturé, édifices culturels, architecture de recherche* (Orléans: HYX, 1996).

Migayrou, F. (ed.), *Nevers, Architecture Principe, Claude Parent, Paul Virilio* (Orléans: HYX, Frac Centre, 2010).

Mills, E. D., *The Modern Church* (London: Architectural Press, 1956).

Moles, A., *Histoire des Charpentiers* (Paris: Librairie Gründ, 1949).

Moore, R. A., "Alchemical and Mythical themes in the Poem of the Right angle 1947-65", *Oppositions* 19/20, (winter/spring 1980), pp. 110–139.

Nora, P. (ed.), *Les lieux de mémoire, II. La Nation, tome 2* (Paris: Gallimard, 1986).

Nussaume, Y. (ed.), *Tadao Ando et la question du milieu* (Paris: Le Moniteur, 2000).

Pauly, D., *Le Corbusier: Drawing as Process* (Yale University Press, 2018). Originally published as *"Ce labeur secret", Le Corbusier et le dessin* (Lyon: Fage éditions, Paris: Fondation Le Corbusier, 2015). Translated by G. Hendricks.

Pauly, D., *Ronchamp, lecture d'une architecture* (Paris: Ophrys, 1980).

Pauly, D., *Le Corbusier: The Chapel at Ronchamp* (Birkhäuser: Basel, 1997).

Petit, J. (ed.), *Le Livre de Ronchamp: Le Corbusier* (Paris: Forces Vives, 1961).

Petit, J. (ed.), *Un Couvent de Le Corbusier* (Paris: Minuit, 1961).

Petit, J. (ed.), *Textes et Dessins pour Ronchamp, Le Corbusier* (Geneva: Coopi, Ronchamp: Association Œuvre Notre-Dame-du-Haut, 1995). Originally published in Geneva: Jean Petit, 1965.

Petit, J., *Le Corbusier lui-même* (Paris: Forces Vives, 1970).

Pevsner, N., *Pioneers of Modern Design* (Harmondsworth: Pelican, 1975).

Pico della Mirandola, G., *On the Dignity of Man* (Indianapolis: Hackett, 1998). Originally written in 1486.

Plummer, H., *Cosmos of Light, The Sacred Architecture of Le Corbusier* (Bloomington and Indianapolis: Indiana University Press, 2013).

Potié, P., *The Monastery of Sainte Marie de La Tourette* (Basel: Birkhäuser, 2001).

Prelorenzo, C. (ed.), *Le Corbusier, Le Couvent de la Tourette* (Marseilles: Éditions Parenthèses, 1987).

Provensal, H., *L'Art de Demain* (Paris: Perrin, 1904).

Purdy, M. "Le Corbusier and the Theological Program" in R. Walden (ed.), *The Open Hand, Essays on Le Corbusier*, (Cambridge: MIT Press, 1986), pp. 286–321.

Rabelais, F., *Œuvres complètes* (Paris: Gallimard, 1951).

Ragon, M., *Histoire mondiale de l'architecture et de l'urbanisme modernes, tome 2: pratiques et méthodes 1911–1985* (Paris: Casterman, 1986).

Ragot, G., *Le Corbusier à Firminy-Vert manifeste pour un urbanisme moderne* (Paris:

Éditions du patrimoine, Centre des monuments nationaux, 2011).

Raymond, A., *An Autobiography* (Vermont: Charles E. Tuttle Company, 1973).

Réau, L., *Iconographie de l'art Chrétien Volume 1* (Paris: Presses Universitaires de France, 1955).

Réau, L., *Iconographie de l'art Chrétien Volume 2* (Paris: Presses Universitaires de France, 1957).

Régamey, P.-R., *Art sacré au XXe siècle ?* (Paris, Cerf, 1952).

Régamey, P.-R. (ed.), *L'Art sacré, "Le Père Couturier"*, 9–10 (1954).

Renan, E., *La Vie de Jesus* (Paris: Calmann-Levy, 1906).

Richardson, P., *New Sacred Architecture* (London: Laurence King Publishing, 2004).

Robin, S., *Églises modernes, évolution des édifices religieux en France depuis 1955* (Paris: Hermann, 1980).

Roche, A.V., *Provençal Regionalism* (Illinois: Northwestern University Studies, 1954).

Rollet, T., *Les Catacombes de Rome. Histoire de l'art et des croyances religieuses pendant les premiers siècles du Christianisme, Volume II* (Paris: Morel, 1881).

Rubin, W., *Modern Sacred Art and the Church of Assy* (New York: Columbia University Press, 1961).

Rüegg, A. (ed.), *Le Corbusier Photographs by René Burri: Moments in the Life of a Great Architect* (Basel: Birkhäuser, 1999).

Saint-Martin, I., preface Boespflug, F., *Art chrétien-art sacré: regards du catholicisme sur l'art, France, XIXe–XXe siècle* (Rennes: Presses universitaires de Rennes, 2014).

Saint Palais, C., *Esclarmonde de Foix: Princesse Cathare* (Toulouse: Privat, 1956).

Samuel, F., "Le Corbusier, Women, Nature and Culture", *Issues in Art and Architecture* 5, 2 (1998), pp. 4–20.

Samuel, F., "A Profane Annunciation: The Representation of Sexuality in the Architecture of Ronchamp", *Journal of Architectural Education*, 53, 2 (1999), pp. 74–90.

Samuel, F., "Le Corbusier, Teilhard de Chardin and the Planetisation of Mankind", *Journal of Architecture*, 4 (1999), pp. 149–165.

Samuel, F., "The Philosophical City of Rabelais and St Teresa: Le Corbusier and Edouard Trouin's scheme for St

Baume", *Literature and Theology* 13, 2 (1999), pp. 111–126.

Samuel, F., "The Representation of Mary in Le Corbusier's Chapel at Ronchamp", *Church History*, 68, 2 (1999), pp. 398–417.

Samuel, F. "Orphism in the work of Le Corbusier with particular reference to his scheme for La Sainte Baume, 1948–1960". Unpublished PhD thesis, Cardiff University (2000).

Samuel, F., "Le Corbusier, Teilhard de Chardin and *La Planétisation humaine:* spiritual ideas at the heart of modernism", *French Cultural Studies*, 11, 2 (2000).

Samuel, F., and Menin, S., *Nature and Space: Aalto and Le Corbusier* (London: Routledge, 2002).

Samuel, F., "La cité orphique de La Sainte Baume", *Le Corbusier: le symbolique, le sacré, la spiritualité* (Paris: Fondation Le Corbusier, Éditions de la Villette, 2004), pp. 121–138.

Samuel, F., *Le Corbusier: Architect and Feminist* (London: Wiley/Academy, 2004).

Samuel, F., *Le Corbusier in Detail* (Oxford: Architectural Press, 2007).

Samuel, F., *Le Corbusier and the Architectural Promenade* (Basel: Birkhäuser, 2010).

Schloeder, Stephen J., *Architecture in Communion: Implementing the Second Vatican Council through Liturgy and Architecture* (Ignatius Press 1998).

Schumacher, T., "Deep Space Shallow Space", *Architectural Review*, vol. CLXXXI, no 1079, 1987, p. 41.

Schuré, E., *Les Grands Initiés* (Paris: Perrin, 1908).

Schwarz, R., *The Church Incarnate* (Chicago: Henry Regnery and Company, 1958) translated by Cynthia Harris. Originally published as *Vom Bau der Kirche* (Heidelberg: Verlag Lambert, 1938).

Scott, W., *Hermetica* (Oxford: Clarendon Press, 1924).

Scully, V., *The Earth, the Temple and the Gods* (New Haven: Yale, 1962).

Serenyi, P., "Le Corbusier, Fourier and the Monastery of Ema", *Art Bulletin*, 49 (1967), p. 297.

Smith Jr., K. and Tansal, R., (eds.), *The Development by Le Corbusier of the Design for the l'Eglise de Firminy, a church in France* (Raleigh: Student Publications of the School of Design, North Carolina State University at Raleigh), Volume 14, no. 2, 1964.

Spate, V., *Orphism: the Evolution of Non-figurative Painting in Paris in 1910–14* (Oxford: Clarendon, 1979).

Sperling, H. and Simon, M., trans., *The Zohar*, (London: Soncino Press, 1933).

Stock, W. J., *European Church Architecture 1950–2000* (Munich: Prestel, 2002).

Stoller, E., *The Chapel at Ronchamp* (New York: Princeton Architectural Press, 1999).

Swietlicki, C., *Spanish Christian Cabala* (Columbia: University of Missouri Press), 1986.

Teresa of Jesus, Saint, *The Interior Castle* (London: Thomas Baker 1912), originally written in 1577.

Teresa of Jesus, Saint, *The Way of Perfection* (London: Thomas Baker 1911), originally written in 1567.

Texier, S. (ed.), *Églises parisiennes du XXe siècle, architecture et décor* (Paris: Action Artistique de la Ville de Paris, Collection Paris et son patrimoine, 1996).

Thomas, L., *André Gide, the Ethic of the Artist* (London: Secker and Warburg, 1950).

Turner, P., *The Education of an Architect* (New York: Garland, 1977).

Virilio, P., *Bunker Archaeology* (New York: Princeton University Press, 1994). Originally published as *Bunker Archéologie, étude sur l'espace militaire européen de la Seconde Guerre mondiale* (Paris: Centre Georges Pompidou, Centre de Création Industrielle, 1975).

Voragine, Jacobus de, *The Golden Legend, vol. 1,* translated by William Granger Ryan (Princeton: Princeton University Press, 1993).

Wilson, S., "La Bataille des 'humbles'? Communistes et catholiques autour de l'art sacré", in Jobert B. (ed.), *Histoires d'art, Mélanges en l'honneur de Bruno Foucart* (Paris: Norma, 2008), pp. 448–466.

Wogenscky, A. *Le Corbusier's Hands* (Cambridge, Mass: MIT Press, 2006). Originally published as *Les mains de Le Corbusier* (Paris, Éditions de Grenelle, 1987). Also French/German edition (Cologne: Verlag der Buchhandlung König, 2000).

INDEX

ILLUSTRATION CREDITS